Philipp Liegl

Business Documents for Inter-Organizational Business Processes

Philipp Liegl

Business Documents for Inter-Organizational Business Processes

Bridging the interoperability-gap between enterprises using current state-of-the-art in business document modeling

Südwestdeutscher Verlag für Hochschulschriften

Impressum/Imprint (nur für Deutschland/ only for Germany)
Bibliografische Information der Deutschen Nationalbibliothek: Die Deutsche Nationalbibliothek verzeichnet diese Publikation in der Deutschen Nationalbibliografie; detaillierte bibliografische Daten sind im Internet über http://dnb.d-nb.de abrufbar.
  Alle in diesem Buch genannten Marken und Produktnamen unterliegen warenzeichen-, marken- oder patentrechtlichem Schutz bzw. sind Warenzeichen oder eingetragene Warenzeichen der jeweiligen Inhaber. Die Wiedergabe von Marken, Produktnamen, Gebrauchsnamen, Handelsnamen, Warenbezeichnungen u.s.w. in diesem Werk berechtigt auch ohne besondere Kennzeichnung nicht zu der Annahme, dass solche Namen im Sinne der Warenzeichen- und Markenschutzgesetzgebung als frei zu betrachten wären und daher von jedermann benutzt werden dürften.

Verlag: Südwestdeutscher Verlag für Hochschulschriften Aktiengesellschaft & Co. KG
Dudweiler Landstr. 99, 66123 Saarbrücken, Deutschland
Telefon +49 681 37 20 271-1, Telefax +49 681 37 20 271-0
Email: info@svh-verlag.de
Zugl.: Wien, TU, Diss., 2010

Herstellung in Deutschland:
Schaltungsdienst Lange o.H.G., Berlin
Books on Demand GmbH, Norderstedt
Reha GmbH, Saarbrücken
Amazon Distribution GmbH, Leipzig
ISBN: 978-3-8381-1389-0

Imprint (only for USA, GB)
Bibliographic information published by the Deutsche Nationalbibliothek: The Deutsche Nationalbibliothek lists this publication in the Deutsche Nationalbibliografie; detailed bibliographic data are available in the Internet at http://dnb.d-nb.de.
  Any brand names and product names mentioned in this book are subject to trademark, brand or patent protection and are trademarks or registered trademarks of their respective holders. The use of brand names, product names, common names, trade names, product descriptions etc. even without a particular marking in this works is in no way to be construed to mean that such names may be regarded as unrestricted in respect of trademark and brand protection legislation and could thus be used by anyone.

Publisher: Südwestdeutscher Verlag für Hochschulschriften Aktiengesellschaft & Co. KG
Dudweiler Landstr. 99, 66123 Saarbrücken, Germany
Phone +49 681 37 20 271-1, Fax +49 681 37 20 271-0
Email: info@svh-verlag.de

Printed in the U.S.A.
Printed in the U.K. by (see last page)
ISBN: 978-3-8381-1389-0

Copyright © 2010 by the author and Südwestdeutscher Verlag für Hochschulschriften Aktiengesellschaft & Co. KG and licensors
All rights reserved. Saarbrücken 2010

Kurzfassung der Dissertation

Papierbasierte Prozesse zwischen Unternehmen werden zunehmend durch automatisierte papierlose Interaktionen abgelöst. Die Durchführung von automatischen Interaktionen erfordert üblicherweise bindende Entscheidungen in juristischer und technischer Hinsicht durch die beteiligten Geschäftspartner. Auf technischer Ebene sind hierbei zwei wichtige Vereinbarungen notwendig. Einerseits müssen sich beide Geschäftspartner auf die einheitliche Abfolge für den interorganisationalen Prozess einigen – die sogenannte Prozesschoreographie. Andererseits muss festgelegt werden, welche exakte Dokumentenstruktur innerhalb dieser Prozesschoreographie ausgetauscht wird. Der Fokus dieser Dissertation liegt auf der eindeutigen Definition von Geschäftsdokumenten für inter-organisationale Geschäftsprozesse. Dabei werden insbesondere sogenannte top-down und bottom-up Standards zur Definition von Geschäftsdokumenten untersucht. Des Weiteren ist die Integration von Geschäftsdokumentmodellen und Prozesschoreographiemodellen Gegenstand der Untersuchung.

Die Forschungsfrage lautet daher, wie notwendige Methoden für die eindeutige Definition von Geschäftsdokumenten im interorganisationalen Umfeld bereitgestellt werden können. Ansätze, wie sie vor allem im intraorganisationalen Umfeld verwendet werden, lassen sich nur teilweise auf die interorganisationale Domäne anwenden. Dies liegt einerseits an der Vielzahl von unterschiedlichen Stakeholdern, welche am Prozess beteiligt sind und deren spezifischen Anforderungen, und andererseits daran, dass Entscheidungen nicht von einer einheitlichen, zentralen Instanz getätigt werden. Für die Definition von interorganisationalen Geschäftsdokumenten setzt der Ansatz in dieser Arbeit auf top-down und bottom-up Standards auf. Dabei werden geeignete Methoden für die eindeutige Definition und das Mapping von Dokumentenstandards sowie für die Ableitung von XML Schema Artefakten von Geschäftsdokumentenstandards zur

Kurzfassung der Dissertation

Verfügung gestellt. Des Weiteren wird der aktuelle Stand der Forschung im Bereich von Geschäftsdokumenten für interorganisationale Geschäftsprozesse vorgestellt.

In Kapitel 1 wird der Übergang vom dokumentenzentrierten elektronischen Datenaustausch (EDI) hin zu automatisierten Business-to-Business (B2B) Geschäftstransaktionen vorgestellt. Dabei wird vor allem auf die spezifischen Anforderungen für die Definition von Geschäftsdokumenten eingegangen, die sich durch die geänderten Bedingungen des B2B ergeben. In weiterer Folge werden der Umfang dieser Arbeit sowie die einzelnen Problemstellungen und deren Lösungen, welche diese Arbeit liefert, kurz vorgestellt. Die vorliegende Arbeit ist so angelegt, dass die einzelnen Kapitel auch eigenständig gelesen werden können, ohne die gesamte Arbeit zu kennen. Dies setzt jedoch ein gewisses Maß an Verständnis der behandelten Technologien voraus. Es wird daher empfohlen die Arbeit Kapitel für Kapitel in aufsteigender Reihenfolge zu lesen. Die einzelnen Kapitel dieser Arbeit verwenden ein durchgehendes Beispiel aus der Abfalltransportdomäne, welches in Kapitel 2 vorgestellt wird.

Eine Übersicht über aktuelle Geschäftsdokumentenstandards im Bereich von B2B wird in Kapital 3 gegeben. Die Core Component Technologie von UN/CEFACT, die ein elementarer Bestandteil dieser Arbeit ist, wird in Kapitel 4 erläutert. Core Components sind wieder verwendbare Bausteine zur eindeutigen Definition von Geschäftsdokumenten, die allerdings nur in einer implementierungsneutralen Form vorliegen. Dadurch wird zurzeit eine größere Verbreitung des Standards noch verhindert. In dieser Arbeit stellen wir drei verschiedene Repräsentationsmechanismen für Core Components vor: ein UML Profil für Core Components (Kapitel 5), eine domänenspezifische Sprache für Core Components (Kapitel 6) und eine OWL (Web Ontology Language) Repräsentation für Core Components (Kapitel 7).

Die Ableitung von XML Schema Artefakten von Core Component Modellen wird in Kapitel 8 behandelt. Um eine weitere Verbreitung der Core Component Technologie zu unterstützen, wurde im Rahmen dieser Arbeit ein Core Component Registry Meta-Modell entwickelt, welches in Kapitel 9 vorgestellt wird.

Der zweite Teil dieser Dissertation behandelt bottom-up Standards. Die Definition von domänenspezifischen Erwei-

Kurzfassung der Dissertation

terungen für bottom-up Standards wird in Kapitel 10 vorgestellt. Ein Mapping eines XML basierten bottom-up Standards zu einem in UML definierten top-down Core Component Modell wird in Kapitel 11 vorgestellt. Die Integration von UML basierten interorganisationalen Geschäftsprozess- und Geschäftsdokumentmodellen ist Gegenstand von Kapitel 12. Bereits bestehende Arbeiten auf dem Gebiet von interorganisationalen Geschäftsdokumenten und eine Abgrenzung zur vorliegenden Arbeit werden in Kapitel 13 vorgestellt. Abgeschlossen wird diese Arbeit mit Kapitel 14, wo eine Zusammenfassung der Arbeit und eine Auflistung von noch offenen Forschungsfragen erfolgt.

Zusammenfassend liefert die vorliegende Arbeit folgende sieben Beiträge zum Stand der Forschung im Bereich von interorganisationalen Geschäftsdokumenten: (1) einen Überblick über aktuelle Geschäftsdokumentenstandards, basierend auf Standard-Clustern; (2) drei Referenzrepräsentationen für Core Components basierend auf UML, domänenspezifischen Sprachen und OWL (Web Ontology Language); (3) eine eindeutige Ableitung von XML Schema Artefakten von UML basierten Core Component Modellen; (4) ein Meta-Modell für eine Core Component Registry; (5) domänenspezifische Erweiterungen für einen XML basierten bottom-up Geschäftsdokumentenstandard; (6) ein Mapping von bottom-up Geschäftsdokumentenstandards zu top-down Geschäftsdokumentenstandards; (7) eine Integration von UML basierten Core Component Modellen in UML basierte Prozesschoreographiemodellen.

Dementsprechend liefert diese Dissertation einen Ansatz, welcher die Definition von interorganisationalen Geschäftsdokumenten erleichtert und ihre Wiederverwendbarkeit durch geeignete Methoden fördert.

Abstract

Automated business-to-business (B2B) interactions between companies are constantly superseding old paper-based processes. This automation of inter-organizational processes requires legal and technical agreements between the participating business partners. In a technical sense a twofold agreement is necessary between business partners. First of all, business partners must agree on a common process choreography, unambiguously defining the exact exchange order of business documents in an inter-organizational business process. Consequently, business partners must agree on the structure of the exchanged business information as well. This thesis focuses on the definition of business documents for inter-organizational business processes and on the integration of business document models into business process choreography models. The two main business document paradigms, on which we elaborate in this thesis, are top-down business document standards and bottom-up business document standards.

The research question, this thesis aims to solve, is how to provide appropriate methods for the definition of business documents for inter-organizational business processes. Due to their special characteristics, such as the involvement of various stakeholders from different companies, the definition of business documents for inter-organizational business processes is not as straightforward as the definition of business documents or data models for intra-organizational business processes. For the definition of inter-organizational business documents we employ two different approaches – a top-down approach and a bottom-up approach. For both approaches we provide appropriate methods for the definition of business documents, the mapping between different business document definitions, and the derivation of XML-based deployment artifacts from business document definitions. Furthermore, we cover state-of-the art in the domain of inter-organizational business documents and inter-organizational business processes.

This thesis starts by giving an introduction to the domain of Electronic Data Interchange (EDI) and shows the transition of data-centric EDI solutions to modern B2B systems in Chapter 1. Thereby, the specific requirements for B2B interactions are elaborated – in particular in regard to the definition of the exchanged business information. Furthermore, we present the scope of this thesis and the problems, to which this thesis contributes to. The Chapters of this thesis are organized in a self-contained manner. Thus, it is possible to read each Chapter without knowing the previous Chapters. However, since a certain knowledge of the domain is generally required, it is recommended to read Chapter by Chapter in an ascending order. We motivate the findings of this thesis using an accompanying example from the domain of pan-European waste transport, which is introduced in Chapter 2.

In Chapter 3 we provide a survey of current state-of-the-art in business document standards. Chapter 4 provides an introduction to UN/CEFACT's Core Components, a top-down business document standard which is key to this thesis. In a nutshell, core components are implementation neutral building blocks for assembling business documents. Although this implementation neutrality is one of the strengths of core components, it hinders a broad diffusion of the standard, since no common representation format for core components is available. To address this issue, this thesis provides three reference representation formats for core components: (i) a UML Profile for Core Components (Chapter 5), (ii) a Domain-Specific Language for Core Components (Chapter 6), (iii) and a Web Ontology Language representation for Core Components (Chapter 7).

The derivation of XML Schema artifacts from core components, which may be deployed to IT systems, is covered in Chapter 8. A successful diffusion of core components may only be achieved if a broad user community has access to the necessary core component definitions. Consequently, we provide a registry meta-model for core components in Chapter 9.

Bottom-up business document standards are subject to discussion in the second part of this thesis. Thereby, domain-

Abstract

specific extensions to bottom-up document standards are introduced in Chapter 10. Consequently, we examine how to map bottom-up standard definitions to core component-based top-down standard definitions in Chapter 11. Finally, we show how to combine business choreography models and business document models in Chapter 12. An overview of related work in the domain of inter-organizational business documents and a comparison to the work presented in this thesis is given in Chapter 13. Finally, Chapter 14 concludes the contributions of this thesis.

In summary this thesis provides the following seven contributions: (1) An overview of business document standards, based on standard clusters; (2) three reference representation formats for core components using the Unified Modeling Language, Domain-Specific Languages, and Web Ontology Language for Core Components; (3) an unambiguous derivation of XML Schema artifacts from UML-based core component models; (4) a registry meta-model for a core component registry; (5) domain-specific extensions for an XML-based bottom-up business document standard; (6) a mapping of bottom-up business document standards to top-down business documents standards; (7) an integration of UML-based core component models in UML-based business choreography models. In short, the overall approach facilitates the definition of business documents in an inter-organizational context and fosters reuse of existing business document definitions.

Contents

Kurzfassung der Dissertation v

Abstract ix

1 Introduction 1
1.1 History of Electronic Data Interchange 2
1.2 From EDI to B2B Electronic Commerce 3
1.3 Scope of this thesis 8
1.4 Contributions of this thesis 9
1.5 Methodological approach 15
1.6 Structure of this thesis 17

2 Introduction of the example: Waste Transport 21
2.1 EUDIN at a glance 22
2.2 Waste management example in this thesis 25

3 An overview of business document standards . 27
3.1 Introduction................................. 27
3.2 Business document standard clusters 28
    3.2.1 Top-Down standardization approaches 30
    3.2.2 Bottom-up standard approaches........... 34
    3.2.3 Hybrid standardization approaches......... 37
    3.2.4 Early mark-up adopters 39
    3.2.5 Integrated standardization approaches....... 41
    3.2.6 Transitioned standardization approaches 43
    3.2.7 Implementation neutral standardization approaches................................. 45
    3.2.8 Converging approaches 48
3.3 A standard comparison 50
3.4 Final assessment 56

4 An introduction to Core Components........ 59
4.1 Introduction and historical background 59
4.2 Core Components 62
    4.2.1 Aggregate Core Component (ACC) 64

Contents

	4.2.2	Basic Core Component (BCC)	64
	4.2.3	Association Core Component (ASCC)	65
	4.2.4	Core Data Types	66
4.3	Business Information Entities	67
	4.3.1	Aggregate Business Information Entity (ABIE)	70
	4.3.2	Basic Business Information Entity (BBIE)	70
	4.3.3	Association Business Information Entity (ASBIE)	71
	4.3.4	From core components to business information entities	72
	4.3.5	Business Data Types	74
4.4	Core Component Library	75
4.5	Final assessment	76

5 A UML Profile for Core Components 79
5.1 Introduction 80
5.2 UPCC – A UML Profile for Core Components 82
5.3 UML Profile for Core Components by example 86
5.4 Final assessment 98

6 A DSL for Core Components 101
6.1 Introduction 101
6.2 The Core Component DSL 105
6.3 Technical considerations of a DSL 111
6.4 Advantages of the DSL compared to UML 113
6.5 Final assessment 116

7 Building a global reference ontology with OWL 119
7.1 Introduction 120
7.2 Reference ontology 123
7.3 Core component ontology 126
7.4 Mapping instances to the core component ontology 127
7.5 Final assessment 131

8 Deriving XML Schema from Core Components 133
8.1 Introduction 134
8.2 Transformation concepts 135
8.3 Final assessment 143

9 A registry for Core Components 145
9.1 Introduction 146
9.2 Introduction to the ebXML registry specification ... 148
9.3 The Core Component Registry Model 149

	9.3.1 Registering conceptual core component models 151
	9.3.2 Registering logical level core component artifacts 154
9.4	Registry Federation 156
9.5	Final assessment 158

10 Extensions for bottom-up standard approaches 159
10.1	Introduction 160
10.2	ebInterface – the core 161
10.3	Alternative strategies for a bottom-up approach ... 163
	10.3.1 Custom section 163
	10.3.2 Redefine 168
	10.3.3 Substitution group 170
	10.3.4 xsi:type overloading 172
10.4	Final assessment 174

11 Mapping bottom-up to top-down standards .. 177
11.1	Introduction 177
11.2	Basic Mapping 178
11.3	Advanced Mapping 181
	11.3.1 Meta-model Layer Mapping 181
	11.3.2 Model Layer Mappings 188
11.4	Implementation and Case Study 191
11.5	Final assessment 191

12 Process choreographies and document definitions 193
12.1	Introduction to UN/CEFACT's Modeling Methodology 194
	12.1.1 Business Requirements View 196
	12.1.2 Business Choreography View 201
	12.1.3 Business Information View – Combining UMM and UPCC models 210
12.2	Deriving code artifacts from UMM 213
12.3	Final assessment 219

13 Related Work 221
13.1	Business Document Standard Overview 221
13.2	Core component concepts 222
13.3	Conceptual business document modeling with UML 224
13.4	Domain-Specific Language Approaches 227
13.5	Semantic approaches 229

Contents

13.6 From conceptual models to XML Schema artifacts . 231
13.7 B2B registry approaches....................... 231
13.8 Bottom-up standard extensions 233
13.9 Mapping business document model to core components 234
13.10 Capturing inter-organizational process requirements 235

14   Conclusion and open research issues 239

List of Figures **247**

Nomenclature **251**

Bibliography **253**

List of Publications **275**

1 Introduction

According to a recent study conducted in Germany [152], around six billion invoices are issued between companies every year. In most cases the issuing company retrieves the necessary data from its IT system, prints the invoice in paper form, and sends it using regular postal service. The receiving company manually processes the incoming invoice and stores the relevant data in its IT system for further processing. According to [152] the average costs of a manually sent invoice are five to seven Euros and the average costs for a manually received invoice are ten to twelve Euros. Assuming a worst case scenario, the manual exchange of invoices causes a total of $114 * 10^9$ Euros in costs.

Manual document processing is one of the major cost traps

You might ask yourself, why these companies do not simply introduce electronic data interchange (EDI) solutions, to lower the significant costs of manual invoice processing. As we outline in this thesis, the introduction of automated interactions between companies is not as easy as it might appear. Before two companies may engage in an automated business interaction, a set of agreements between the participating business partners has to be made. These agreements have to be achieved on the business and the IT level. In particular on the IT level, companies will most likely face the following questions (among others):

EDI to the rescue?

- There is a multitude of different business document standards out there – which one should I choose?
- Which business document standard does my counterpart support and is it compatible with mine?
- In what exact exchange order do I have to send business documents to my business partner?

With this thesis we aim to answer these questions and provide appropriate scientific methods for the introduction of automated business interactions between companies. Before we further elaborate on the details of automated business-to-business interactions, we briefly take a look into the past of electronic data interchange.

1.1 History of Electronic Data Interchange

The beginning of Electronic Data Interchange

The first attempts towards electronic data interchange go back to the time of the Berlin Airlift in 1948 [150]. Ed Guilbert, who was responsible for the air support traffic to Berlin, was confronted with numerous paper-based business transactions and sought for an automated solution. These concepts, however, were not implemented. Later, large companies such as Ford started to implement their own proprietary interchange formats to automate their processes. However, most of these standards weren't harmonized on an industry level and as a result several, partly redundant and incompatible interchange standards were developed.

Consolidation phase of EDI standards

An important step towards a consolidated EDI standard definition for North America was achieved in 1983, when the American National Standards Institute (ANSI) published the first five ANSI X12 standards [6]. Previously, several industry branches had developed their own EDI standards, which were limited to a specific industry. A similar situation could be observed in Europe, where the United Nations Economic Commission for Europe (UN/ECE) decided to develop an internationally valid standard for EDI, based on the best features of ANSI X12 and other European initiatives. Eventually, these efforts resulted in the Electronic Data Interchange For Administration, Commerce, and Transport (EDIFACT) [163] standard, which was first released in 1988.

Value added networks

In the early days of EDI, the availability of network connections between enterprises was rather scarce and the Internet as we know it today did not exist. EDI messages were exchanged between different companies via value added networks (VAN). In such VAN environments the participating business partners paid a fee for the exchange of EDI messages. Furthermore, the operation of IT systems, capable of parsing and processing EDI messages, was expensive and only large companies could afford the costs. With the inception of the Internet and the broad availability of network connections and computing power at low cost, the field of EDI underwent a significant change.

1.2 From EDI to B2B Electronic Commerce

Since the advent of the EDIFACT standards around 25+ years ago, the challenges for electronic data interchange have changed considerably. In the early days of electronic data interchange, the main drivers for the implementation of EDI solutions were the optimization of inter-organizational document exchanges and the reduction of errors, occurring during manual processing of business documents. Errors due to manual processing of business documents mostly occur in case of media breakages, i.e., the conversion of a paper document to an electronic representation, usually done by a human. Although these objectives are still valid today, the scope of EDI has broadened. Today, we observe a transition from data centric enterprise relations towards the realization of complex inter-organizational business processes. Consequently, the term electronic data interchange (EDI) is superseded by the term business-to-business (B2B) collaborations or interactions.

Moving beyond pure data centric standardization

The increased networking of today's enterprises has led to a new level of flexibility in terms of finding potential business partners. An enterprise seeking transport services does not contact the next transport service provider in town, but may choose from a multitude of different service providers by searching the Internet. Furthermore, business processes tend to be designed in a finer grained manner to be able to split them up between different roles. Whereas, for instance, in former days the entire sales process was realized in-house by a dedicated sales department, outsourcing and offshoring policies may place the responsibilities for the sales process on different sub-contractors.

Increased competition for a business partner

Typically, an enterprise will try to get the cheapest suppliers, sub-contractors, sales agents, etc. as possible to lower costs and increase profit margins. Thereby, an enterprise usually builds on long running business relationships between suppliers, production companies, and sales forces. However, in recent years a change in the general attitude on how business is conducted between companies could be observed. Business relationships are shorter-lived and business partners, participating in a business transaction, are replaced easier and faster.

1 Introduction

Higher process flexibility

Generally, business relationships move away from isolated bi-lateral document exchanges between business partners to a more networked environment. Tapscott et al. [161] define *Business Webs* as a distinct network of suppliers, distributors, commerce service providers, and customers that link via the Internet and other electronic media to produce value for end-customers and for one another. According to Van Heck et al. [179] modern business is conducted through a rapidly formed network with anyone, anywhere, anytime regardless of different computer systems and business processes. This scenario is also known as *Smart Business Networks*. To cope with the requirements of these networked environments, an increased level of flexibility is expected from business partners. Furthermore, the traditionally intra-organizational focus of business processes must change to an inter-organizational one.

Business/IT alignment with service oriented architectures

In a nutshell, modern business processes must be designed in a flexible manner to support changing business conditions. Accordingly, the IT applications of the different companies must be designed in a flexible manner too, to be able to quickly adapt to changing company goals. This paradigm is also known as business/IT alignment. Service oriented architectures (SOA) are a promising solution for solving this business/IT alignment problem. Prior to its use in IT, the notion of a *service* has been established in the business administration domain, referring to a value exchange as a business economic activity [195]. In a SOA environment services expose company internal business functionality through well defined interfaces to other business partners via a network. Thus, new business processes may be easily assembled by reusing existing services. In former days, change requests to the IT resulted in rigorous reengineering tasks of existing IT implementations. Nowadays, service oriented IT departments face the challenge of aligning their service interfaces. This term is also known as service alignment and refers to the reconcilement between business partners to provide complementary services. An appropriate interlink between business and IT has to be found to allow for a better alignment of processes and IT requirements.

Abstracting from complex implementation details

In particular in inter-organizational business processes several stakeholders are involved in the collaborative agreement on a common structure of the inter-organizational busi-

1.2 From EDI to B2B Electronic Commerce

ness process and the structure of the business documents, exchanged in the inter-organizational process. Often the technical skills of the different stakeholders vary, since for instance not everybody is familiar with XML-based document or process definitions. In order to overcome knowledge heterogeneities among different stakeholders, business requirements are captured on an implementation neutral level using appropriate models. Thereby, a model abstracts from technical implementation details and provides a conceptual view on business documents and business processes. In a consecutive step the created models may be used in a model-driven manner to derive technical deployment artifacts such as XML Schema definitions. The benefits of such a model-driven approach are thus twofold. On the one hand, non-technical experts may also be involved in the decision making process of an inter-organizational business process. On the other hand, changing business requirements may be reflected in conceptual models and the necessary deployment artifacts for IT systems may be conveniently derived from these conceptual models. Thus, changing business requirements may be integrated in the respective IT systems in a faster and easier manner. Obviously, electronic data interchange projects have to go beyond simple data standardization approaches and have to consider model-driven approaches for inter-organizational processes as well.

In the early days of EDI, only a limited set of business document standards and standardized business message types were available. Starting in the late 1980ies, more and more interchange standards were developed and the inception of XML brought an additional boost to business document standard development. Today, a company seeking to introduce a business document standard is facing a multitude of different standards to choose from. However, the integration of a business document standard in an IT system must be carefully planned, since considerable costs may arise if the wrong standard is chosen. Typically ERP software (Enterprise Resource Planning) is responsible for processing instances of a certain business document standard. Parameters, such as release iterations of a standard or backward compatibility of a standard, must be carefully taken into account to avoid expensive customization costs of ERP software in case of, e.g., a standard update. An IT

Multitude of different business document standards

analyst, responsible for the inception of a new business document standard format, requires a profound survey pointing out implementation crucial facts such as business messaging compatibility, technology features, potential user groups, and acceptance per standard.

Moving beyond the delimiter age — We conclude that a large heterogeneity in regard to the used business document standards in the industry exists today. Thus, the original idea of harmonization between different data formats as it was planned by EDIFACT is undermined. The multitude of available business document standards, whose original goal was to overcome data heterogeneity, is itself causing heterogeneity. As shown in scenario A on the left hand side of Figure 1.1, the number of necessary mappers between business document standards grows significantly with the participating business partners (assuming every partner uses a different standard).

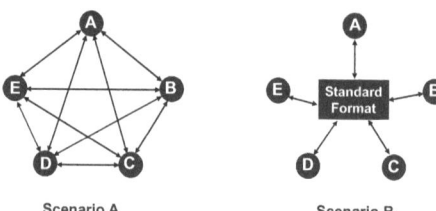

Figure 1.1 Single business document standard

One solution would be the introduction of a single data format, upon which all participating business partners agree (scenario B in Figure 1.1). Originally, this was the idea pursued by the different EDIFACT standards. However, through extensive sub-setting and domain-specific message implementation guides (MIG), the original idea of one single standard was soon abandoned.

EDIFACT still has a considerable market share — Furthermore, the delimiter-based approach of EDIFACT, which was innovative and new 25+ years ago, does not comply with current state-of-the-art B2B requirements. In delimiter-based standards the different standard elements are separated using a defined set of ASCII characters. In particular service oriented architectures generally prefer markup-based standards, where content and document structure are separated using designated markup-tags, which may be arbitrarily defined. Markup-based standards provide a new level of flexibility in the definition of new document formats

1.2 From EDI to B2B Electronic Commerce

and integrate well with model-driven approaches. Thus, a new approach for the definition of a single business document standard is needed, overcoming limitations of traditional delimiter-based approaches. However, note that EDIFACT is still a very popular exchange format. According to a study conducted in Germany and the U.S., 52% of all enterprises in Germany and 75% of all enterprise in the U.S. use EDIFACT technology to transfer structured business data [175].

Today, not only large companies participate in automated business-to-business interactions, but more and more small and medium-sized enterprises (SME) aim at participating in B2B scenarios as well. Top-down business document standards, such as EDIFACT, were developed with the prerequisite to meet as many different requirements as possible. Thus, most of the top-down standard definitions are quite complex and contain a multitude of optional elements to cope with various requirements. If two business partners want to use, e.g., EDIFACT for the exchange of business documents, a prior agreement on a subset of the EDIFACT message is necessary, requiring adaptations of the IT systems processing the different business document types. However, in particular small and medium-sized enterprises need business document standards, which may be used without prior agreements on standard sub-sets.

EDI for everybody

Unfortunately, small and medium-sized business partners are usually forced by their larger business partner to use the business document standard and its subset, which the larger business partner is using. However, this presupposes that an SME has an ERP system which is customizable to import and export the business document format, the large business partner dictates. In particular SMEs often cannot afford such customizable ERP solutions, but rely on configurable commercial-of-the-shelf-software (COTS). These COTS systems may contain standardized interfaces for the import and export of a certain standard definition. However, in contrast to top-down standard definitions such as EDIFACT, these interfaces may only process standards which do not require prior agreements between the different business partners. Thus, the increasing participation of SMEs in automated B2B interactions demands for a new definition of business document standards, where only the most

Need for bottom-up business document standards

important requirements of the participating business partners are reflected in an unambiguous manner, without the necessity to define partner specific sub-sets prior to an exchange. We refer to such standard definitions as bottom-up business document standards. Even if an agreement on a core bottom-up standard definition has been found, certain business cases may require partner specific extensions to the business document standards. These partner specific amendments must be defined without interfering with compatibility at the core standard level. The requirements of modern EDI impose additional challenges on business document standardization.

Meeting the requirements of today's B2B

This thesis provides solutions for the new challenges, dynamic B2B interactions impose on an enterprise. In the following Section we highlight the two main areas of business-to-business interactions, this thesis contributes to.

1.3 Scope of this thesis

Common business document exchange format

Business-to-business interactions between two business partners demand for a twofold agreement. As shown in Figure 1.2, an automated B2B interaction requires a common agreement on the exchanged business documents and a common agreement on the exact exchange order of the different business documents (= process choreography). In this thesis we concentrate on methods for defining a common business document exchange format for an inter-organizational business process. We first give a survey of current state of the art in business document standards. Consequently, we elaborate on the two main paradigms for business document standardization: top-down business document standardization and bottom-up business document standardization.

Figure 1.2 Scope of this thesis

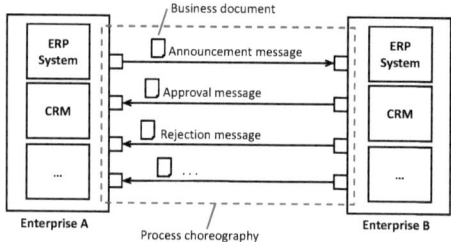

Apart from a common agreement on the structure of the exchanged information, business partners in an inter-organizational business process must also agree on an exact exchange order of business documents. We refer to this exchange order as a global business process choreography. In this thesis we examine how business choreography models may be combined with business document models to unambiguously define an inter-organizational business process. Furthermore, we employ model-driven concepts to derive deployment artifacts for IT systems from conceptual business process and business document models.

Exact exchange order of business documents

1.4 Contributions of this thesis

As outlined before, this thesis addresses the domain of B2B interactions between enterprises. With the increasing cross-linking of business processes from different enterprises through the use of service oriented architectures, seamless interoperability between different enterprises becomes a crucial success factor. Although several standardization initiatives were founded over the years, seamless interoperability between different business partners is still an unresolved issue. This thesis tackles several problem areas from the domain of inter-organizational business document and business process definitions. Figure 1.3 gives an overview of the different contributions of this thesis.

Overview of contributions

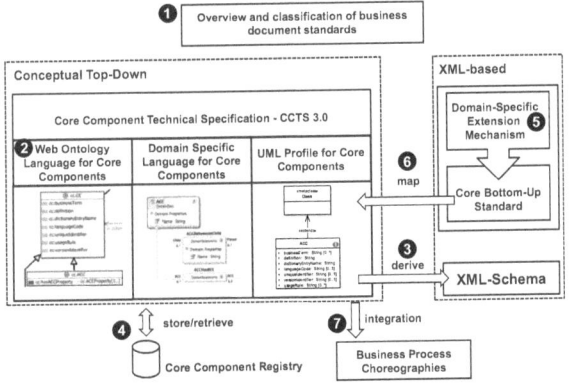

Figure 1.3
Overview of the contributions of this thesis

1 Introduction

Problem 1: Missing overview and classification of business document standards

Since the beginning of electronic data interchange, several business document standardization initiatives were founded. Over the years several business document standards surveys have been published, with the goal to help business document modelers to choose the right business document standard definition for a particular business case. However, most of the different surveys and publications are either quite generic [43], outdated [91] [143], or focus on entire e-Business frameworks rather than on single standards [117] [86]. Furthermore, due to the abundance and inherent heterogeneity of most of the standard definitions, no single survey covering all of the different standards is currently available. Thus, most of the surveys cover only a specialized part of the entire business document standards.

Contribution 1: Business document standard survey based on standard clusters

In this thesis we do not provide yet another business document standard survey. Instead of examining single standard definitions, we introduce standard clusters aggregating business document standards of a certain type. Consequently, we base our standard survey on these standard clusters. Our survey distinguishes between eight different business document standard clusters namely (i) top-down approaches, (ii) bottom-up approaches, (iii) hybrid approaches, (iv) early mark-up adopters, (v) integrated approaches, (vi) transitioned approaches, (vii) implementation neutral approaches, and (viii) converging approaches. Based on these clusters, we provide an assessment in regard to business messaging compatibility, technology features, potential user groups, as well as acceptance. The provided survey intends to be a guide for a business analyst or technologist, responsible to chose a certain business document standard.

Thesis focuses on top-down and bottom-up standards

Problem 2: Missing implementation for core components

In this thesis we in particular focus on top-down and bottom-up business document standards, since they represent the two predominant standard paradigms. Most of the other standard clusters may to different extends be associated with the findings for top-down and bottom-up business document standards.

As part of the Electronic Business XML (ebXML) initiative [124] *core components* were developed. Core components are reusable building blocks for assembling business documents in an interoperable manner. This is achieved by defining core components independent of any business context. If used in a certain business scenario, a core com-

1.4 Contributions of this thesis

ponent becomes a *business information entity*. In contrast to core components, business information entities are context specific and tailored to a certain application domain. Business information entities are always derived from core components by restriction to maintain traceability of business information entities back to their common semantic basis. Although the core component mechanism provides a powerful approach for the definition of interoperable business documents, it has one significant shortcoming: core components and business information entities are defined in an implementation neutral manner.

First, the Core Component Technical Specification (CCTS) [170], which defines the meta-model for core components, is defined in a non-formal manner using English prose. Second, predefined core components are provided to business document modelers in a Core Component Library (CCL) [173]. However, the CCL is currently just a single spread sheet file.

We conclude that representation formats for core components must be provided to allow for a wide-spread adoption of the core component technology. In this thesis we tackle the problem by providing three different reference formats for core components: (i) a UML Profile for Core Components (UPCC) (ii) a Domain-Specific Language (DSL) for Core Components and (iii) a Web Ontology Language implementation for Core Components.

Implementation neutral core component concepts are transferred to a formalized UML representation by providing a UML Profile for Core Components (UPCC). Using the UML profile mechanism, we tailor the generic UML meta-model to the specific needs of core component based business document modeling. Based on the UML Profile, a business document modeler is able to assemble core component models in an easy manner. The UML-based business document model may then be validated according to the constraints, specified in the UML Profile for Core Components. The valid core component model is the basis for further processing such as the derivation of deployment artifacts for a SOA.

Contribution 2a: UPCC – UML Profile for Core Components

Contribution 2b: Domain-Specific Language for Core Components

With the concept of Domain-Specific Languages (DSL) for Core Components we follow a similar approach as with the UML Profile for Core Components. However, instead of tailoring the generic UML meta-model to business docu-

1 Introduction

ment modeling specifics, we define our own meta-model using Domain-Specific Languages. The result is a streamlined modeling environment, entirely dedicated to core component modeling. The benefits for a business document modeler are the same as with the UML Profile for Core Components – easy validation of core component models and further processing of core components models to generate deployment artifacts for a SOA. Furthermore, we elaborate on the specific advantages of a DSL compared to the Unified Modeling Language.

Contribution 2c: Web Ontology Language for Core Components

We provide a third implementation for core components using the Web Ontology Language (OWL) [183], to leverage benefits of Semantic Web Technologies. First, the essential core component concepts as defined in the Core Component Technical Specification (CCTS) are represented using OWL. Second, core components and business information entities are described using OWL to form a common document model. This common document model may be used to map arbitrary business document standards to and from the core component representation. Compared to other mapping approaches, the Web Ontology Language representation for core components allows the use of semantic technologies such as reasoners and ontological mappings facilitating the standard mapping process.

Problem 3: From conceptual business document models to deployment artifacts

As shown on the left hand side of Figure 1.3, core components are defined in a top-down manner on a conceptual level. Using the UML and DSL-based reference implementations provided in this thesis, conceptual core component models may be easily communicated between business document modelers. Furthermore, conceptual core component models provide a formalized representation of the core component meta-model, allowing for instance the validation of core component models. However, for the definition of business service interfaces in a service oriented environment, XML Schema representations of core component models are needed. The XML Schema definitions may be imported into Web Service interfaces (e.g., WSDL) and unambiguously define which type of XML instances a certain interface accepts. Thus, appropriate derivation mechanisms must be found, allowing the generation of XML Schema artifacts from conceptual core component models.

1.4 Contributions of this thesis

In this thesis we provide a method for an unambiguous mapping between model based core component technology and deployment artifacts for a SOA. Thereby, a conceptual UML-based core component model is taken as the basis for generating XML Schema artifacts for a SOA in a model-driven manner. Using the model-driven approach, we are able to leverage benefits for both – the business and the IT. Business document modelers may easily communicate conceptual core component models, representing SOA interfaces, between different stakeholders. IT departments may use the formalized core component models and derive deployment artifacts such as XML Schema for the configuration of SOA interfaces.

Contribution 3: Deriving XML Schema from conceptual core component models

Currently, core components are harmonized and standardized by UN/CEFACT and released in a Core Component Library (CCL) twice a year. The core component library represents the common semantic basis for all business information entities. Unfortunately, the library is based on a regular spread sheet and therefore automated tool integration is difficult. To fully leverage the benefits of core components, a storage and retrieval facility provided by a registry is needed.

Problem 4: Missing specification for a core component registry

In this thesis we provide a meta-model for a core component registry, based on the Electronic Business XML (ebXML) registry specification [119]. The meta-model is the first step towards a successful implementation of a registry and defines which metadata and content may be stored in the registry and how the different artifacts are related to each other. Furthermore, we exemplarily show how business information entity artifacts may be mapped to the registry. Additionally, we introduce a registry federation concept for the core component registry, enabling interoperability on different levels such as international, national, and industry specific levels.

Contribution 4: A core component registry model based on ebRIM

Top-down business document standards, such as the core components initiative, aim at the inclusion of as many different stakeholder requirements as possible. This results in a standard which essentially is a superset of all requirements of the involved stakeholders. In contrast, bottom-up standards only include the most important requirements on which the different stakeholders agree. The result is a stream-lined core standard definition, which may be incorporated in software in an easier way than complex top-down standards.

Problem 5: Missing mechanisms for domain-specific extensions of bottom-up standard definitions

1 Introduction

However, the core standard definition may not cope with domain-specific requirements, some of the involved stakeholders may demand. Therefore, the core standard must provide a set of well defined extensions points, allowing domain- or user-specific amendments to the core standard definitions. Extensions must be defined in such a way that they do not alter the core standard, because this would violate the principle of guaranteeing interoperability at the core level at any time. Thus, it is necessary to examine different extension mechanisms as provided by the XML Schema specification and assess their applicability for the definition of bottom-up standard extensions.

Contribution 5: Study on domain-specific extension mechanisms for bottom-up standard definitions

In this thesis we examine extension approaches for the bottom-up business document standard *ebInterface*, a standard for electronic invoicing, led by the Austrian Federal Economic Chamber. Based on the XML definition of ebInterface, we examine the different XML Schema extension mechanisms and assess their applicability for the definition of bottom-up extension points according to four criteria: (i) core schema integrity (ii) core schema compatibility (iii) extension control and (iv) guarantee of validity of extensions.

Problem 6: Missing link between bottom-up standards and top-down standards

The core component standard, which is an integrative part of this thesis, may be used in a two-fold manner. In a forward engineering approach a new conceptual business document model, based on core components, is created. The resulting conceptual business document model may further be used to drive deployment artifacts for a SOA in a model-driven manner. However, in certain cases existing bottom-up standards may be mapped to a common core component model, serving as the interchange format between two or more different business document standards. Mapping mechanisms must ensure that the semantics of the standard which is going to be mapped and the semantics of the used core components are preserved correctly.

Contribution 6: Mapping heuristics from bottom-up to top-down document standards

For an unambiguous mapping from a bottom-up business document standard to a core component-based business document definition, mapping rules are necessary. UN/CEFACT already provides rules for mapping conceptual core component models to XML Schema artifacts in their Naming and Design Rules (NDR) [171]. Thus, if an XML-based bottom-up document standard is to be mapped to a conceptual core component model, the Naming and Design Rules of

UN/CEFACT may simply be inverted. However, the NDR cover only a small subset of all elements available in the XML Schema standard. Thus, in case any arbitrary XML Schema is mapped to a conceptual core component representation, additional mapping rules are necessary. In this thesis we examine mapping rules and mapping heuristics for advanced XML Schema concepts.

As already outlined, the successful implementation of inter-organizational business processes requires a two-fold agreement: (i) a common agreement on the exact information being exchanged between two business partners and (ii) an agreement on the exact exchange order of the business information. If the requirements for both are captured in an unambiguous and conceptual manner, the resulting business document and business process models may be used to derive artifacts for a service oriented architecture in a model-driven manner. Currently, approaches for the definition and derivation of deployment artifacts from business process and business document models exist in an isolated manner. Thus, no integrated approach covering both, the business process and the business information perspective, exists.

Problem 7:
Providing an integrative approach for the definition of a SOA

In this thesis we use UN/CEFACT's Modeling Methodology (UMM) [174], a UML-based methodology to uniquely capture requirements of inter-organizational business processes. We show how conceptual business document models, based on the UML Profile for Core Components and business choreography models, based on UMM, may be combined. The resulting conceptual model uniquely and unambiguously defines the requirements of the exchanged information and the information exchange itself. We exemplarily outline how the integrated business document/business process model is used to derive deployment artifacts for a SOA.

Contribution 7:
Service Engineering with UMM [174] and UPCC [172]

1.5 Methodological approach

In this thesis we employ a *conceptual* and *constructive* methodological approach for our research. Our objective is to develop methods and models for the unambiguous definition of inter-organizational business document requirements. Thereby, we go beyond state-of-the-art and provide implementations on a prototypical level.

1 Introduction

Research question

The research question, which this thesis aims to answer states as follows:

> How may we unambiguously capture the collaborative space in B2B interactions in regard to the exchanged information?

Following our central research question we aim to validate the following hypotheses in this thesis.

Hypothesis 1
Hypothesis 1. A comparison of different business document standards must be provided to allow decision makers in the field of business document modeling to decide upon the most relevant business document standard for a certain domain. Thereby, it must be evaluated whether it is possible to provide a survey based on business document clusters instead of single business document standards.

Hypothesis 2
Hypothesis 2. Since core component concepts are defined in an implementation neutral manner, we must provide pertinent representation mechanisms in order to allow for an easy integration into business document modeling tools. It must be evaluated, whether core components may be represented using the Unified Modeling Language (UML), Domain-Specific Languages (DSL), and the Web Ontology Language (OWL).

Hypothesis 3
Hypothesis 3. The current Core Component Library (CCL) is realized using regular spreadsheet files, thus obstructing seamless integration into core component modeling tools. To overcome this limitation it must be analyzed, whether we are able to adapt the electronic business XML (ebXML) registry specification to support storage and retrieval of core component related artifacts.

Hypothesis 4
Hypothesis 4. Bottom-up business document standards comprise a minimal subset of the most important requirements of all involved stakeholders. Domain-specific extensions are realized using dedicated extension points in the business documents. The different extension mechanisms of XML Schema must be evaluated and their applicability for the definition of domain-specific extensions must be evaluated.

Hypothesis 5
Hypothesis 5. In order to close the gap between top-down business document standards and bottom-up business document standards, a possible mapping of bottom-up business document models to a core component based top-down

business document model shall be evaluated. It must be verified, whether an unambiguous mapping without any loss of information is possible.

Hypothesis 6. Finally, it must be evaluated how UN/CEFACT's Modeling Methodology and UN/CEFACT's Core Components may be combined to unambiguously capture the business process and business document requirements in an inter-organizational business process.

Hypothesis 6

The technical feasibility of the work, presented in this thesis, has been validated using prototypical implementations. Furthermore, the conceptual modeling approaches, introduced in this thesis, are successfully used within UN/CEFACT for the unambiguous representation of core component artifacts. The future evaluation of our research results concentrates on additional real-world case studies.

Evaluation of this thesis

1.6 Structure of this thesis

This thesis is a result of several years of research in inter-organizational business document and business process standardization. The foundations of each of the different chapters of this thesis have been published at international conferences and in international journals. In this thesis we provide a consolidated summary of our various contributions. For a complete reference of all relevant publications please see the publication list at the end of this thesis. The Chapters of this thesis are organized in a self-contained manner. Thus, it is possible to read each Chapter without knowing the previous Chapters. However, since a certain knowledge of the domain is generally required, it is recommended to read Chapter by Chapter in an ascending order.

Chapter 2: Introducing of the accompanying example

The contributions, as outlined in the previous Section, all use the same accompanying example from the domain of European cross-border waste transport. In Chapter 2 we briefly introduce the basic concepts of the EUDIN (European Data Interchange for Waste Notification Systems) project, from which the accompanying example has been taken.

Chapter 3: Business document standard survey

In Chapter 3 we introduce our business document standard survey, which we conducted as part of this thesis. We show the basis business document standard clusters and explain the specifics of the different business document stan-

1 Introduction

dardization approaches such as top-down, bottom-up, hybrid-standardization, etc. Finally, we give an assessment aiding a business document modeler in choosing the right business document standard.

Chapter 4: Introduction to core components
Since core components are an integral part of this thesis, the basics of the Core Component Technical Specification (CCTS) [170] are explained in Chapter 4. In particular the complex naming principles of core components and business information entities are outlined in detail.

Chapter 5: UML Profile for Core Components
Chapter 5 outlines the UML Profile for Core Components (UPCC) [172]. We first introduce the theoretical foundations of the UPCC standard, which was developed as part of this thesis and has been submitted to UN/CEFACT for standardization. In a second step we introduce the different libraries of the UPCC; using an accompanying example from the waste management domain.

Chapter 6: DSL for Core Components
In Chapter 6 we introduce the Domain-Specific Language (DSL) for Core Components and specifically elaborate on the technical considerations which led to the development of the DSL. Furthermore, we compare the advantages and disadvantages of Domain-Specific Languages and the Unified Modeling Language (UML) for core component modeling.

Chapter 7: Web Ontology Language for Core Components
A Web Ontology Language representation for Core Components is introduced in Chapter 7. We show how to build our global reference ontology based on the concepts from the Core Components Technical Specification (CCTS). Based on this global reference ontology, a common business document model is provided. Consequently, we show how to map two exemplary business document standards to the common document model.

Chapter 8: Deriving XML from Core Components
Chapter 8 shows how a conceptual core component model, based on UML, may be used to derive XML Schema artifacts for a service oriented architecture in a model-driven manner. We use the UML model from Chapter 5 to outline the derivation of XML according to the Naming and Design Rules (NDR) [171] of UN/CEFACT.

Chapter 9: Registry for Core Components
A meta-model for a core component compliant registry is introduced in Chapter 9. We first introduce a registry model, based on the Electronic Business XML (ebXML) registry specification [119] and consequently show how to map business information entity artifacts to the registry model.

1.6 Structure of this thesis

Finally, we discuss how registry federation concepts may leverage interoperability benefits at different levels.

In Chapter 10 we discuss the necessity to provide extension points to bottom-up standard definitions. We examine different built-in extension mechanisms of the XML Schema specification and assess their applicability to define domain-specific amendments to a bottom-up standard definition. We provide an example using the Austrian e-Invoice standard *ebInterface*.

Chapter 10: Bottom-up standard extensions

If bottom-up standards are mapped to a top-down conceptual core component model, a set of mapping issues arise. In Chapter 11 we examine basic and advanced mapping mechanisms between bottom-up and top-down standards. Where no clear mapping may be provided, we examine mapping heuristics.

Chapter 11: Mapping bottom-up to top-down standards

In Chapter 12 we introduce UN/CEFACT's Modeling Methodology (UMM), a business process based approach for the unambiguous definition of inter-organizational process choreographies. We show how the UML Profile for Core Components (UPCC) and UMM may be combined to provide an integrated model-driven approach for the definition of SOA deployment artifacts.

Chapter 12: Business document models and business process models

An overview of related work in the domain of inter-organizational business documents and a comparison to the work presented in this thesis is given in Chapter 13. For each contribution of this thesis a dedicated related work section is provided.

Chapter 13: Related work

Finally, we conclude the thesis in Chapter 14 by providing concluding remarks and an overview of open research issues, which have not been targeted by this thesis.

Chapter 14: Conclusion and open issues

2 Introduction of the example: Waste Transport

The examples, presented in this thesis, are motivated using a real world example from the waste management domain in the European Union. With the introduction of the European Union (EU), free movement of persons, goods, and services without restrictive border controls was established in Europe. However, the free transport of particular goods is still restricted within the European Union. This includes hazardous materials such as chemical products, products from the defense industry, but also everyday materials such as simple waste. If cross-border waste transports are conducted in the EU, mandatory transport documents must be exchanged between the participating parties, including the export and import authorities of the respective countries.

Accompanying waste management example

Today, the exchange of these transport documents is done in a paper-based manner. This results in thousands of different paper documents being exchanged between the different business partners. If a business partner receives a paper-based document, it is manually processed by a human and the information is entered in an IT system. Consequently, if a new document is sent to another business partner, the necessary paper-based form is generated out of the IT system. Again the recipient of the paper form manually processes the received information and so on. This media-disruptive process is error-prone and inefficient. Additionally, efficient monitoring of the different waste transports by the competent authorities in the export, transit, and import countries is not possible.

Moving beyond manual document processing

In 2000 Belgium and the Netherlands started a project called EUDIN (European Data Interchange for Waste Notification Systems), aiming to replace the current paper-based solution with an efficient EDI solution. In 2001 Germany and Austria joined the project consortium. EUDIN uses two key technologies: UN/CEFACT's Modeling Method-

UN/CEFACT's Core Components and UN/CEFACT's Modeling Methodology in action

2 Introduction of the example: Waste Transport

ology [174] for the definition of the process choreography between the participating business partners and UN/CEFACT's Core Components [170] for the definition of the exchanged business documents.

2.1 EUDIN at a glance

The EUDIN initiative   Currently four of twenty-seven EU-member country states, namely Belgium, The Netherlands, Germany, and Austria, participate in the EUDIN initiative. The overall goal is to develop a standardized interface for the exchange of data between European member states meeting the requirements of the European Waste Shipment Regulation 259/93 EC. Thus, the EUDIN initiative may be seen as a first step towards the introduction of a standardized European interface for the transmission of waste and environmental related data between European countries.

Simplified and adapted EUDIN model   According to the regulation 259/93 EC, a waste transporter who plans to ship waste to, from, or through a member country of the European Union must notify the waste transport to the competent authorities of the export, transit, and import countries. Figure 2.1 gives an overview of a reference waste transport between two EU member countries. An exporter announces the waste transport to the export authority. The export authority announces the transport of waste to the import authority of the import country, which in turn informs the importer. In case the waste transport goes through transit countries, additional intermediary export and import authorities of the respective transit countries are added to the process. In this thesis we use a simplified and adapted EUDIN model as accompanying example. As outlined in Figure 2.1 we limit our discussion to four actors and two business transactions between the different actors.

Figure 2.1 EUDIN example use case

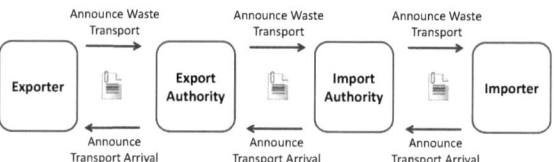

2.1 EUDIN at a glance

After the waste transport has been successfully announced and approved by the different authorities, the actual transport of waste takes place. As soon as the waste arrives at its target destination, the information flow goes backward to the exporter, i.e., the arrival of the transport is announced from the importer back to the exporter through the import authorities and the export authorities.

The goal of EUDIN is to realize the entire waste transport announcement process in an electronic manner, as described in Figure 2.1. The exchange of digital notification documents is achieved between the different participating partners in an automated manner and through standardized interfaces with as little human intervention as possible. Thereby, the different waste transporters are able to announce their various transports over the Internet. The competent authorities, involved in the transport process, are provided with the opportunity to register the different notifications in their back-office systems in an automated manner. Thus, waste transports may be approved or rejected electronically and other authorities as well as exporter and importer are informed automatically.

Realizing the waste transport process in an electronic manner requires an agreement on the exchanged information between the different stakeholders. Before the introduction of an electronic data interchange, regular paper forms were exchanged among stakeholders. Figure 2.2 gives an overview of a waste transport form as it is still in use today. The challenge for the EUDIN project was to find an equivalent electronic representation for the old fashioned paper-based form as shown in Figure 2.2. The EUDIN project consortium decided to build the business document specification on UN/CEFACT's Core Components Technical Specification (CCTS) [170]. *Necessity for a common business information definition*

It soon became evident that a pure data-centric standardization approach is not sufficient for a successful realization of the EUDIN project goals. EUDIN requires a process-centric approach, where apart from the exchanged business document information, the inter-organizational processes between the different partners are unambiguously defined as well. Thus, the EUDIN scenario requires that all involved business partners agree on a common process choreography. A process choreography describes the exact exchange or- *Necessity for a common process choreography*

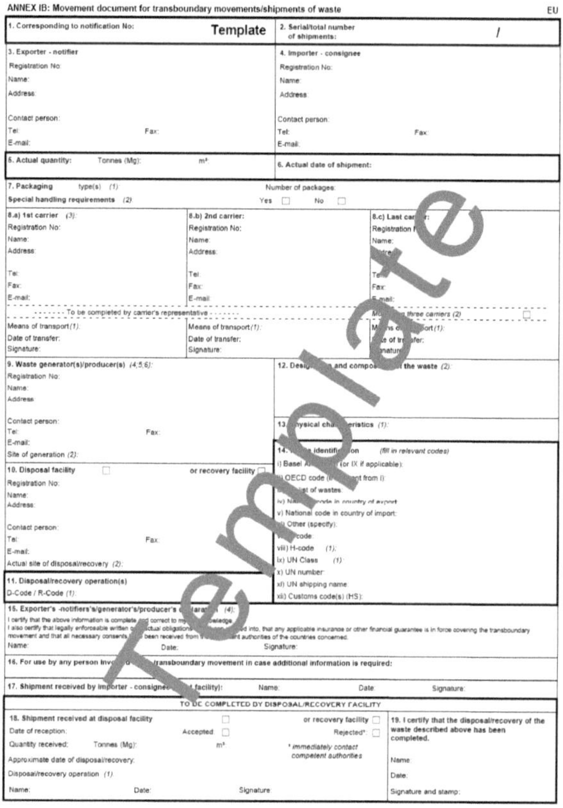

Figure 2.2
EUDIN paper form

der of different business documents in a precise and unambiguous manner, e.g., that a waste transport must first be announced before a waste transport arrival may be communicated. According to a process choreography, the different interfaces of each business partner may be configured.

Global vs. local choreographies

However, if each business partner describes his own process choreography in isolation, the resulting interface definitions are unlikely to match. Thus, the EUDIN project aims at the definition of a *global business process choreography*, where the exact exchange order of business documents between partners is described from a global perspective. Using the commonly agreed upon *global business process choreography*, each involved business partner may derive his *local business process choreographies* to configure the respective

IT systems. Thereby, a *local business process choreography* comprises only those processes of a company, which are visible to the outside world, and abstracts from any company internal details. Since the *local business process choreographies* of each business partner are derived from the commonly agreed *global business process choreography*, it is guaranteed that they are complementary to each other.

The benefits delivered by the EUDIN initiative are manifold and both, the participating administrations as well as the participating business partners, benefit from the electronic waste transport announcements.

The participating administrative entities such as the export authorities and the import authorities will benefit from streamlined and faster administration processes. Since the paper-based notification and announcement processes are replaced by automated electronic processes, several process enhancements will be possible. Apart from apparent error and cost reductions, additional positive side effects occur. Since the electronic processes are implemented from the exporter to the importer along the entire supply chain, a full control over the process and traceability of waste announcements is possible. Furthermore, the increased process transparency enables better fraud control for the authorities.

Streamlined administration processes

Similarly, enterprises involved in the waste transport supply chain also benefit from the newly introduced electronic process. Enterprises may abandon error prone paper-based processes and integrate the new inter-organizational waste transport announcement process directly in their back-office IT systems. Thus, waste transport announcements may be communicated to the necessary authorities in a faster and more reliable manner. Consequently, the necessary waste transport approvals or waste transport rejections are issued faster by the respective authorities.

Streamlined inter-organizational processes

2.2 Waste management example in this thesis

In this thesis we take the waste management scenario of the EUDIN project as an accompanying example for our investigation of business document definition approaches in a service oriented environment. For demonstration purposes we make two facilitating assumptions (i) we do not consider

Simplified waste management example

2 Introduction of the example: Waste Transport

transit countries for the process choreography part – thus, export authorities and import authorities communicate directly; (ii) our example does not consider the information flow related to the disposal of waste in the target country.

In regard to the exchanged business document information, we assume a waste movement form, used to announce a waste transport, as shown in Figure 2.3. A waste movement form consists of several waste consignments. For each waste consignment multiple consignment items are defined. Each consignment item has a dispatch and delivery party as well as shipping marks. Additionally, import, export, and transit countries are associated with a waste consignment item. Note that the business document information as shown in Figure 2.3 has been arbitrarily chosen to better visualize core component concepts in this thesis and is not used in real world EUDIN processes.

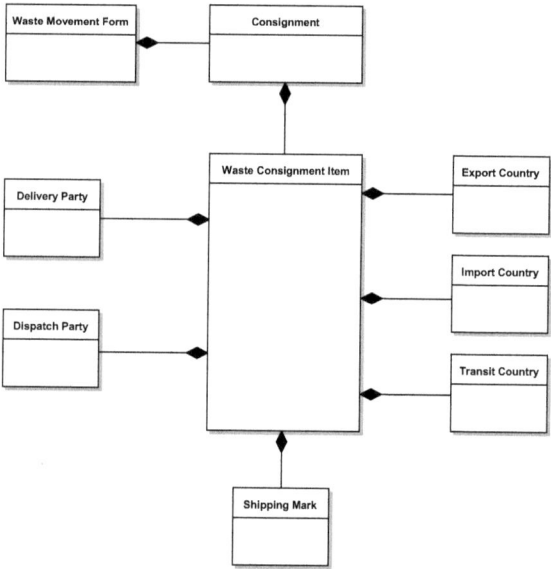

Figure 2.3
EUDIN – example waste movement form

3 An overview of business document standards

If two business partners want to engage in an automated business interaction, they first agree on a common exchange format. Instead of choosing a proprietary document format, the business partners may choose an already standardized business document format for the exchange of business information. In the last 25+ years a multitude of different business document standards have been developed. Each of the different standards has its strengths and weaknesses and is either better or worse suited for a certain application domain or scenario. Due to the multitude of available standards no general survey, covering all of the available standards, may be provided. To overcome this limitation we provide a new approach for a business document standard survey, based on standard clusters. Thereby, a standard cluster aggregates different business document standards of a certain type.

Today hundreds of different business document standards exist

The remainder of this Chapter is structured as follows: Section 3.1 introduces the main drivers behind business document standardization and Section 3.2 introduces the business document standard clusters, together with a representative example from each cluster. Section 3.3 provides an evaluation of each standard cluster in regard to technical implementation, business messaging conformance, as well as target groups and acceptance criteria. Finally, Section 3.4 concludes the Chapter with a final assessment.

3.1 Introduction

The importance of compatibility has already been recognized long before the advent of computer systems and networks. In physical networks such as railroads, telephone systems, and electronic distribution networks compatibility is a critical success factor. According to [71] it was Thomas

Standards are driven by different objectives

3 An overview of business document standards

Edison's ability to think in terms of whole systems rather than in terms of single generators, which led to his success in the electricity business. Similarly, successful electronic business transactions between arbitrary business partners may only be established if standardized and interoperable system interfaces are provided. According to Feng [35] we refer to *standardization* as *the process by which explicit specifications for the form or function of a particular technology are created*. These specifications, as a result, are called *standards*. Feng identifies five different objectives for the development of standards: (1) uniformity in production, (2) compatibility between technologies, (3) objectivity in measurement, (4) standards as a means of justice, and (5) as a form of hegemony.

Compatibility as the main driver for business document standardization

In particular in the field of electronic business the different standardization approaches aim at facilitating the electronic interchange of business data between heterogeneous systems and platforms. Thus, we identify the compatibility between technologies as the main driver for the development of business document standards. A multitude of different business document standards has been developed over time with the goal to achieve compatibility between technologies. In the following we give an overview of current state-of-the-art in electronic business document standards and provide a classification matrix using predefined standard clusters. The classification matrix helps an IT analyst to decide upon the applicability of a given business document standard in certain application scenarios. We assess each standard cluster in regard to business messaging compatibility, technology features, potential user groups, and acceptance per standard.

3.2 Business document standard clusters

Delimiter-based vs. markup-based business document standards

A standard cluster represents a family of related business document standards, sharing certain characteristics. As a starting point, Figure 3.1 gives a non-exhaustive overview of the most important standard definitions, together with a timescale.

We identify two major groups of business document standards: delimiter-based standards and markup-based stan-

3.2 Business document standard clusters

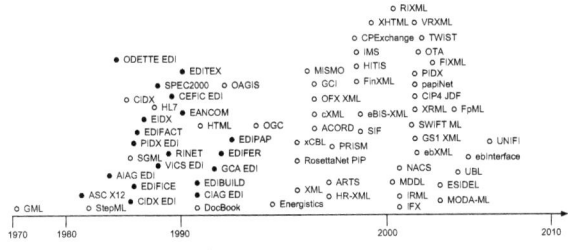

Figure 3.1
Overview of different standards

dards. Delimiter-based approaches use standard ASCII characters to separate different data elements, segments, and messages. The two most important delimiter-based standard definitions are UN/EDIFACT [163] and ANSI X12 [6]. Delimiter-based standards were particularly developed in the eighties and early nineties of the last century, as outlined by the cloud of black dots on the left hand side of Figure 3.1. Currently, several EDIFACT dialects for specific industries exist on the market, e.g., EDIBUILD [28] for the construction industry or ODETTE EDI [130] for the automotive industry. A comprehensive introduction to EDIFACT standards is provided by [12] and [61].

An important development step for the domain of business document standardization was the introduction of IBM's Generalized Markup Language (GML) [72], developed in the early 1970s. Later, GML was the basis for the development of the Standard Generalized Markup Language (SGML) [77], which was the foundation for two other prominent markup languages – Hypertext Markup Language (HTML) and eXtensible Markup Language (XML). A markup language-based document distinguishes between two different information sets: *markup* and *content*. With the application of simple syntactic rules, the markup may be distinguished from the actual content. In particular the development of XML in the late 1990s revolutionized the way how business document standards were developed. From this point on, almost all of the known business document definitions were based on XML. In Figure 3.1 markup-based document standards are denoted by white dots. The strong transition of delimiter-based standards to markup-based standards underlines the significance of XML for business document standardization. White dots in the cloud of black

The introduction of XML brought several changes to business document standardization

3 An overview of business document standards

dots on the left hand side of Figure 3.1 are either standards based on general markup languages, e.g., SGML, or standards which were initially defined in a delimiter-based manner, but were later transferred to an XML-based syntax, e.g., HL7 (Health Level Seven) [49] or CIDX (Chemical Industry Data Exchange Standard) [19].

Introducing standard clusters

In the following we abstract from single standard definitions and use standard clusters. Thereby, each standard cluster aggregates business document standards, sharing certain characteristics. As shown in Table 3.1, we identify eight standard clusters along with a representative standard example. Each standard cluster has been chosen under the prerequisite that (i) it provides a sufficient size, justifying an examination and (ii) the cluster and its members provide an adequate distance to the other clusters.

Table 3.1 Identified Standard clusters

(1)	Top-down standard approaches	UN/EDIFACT [163]
(2)	Bottom-up standard definitions	ebInterface [8]
(3)	Hybrid approaches	Universal Business Language (UBL) [121]
(4)	Early mark-up adopters	Open Applications Group Integration Specification (OAGIS) [131]
(5)	Integrated approaches	Electronic Business XML (ebXML) [124]
(6)	Transitioned approaches	Health Level Seven (HL7) [49]
(7)	Implementation neutral approaches	Core Component Technical Specification (CCTS) [170]
(8)	Converging approaches	Universal Financial Industry Message Scheme (UNIFI) [79]

Each of the clusters represents a family of related business document standards, categorized according to their technical features. Note that business document standards, due to their diversity, may be included in several clusters at the same time. In the following, the different clusters together with an accompanying example are outlined. For each cluster we introduce the specific advantages and disadvantages.

3.2.1 Top-Down standardization approaches

Inclusion of as many requirements as possible

Top-down standardization approaches are mostly driven by a single entity or organization, supervising the standard – we refer to such an organization as standardization body. Stakeholders of the standard such as interest groups, businesses, as well as individuals submit their requirements to

3.2 Business document standard clusters

the standardization body, which includes them into the standard definition. The goal of a top-down approach is to meet as many stakeholder requirements as possible by including all necessary elements. Figure 3.2 gives an overview of a top-down standardization approach. Thereby, the standardization body consolidates the different requirements and eventually releases a core standard definition. Mathematically, such a standard definition results in a union of different requirement sets. Usually, a top-down standardization approach leads to a rather complex standard definition, since a lot of different elements are included. Nevertheless, a top-down approach provides a maximum of flexibility for different application domains. In most cases the different requirements are consolidated at meetings, which the standardization bodies organize on a regular basis. New releases or updates to the standard definitions are typically made available to the public after such meetings.

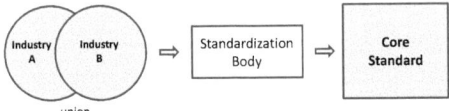

Figure 3.2
Top-down standardization

Since top-down standards represent a union of different requirements of all involved stakeholders, businesses may easily find necessary elements in the standard definition. In case a certain element is missing, standardization organizations provide predefined procedures for the inclusion of new elements. These requests are often referred to as standard maintenance requests (SMR) or data maintenance requests (DMR), and they often differ between standardization organizations. One elementary goal of every standardization effort is to reach a maximum of acceptance in potential user communities. Due to their generic nature, top-down standardization efforts are likely to achieve a high acceptance in their respective user communities.

In general, top-down approaches contain a multitude of optional elements, making their integration into existing applications difficult. A recipient of a top-down business document instance is not required to be able to process all of the specified elements in the business document standard. In most scenarios only a small subset of the provided features of a top-down standard is needed for actual implemen-

Top-Down standards are extensive and complex

tation. Message implementation guides (MIG) have been introduced to overcome the limitation of too complex top-down standards. A MIG restricts the amount of allowed elements in a standard definition to a subset of elements, agreed upon by a certain user group. Figure 3.3 gives on overview of the message implementation guide concept.

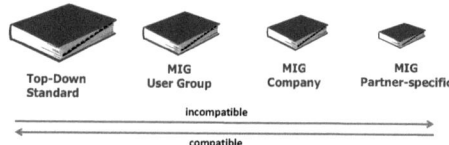

Figure 3.3
Message implementation guide

MIGs are introduced on several levels of granularity, such as user groups or even on a partner-specific basis. Message implementation guides may potentially undermine the overall concept of top-down standards. If too many MIGs are introduced, incompatibilities between MIG restricted documents may arise. However, every MIG restricted document is compatible to the original document it is based on. The MIG on the right hand side of Figure 3.3 restricts the top-down standard the most and thus provides the least level of interoperability. Different MIGs on the same level (e.g., MIG Company in Figure 3.3) are in most cases incompatible. Additionally, requirements reflected in top-down standards may change on a regular basis, since a multitude of different stakeholders is involved. Updates to the standard, reflecting these changes, have to be released regularly. For a business using a top-down standard, the different standard versions impose an additional obstacle towards seamless interoperability.

Examples for top-down standards

Currently, a multitude of different top-down standardization approaches exists on the market. Probably the most commonly known approach is the UN/EDIFACT standard [163], developed and maintained by the United Nations Centre for Trade Facilitation and Electronic Business (UN/CEFACT). The standard itself is one of the oldest in use in different industries, but still has the highest level of acceptance. New updates for the standard are released twice a year and referred to as UN/EDIFACT directories. Another well known top-down implementation is ANSI ASC X12 [6], pre-dominant mainly on the North American market.

3.2 Business document standard clusters

UN/EDIFACT As an example for a top-down standard we introduce UN/EDIFACT [163]. The United Nations Electronic Data Interchange for Administration, Commerce, and Transport (UN/EDIFACT) standard is developed by the United Nations and its member countries. The standard itself consists of syntax rules, used to structure data (referred to as EDIFACT), and standard messages, stored in directories allowing cross-country and cross-industry data exchanges (referred to as UN/EDIFACT directories). Generally, the standard itself is referenced by the term UN/EDIFACT. Note that the syntax rules of EDIFACT are standardized by the ISO standard 9735.

UN/EDIFACT is one of the most prominent top-down standards

Top-down standards provide a generic concept for the representation of business documents. Thus, a business document modeler may easily find the required business messages and elements in the standard definition. Furthermore, top-down standards such as UN/EDIFACT are well accepted and have been tested and evaluated thoroughly during the last 25+ years of application.

Advantages

However, top-down definitions are complex and business service interfaces, capable of processing top-down business document messages, are costly to implement. A business service interface is defined as a piece of software processing incoming business document messages and passing the required information to the internal software of a company. A business service interface is typically responsible for validation of sequence, grammar, and syntax of an incoming business document. In most cases only big players can afford to establish such business service interfaces. Small and medium-sized enterprises often lack the software prerequisites to implement the pertinent interfaces and are therefore not able to participate in B2B interactions using top-down standards.

Shortcomings

We conclude that in general all of the different delimiter-based standard definitions are following a top-down principle (ANSI X12 [6], UN/EDIFACT [163], etc.). The core components approach, which is central to this thesis and will be introduced in Chapter 4, also follows a top-down approach.

Although they are very powerful and generic, top-down standards may require a considerable effort for the realization of a compliant business service interface. In our study

From top-down to bottom-up standards

3 An overview of business document standards

we observed an upcoming trend in recent years towards the use of bottom-up standard definitions.

3.2.2 Bottom-up standard approaches

Focus on the most important requirements

In contrast to a top-down approach, which comprises a superset of the requirements of all stakeholders, a bottom-up standard focuses on the definition of a core set of elements. Bottom-up standards are defined by the inclusion of the most important elements, which may be used by the involved business partners. Thus, only a few data elements in a bottom-up standard are defined as being optional. Additionally, no agreement on a subset of the bottom-up standard is needed, prior to an automated business document exchanged. The recipient of a bottom-up standard message must in any case be able to understand all elements of the core definition (even the optional ones). This is a major difference compared to top-down standard definitions.

Focusing on a core set of requirements

Figure 3.4 gives an overview of the core idea of a bottom-up standardization approach. Different stakeholders agree on a core set of requirements, which are then reflected in a core standard definition. Mathematically, such a standard definition results in an intersection of different sets. Bottom-up business document standards are conciser than top-down approaches. However, not all needs of the different stakeholders will be met by the bottom-up standard definition, which only covers a core set of all requirements. Certain industries might require additional elements, necessary for a successful implementation of an electronic business transaction. Thereby, extension mechanisms for the standard definition are used to allow domain-specific standard extensions. As shown on the right hand side of Figure 3.4, extensions are plugged into the core standard definition, thus allowing domain-specific amendments. The idea of an extension is to add domain-specific amendments to the standard, without altering the core definition. We further investigate this issue in Chapter 10 of this thesis.

Figure 3.4 Bottom-up standardization

3.2 Business document standard clusters

A bottom-up approach has several advantages in comparison to a top-down approach. The restriction of defining a core set of elements, reflecting the most important requirements of all participating parties, results in a lean and precise standard definition. In case domain-specific requirements have to be reflected in the standard, extension mechanisms may bridge the gap. Even if both parties are using different extension mechanisms (e.g., Party A uses a telecom specific extension and Party B a semi-conductor specific extension), interoperability on the core level is always given. Note that domain-specific extensions are maintained by the standardization body as well, thus avoiding an uncontrolled growth of standard extensions.

Advantages of bottom-up standards

One of the major challenges of bottom-up standards is to define what to include in the core standard definition and what to omit. Essentially, finding an agreement on the elements to be included in the core definition often results in long discussions between the involved stakeholders. Often no agreement may be found and several stakeholders and their requirements are left unsatisfied. Even though additional requirements may be reflected using the extension mechanism, the definition of the extensions is a technical challenge yet to be solved. In general, bottom-up business document standard definitions are not as common as top-down definition approaches.

What to include in the standard definition and what to omit?

Among the many different available bottom-up standard definitions, we examined the ebInterface standard [8], an unambiguous e-Invoicing standard for the Austrian market. The goal of ebInterface is the definition of a core standard, including the most important elements for electronic invoices. An agreement on the standard was made by twelve COTS (commercial-of-the-shelf-software) vendors under the supervision of the Austrian Federal Economic Chamber. Another example for a bottom-up approach is the electronic payment standard (EPS) [32] [42], which is used as a simple and secure payment method. The basis for this standard is formed by the Electronic Payment Initiator standard (ePI) [33], specified by the European Committee for Banking Standards in 2003. Note that EPS comprises only those elements needed for national transactions, and thus uses a subset of ePI.

Examples for bottom-up standards

3 An overview of business document standards

Introducing the Austrian e-Invoice bottom-up standard ebInterface

ebInterface   As an example for a bottom-up standard we introduce ebInterface, an XML-based standard for electronic invoices. The ebInterface standard resulted out of a joint effort started by AustriaPRO, which is an association affiliated with the Austrian Federal Economic Chamber. Several Austrian ERP vendors and other stakeholders agreed upon a common electronic invoice standard, consisting of commonly used invoice elements in Austria.

Advantages   As a bottom-up approach ebInterface is less overloaded and ambiguous than top-down approaches. Due to the lean design of ebInterface, ERP vendors may implement interfaces for the import and export of ebInterface compliant messages in their software. Thus, in particular small and medium-sized enterprises, which heavily depend on COTS solutions, are the major target group of the ebInterface standard. Nevertheless, large enterprises may also employ bottom-up standard definitions, in particular for business interactions with small and medium-sized companies.

Shortcomings   The ebInterface standard covers only a rudimentary set of elements and thus needs to provide extension mechanisms to support additional use cases as well. Currently, the standard contains a custom section, where any user-specific content may be added. Thereby, it is entirely up to the business document modeler to decide which elements are included in the custom section. The loose extension specification leads to a multitude of incompatible user-specific amendments. Furthermore, important aspects such as core schema integrity and compatibility as well as a central control of extensions may not be ensured. Consequently, current research focuses on the definition of well defined extensions points to overcome uncontrolled growth of user-specific standard amendments. In Chapter 10 of this thesis we evaluate extension mechanism for bottom-up standards using the ebInterface standard as accompanying example.

Bottom-up standards are in particular useful for smaller companies, since they require significantly less implementation effort than top-down approaches. In general, bottom-up approaches are a rather new concept and thus not so many standards are available at the moment.

3.2.3 Hybrid standardization approaches

Hybrid standardization approaches have been developed to overcome the limitations of top-down and bottom-up standards and to unite the advantages of both worlds. On the one hand, a hybrid standard tries to include as many requirements as possible, thus aiming at a union of different industry needs. On the other hand, a hybrid approach provides extension mechanisms to integrate additional elements, originally not reflected in the standard (cf. extensions on the right hand side of Figure 3.5). Thus, hybrid approaches combine a best-of-breed of both worlds.

Merging best-of-breed of both worlds

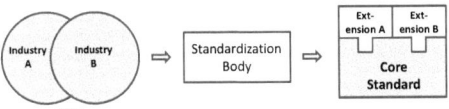

Figure 3.5 Hybrid standardization

Due to the inclusion of different requirements, hybrid standards are generic, thus meeting the needs of a variety of business document modelers. Even if a required element is not reflected in the standard, the extension mechanism may be used to include the missing artifact.

However, simply combining top-down and bottom-up approaches eventually does not result in a superior standard, but is accompanied by a set of shortcomings as well. Most hybrid approaches do not have a standardized way to define extension points, such as bottom-up approaches, but leave it up to the document modeler what to additionally include in the document. Such an openness may lead to numerous, incompatible, and most likely redundant document extensions. Nevertheless, standardized extension mechanisms, as used in bottom-up standards, may be applied to hybrid standard definitions as well.

An example for a standard definition, combining top-down and bottom-up standardization elements, is the Universal Business Language (UBL) [121], developed by OASIS. Depending on the viewpoint, other standard definitions such as Health Level Seven (HL7) [49] and Human-Resources XML (HR-XML) [60] may also be accounted as being part of the hybrid standard family, since they are defined in a top-down manner, but provide additional extension mechanisms for domain-specific amendments.

Examples for hybrid standards

3 An overview of business document standards

Introducing the Universal Business Language (UBL)

Universal Business Language (UBL) In our survey we introduce UBL [121] as an example for a hybrid standard. UBL is a library of royalty-free standard electronic business documents based on XML. Currently, UBL consists of 31 different document types, pursuing a top-down definition approach, i.e., an inclusion of as many different requirements as possible. As Ken Holman pointed out in a mail to the UBL developers list [59], the current version of the UBL *purchase order* covers 830,338 different elements in context and 2,171,455 attributes when flattening the document structure and taking the combinatorial issues of qualified elements into account. Obviously, it is difficult to successfully implement standard definitions allowing such a multitude of elements. UBL also has an extension mechanism provided through an optional container element named *UBLExtensions*. Within this optional container any non-UBL data elements may be included, whereby it is entirely left to the business document modeler what to include in the optional container.

Advantages

The UBL standard specification has been based on the data definition approach from the Electronic Business XML (ebXML) [124] initiative, which is considered as a major benefit of the entire standardization initiative. UN/CEFACT (United Nations Center for Trade Facilitation and Electronic Business), one of the co-founders of the ebXML initiative, and the UBL technical committee from OASIS agreed on a common strategy where the UBL standard will eventually be integrated into UN/CEFACT's standard family. Thus, UBL provides a foundation of predefined elements, based on the UN/CEFACT specifications. Additionally, in case user-specific requirements have to be integrated into a UBL-based message, UBL's flexible extension mechanism may be used. Hence, UBL manages to overcome the often criticized shortcoming of top-down standards: lack of user-specific extensions.

Shortcomings

However, UBL has a set of shortcomings as well. First, the UBL initiative is very similar to UN/CEFACT's Core Component initiative. Thus, redundant work is performed and both initiatives are not very well aligned. Although UN/CEFACT and OASIS have agreed upon a cooperation during the UN/CEFACT Forum meeting in 2007, no significant steps towards an integration of UBL into UN/CEFACT

3.2 Business document standard clusters

have been performed by the end of 2009. Additionally, as already outlined in the introduction, UBL has a quite overloaded structure similar to top-down standards, thus obstructing integration in particular for SMEs.

For this standard cluster we conclude that hybrid business document standards provide a good compromise if a generic standard is required, while still allowing domain-specific amendments. Nevertheless, the implementation of interfaces for hybrid standards may cause considerable implementation effort.

3.2.4 Early mark-up adopters

As shown in Figure 3.1, the 1990ies brought a strong transition from delimiter-based standards to markup-based standard solutions. Of particular interest to our survey are early adopters of the mark-up technology – those who started to use XML for their business document standard definitions first. Since the early mark-up adopters were among the first to employ the newly created XML specification, we are going to examine what kind of leverage effect the early adoption had. As an example for an early mark-up adopter we introduce the Open Applications Group Integration Specification (OAGIS) [131], which is an effort to provide a canonical business language for information integration. Another initiative, which used XML in an early stage, was the XML Common Business Library (xCBL) [21]. Meanwhile, the initiative has been ceased and the xCBL efforts have been integrated into the Universal Business Language initiative. Furthermore, the Chemical Industry Data Exchange Standard (CIDX) [19] and the Health Level Seven (HL7) [49] initiative were among the first users of XML.

Examining the benefits of early XML adoption

OAGIS OAGIS is developed by the Open Applications Group (OAGi) and was inaugurated by several major companies, most of them in the IT sector. It was one of the first approaches using XML for defining business document standards. The main goal of the approach was an optimization of the integration of applications, both inside of a company and between different enterprises. This was achieved by crafting standards where necessary and by recommending standards where they already existed.

Introducing OAGIS

The pillars of OAGIS

Conceptually, the OAGIS standard includes five distinctive parts. As a reference for potential systems and applications using OAGIS, an architecture specification of OAGIS is provided. Furthermore, typical business software components are described. The communication patterns between different business partners are outlined using scenario diagrams. Additionally, the standard contains a list of application programming interfaces (API) of all components and a common data dictionary. According to the OAGIS standard, all participating applications communicate by sharing Business Object Documents (BOD).

Advantages One major advantage of the OAGIS standard is the variety of companies that are members of the OAGi. In fact, in some business sectors OAGIS has reached a high level of adoption. Since OAGIS was among the first markup language adopters, the standard has considerable popularity in certain industries. For example, in the automotive industry OAGIS has become an important business language, since it is used and promoted by many leading companies in this sector in the US.

Shortcomings Although OAGIS is very popular in certain sectors (such as the automotive industry), it is still not widely accepted in other business sectors. Thus, in the field of business document standardization an early appearance on the market does not necessarily lead to a high rate of adoption. Nevertheless, some benefits may be leveraged as the example of OAGIS in the automotive sector has shown. In regard to the implementation complexity of OAGIS, the integration of Business Object Documents (BOD) requires substantial efforts.

We conclude that whether XML has been adopted earlier or later by a standardization organization does not influence the general acceptance of a standard. In general, enterprises tend to utilize standards that best fit their needs and the needs of their business partners. This is done regardless of how long the standard has been on the market. However, being on the market for a longer time implies higher standard maturity. Higher maturity of a standard may positively influence the tendency towards adoption by an enterprise.

3.2.5 Integrated standardization approaches

One of the lessons learned from the EDIFACT initiatives was that finding an agreement on the exchanged data only, is not sufficient to establish automated electronic transactions between enterprises. Businesses must also agree on a common process choreography, before they are able to engage in automated business transactions. A process choreography comprises the exact order in which electronic business transactions are executed. We refer to standardization approaches covering both, the business process perspective and the business document perspective, as integrated approaches. The most promising approach was released in 2001 and named Electronic Business XML (ebXML) [120]. ebXML did not only consider the data perspective of an electronic business transaction, but also considered the process perspective, messaging issues, as well as storage and retrieval of process and document definition artifacts.

Going beyond simple data-centric standardization

Several other standardization efforts consider business processes as well. The Universal Business Language (UBL) [121] provides conceptual models outlining the potential application scenarios of the defined business documents. Similarly, the current version of the Financial product Markup Language (FpML) [39] contains a dedicated part for business process architecture. Other comparable efforts include RosettaNet [146], which is considered to follow a similar approach as ebXML in terms of its focus on providing an overall B2B infrastructure. However, RosettaNet's field of application is limited to the domain of computer electronics, electronic components, semiconductor manufacturing, and telecommunications. Furthermore, we already mentioned another integrated, but more lightweight approach – OAGIS. We conclude that the most promising approach remains the Electronic Business XML (ebXML) [120] standard.

Examples for integrated approaches

ebXML The ebXML initiative was a joint effort between the two standardization organizations UN/CEFACT and OASIS with the goal to overcome the known problem of traditional EDI standards such as EDIFACT. The decision was to define an integrated B2B framework, having a strong business process focus.

Electronic Business XML at a glance

Figure 3.6
ebXML architecture

As shown in Figure 3.6, the ebXML framework consists of five complementary components [120]: registry, messaging, collaboration protocol profiles and agreements, business process specifications, and core components (CC). The ebXML messaging (ebMS) builds upon SOAP and other Web Services standards to realize a secure and reliable messaging. An ebXML registry (ebRIM/ebRS) [119] is a central site, supporting the discovery of potential business partners. The registry is responsible for managing collaboration partner profiles, business process specifications, and core components. A collaboration protocol profile (CPP) comprises information about the capabilities of a certain business partner and references collaborative business processes that are supported by the given party – in which role and by which technical infrastructure. A collaboration protocol agreement (CPA) is basically an intersection of two collaboration protocol profiles, corresponding to an agreement between two business partners. In ebXML, the choreography of a collaborative business process is specified using the business process specification schema (BPSS). BPSS is an XML-based and machine-understandable format intended to be processed by message handlers supporting ebXML messaging. Finally, core components (CC) are used to specify the business information that is exchanged within a business collaboration. We further detail the concepts of core components in Chapter 4 of this thesis.

Advantages In a nutshell, the five pillars of ebXML aim at providing an overall B2B infrastructure. Unlike other B2B standards, focusing on business document types only, the framework also deals with aspects like commonly agreed collaborative business process models, business partner profiles, business partner discovery, messaging infrastructure, etc. One the one hand, this may be considered as a distinctive advan-

3.2 Business document standard clusters

tage of the ebXML framework compared to other approaches. On the other hand, the broad focus of ebXML requires a relatively high implementation effort. Thus, it was one of the goals – and also a critical success factor – of the ebXML initiative to gain broad support by tool vendors. It was envisioned that tool vendors provide commercial-of-the-shelf software (COTS) for ebXML, allowing also small and medium companies (SME) to buy affordable e-business solutions. Unfortunately, this vision has not turned into reality.
Until today, tool support for ebXML remains rather low, resulting in a general low acceptance of ebXML. A detailed overview of ebXML's history including a critical evaluation is given in [114].

Shortcomings

In general, we conclude that integrated approaches, due to their complexity and poor tool support, have a rather low acceptance in the industry. However, if they are realized in a successful manner, their mightiness goes beyond those approaches considering only business documents. Although extensive integrated approaches, covering several areas such as registry, messaging, collaboration profiles, etc. are still unsuccessful, a clear trend towards the unambiguous definition of business processes between enterprises may be observed. Chapter 12 of this thesis further elaborates on this trend and introduces UN/CEFACT's Modeling Methodology, a method to unambiguously capture inter-organizational business process requirements and business document requirements together in one UML model.

3.2.6 Transitioned standardization approaches

The introduction of XML was both, a salvation for the ones and a plague for the others. Standardization organizations quickly adapted the new markup language and started to implement their standard definitions based on XML. Existing delimiter-based standards either had to provide an XML equivalent for their standard or transition their entire standard definition to XML, to keep up with the pace of XML. Although several of the delimiter-based standards are well established and still in use today, others successfully transitioned their standard definitions to XML. We identify that the current architectural style of service oriented architectures (SOA) generally prefers XML-based standards, since

From delimiter-based standards to XML-based standards

they are easier to integrate in existing SOA concepts such as BPEL (Business Process Execution Language) [122]. However, companies which already have delimiter-based interfaces are reluctant to abandon their stable and tested interfaces. In addition, a service oriented architecture does not mandate how the payload of a service invocation or answer must be structured. In principle any business document representation format of choice may be transferred – including EDIFACT. Several standardization organizations provide their standard definitions in both formats – EDIFACT and XML – to support legacy implementations, while also providing a contemporary standard format. This standard duality imposes additional challenges on a standardization organization. On the one hand, they still have to provide updates for the EDIFACT definitions to support legacy implementations. On the other hand, new standard amendments have to be integrated in both formats – EDIFACT and XML – likewise. Additional maintenance effort is the result.

Examples for transitioned approaches An example for a transitioned approach is the Health Level Seven (HL7) [49] standard from the health care domain. HL7 is developed and maintained by a not-for-profit organization named Health Level Seven. Another prominent example for a transitioned standard is the Chemical Industry Data Exchange (CIDX) [19] standard. However, CIDX has already abandoned the delimiter-based syntax and focuses entirely on XML. We conclude that specialized standards, developed entirely either on XML or EDIFACT and focusing on certain industries and application domains, will prevail.

Introducing Health Level Seven **HL7** The first version of the HL7 standard, referred to as version 2, followed the paradigm of a delimiter-based approach to encode health care information. With the availability of XML it was desirable to utilize XML as the new format for information exchange. Therefore, an according XML representation of the delimiter-based HL7 standard, starting from version 2, was developed. Currently, two different formats (delimiter-based and XML-based), representing equivalent information, are available. The core of the new version 3 is the Reference Information Model (RIM),

3.2 Business document standard clusters

which serves as the basis from which all of HL7's information models for specific clinical situations are derived from.

Having the RIM of HL7 version at hand, a formal methodology is provided, allowing to model elements and messages in a precise manner. Furthermore, using the RIM as a source for deriving other information models allows keeping consistency.

Advantages

One consequence, as a result of the paradigm switch from a delimiter-based format (version 2) to a common information model (version 3), is the incompatibility of version 2 and version 3. If both approaches are to be supported by an application, additional implementation effort is necessary. With the transition of delimiter-based concepts to XML often flaws and overloaded structures in the standard were transformed to the new syntax as well. Oftentimes these obvious flaws were not omitted to ensure backward compatibility of standard definitions. Thus, XML-based solutions which started from scratch are in general conciser and leaner than transitioned approaches.

Shortcomings

We conclude that transitioned standardization approaches are facing additional maintenance effort, since they have to maintain two separate standard definitions in different representation formats. Whether a standard may entirely be transitioned to an XML representation strongly depends on the user community of the standard. Until delimiter-based systems are still around in the IT departments, legacy support will most likely be provided by the different standardization organizations. In the long-haul, transitioned standardization approaches will abandon the delimiter-based syntax and focus entirely on XML.

Additional maintenance effort

3.2.7 Implementation neutral standardization approaches

In principle all business document standard definitions are bound to a specific implementation syntax. As we have seen, in most cases this syntax is either some sort of delimiter-based format or involves markup to separate different elements. Even if the common syntax is in most cases XML, the underlying XML Schema of each standard is different and, thus, no standard is like the other. Since no common base for all of these standards is provided, incompatibilities are inevitable. In the particular case of business document

Abstracting from the implementation syntax

3 An overview of business document standards

Following the Open-edi through implementation neutral definitions

standardization, these incompatibilities occur on the semantic level as well as on the syntax level.

Implementation neutral standardization approaches aim at specifying a common document definition on a generic and conceptual level without considering any specific implementation syntax. Thereby, the common document definition provides a semantic basis on an implementation neutral level. With this approach implementation neutral definitions follow the concepts of the Open-edi reference model [78]. According to the Open-edi reference model a business transaction, where business documents are exchanged between business partners, is viewed from a two-fold perspective. The business operational view (BOV) abstracts from technical implementation details and focuses on business aspects of a transaction. In contrast, the functional service view (FSV) considers technical implementation details such as exchange formats. In a model driven approach artifacts from the business operational view may be used to derive artifacts for the functional service view such as XML Schema. We further detail these concepts in Chapter 8.

The advantages of such a model-driven approach are manifold. The conceptual model may be used to derive arbitrary implementation specific artifacts. Since all artifacts are derived from a single conceptual model, the different artifacts share a common semantic basis. Based on this semantic basis, mapping mechanisms between different standard definitions may be implemented in a reusable and scalable manner.

Examples for implementation neutral standards

One of the most important implementation neutral approaches for the standardization of exchanged business document information is the Core Components approach by UN/CEFACT [170]. Another implementation neutral standard definition approach is the Context Inspired Component Architecture (CICA) [7] developed by the American National Standards Institute (ANSI). CICA aims at defining a collection of reusable components, designed to fulfill cross-domain and cross-country business document requirements.

Core Components at a glance

CCTS As a representative example for this cluster we introduce the well known implementation neutral standardization approach named UN/CEFACT's Core Components

3.2 Business document standard clusters

Technical Specification (CCTS) [172]. Core components are reusable building blocks for assembling business documents. The standard distinguishes between two elementary concepts: core components and business information entities. First, a business document is defined on a context neutral and generic level with reusable building blocks – we refer to such building blocks as core components. Due to their context neutrality and generic nature, core components may be used in any given business scenario. Before a business document based on core components is used in a certain business scenario, the business document modeler tailors the different core components to the specific needs of the application domain. In this step, core components become business information entities. A business information entity is created from a core component by leaving out attributes, which are not necessary for the application domain. Note that no new attributes may be added to the business information entity. Thus, a business information is derived from a core component by restriction. Core component definitions as well as certain business information entity definitions are stored in a central library. We refer to this library as the *Core Component Library*.

Advantages

Since all business information entities are derived from predefined core components, interoperability is guaranteed, as long as the business information entities are derived from the same core component. Nevertheless, the major advantage of the core component approach is that the concepts are defined on an implementation neutral level. In principle any appropriate representation may be used to build core component compliant business document models. In this thesis three exemplary implementation formats for core components are introduced: A UML Profile (cf. Chapter 5), a Domain-Specific Language (cf. Chapter 6), and a representation format using Web Ontology Language (cf. Chapter 7).

Shortcomings

The shortcomings of the CCTS do not lie in the specification itself, but rather in the library concept which is used for core components. Since any business document definition must be based on a core component, the existence of the appropriate core component in a global library, maintained by UN/CEFACT, is a prerequisite. If a necessary core component is not available in the library, a core component user

3 An overview of business document standards

may submit a new proposal for inclusion of a core component to UN/CEFACT. A dedicated data harmonization group within UN/CEFACT ensures that no duplicate core component information is included in the core component library. The harmonization process, however, takes some time and a business partner might not want to wait for so long. To overcome this limitation, core component registries may not only be established on a global level, but on a country or industry specific level as well. Thus, if adherence to the global core component library is not desired, a country or industry specific core component library may be set up. For a detailed discussion on the necessary concepts of core component libraries see Chapter 9 of this thesis.

Core Components as the most advanced approach for the definition of business documents

Implementation neutral standard definitions are a promising approach towards achieving a common semantic data model on which different document definitions are based. Furthermore, the concept of business information entities helps to overcome the problem of overloaded top-down definitions. Only those elements are included in an industry specific message, which are really needed and adherence to the generic core component base is provided. We conclude that currently the approach pursued by UN/CEFACT's Core Components initiative is the maturest implementation neutral technology available.

3.2.8 Converging approaches

The multitude of redundant standard definitions requires a convergence to a single solution

In several industry domains such as the financial sector a multitude of different standards have been developed over the years. A lot of these standards cover the same problem domain and oftentimes concepts are defined in a redundant manner in different standard definitions. Thus, several industries started to converge their existing approaches towards a single standard definition. One obstacle of converging standards is that standards cannot be converged from one day to the other. Therefore, a convergence plan must be provided allowing for the coexistence of the different standards which have to be converged, at least in the initial phase. Nevertheless, in the long term all the different standard definitions under consideration in the given domain have to be converged to the newly introduced standard definition. We have already introduced a prominent example for a converging standard. ebXML [124] may be seen as a

3.2 Business document standard clusters

converging standardization approach (if not as *the* converging standardization approach), because it aimed at a cross-industry and cross-border standard consolidation. However, we already outlined that ebXML has several deficits in regard to its acceptance in the industry. A more successful example for a converging standardization approach is the Universal Financial Industry Message Scheme (UNIFI).

UNIFI The objective of the UNIFI [79] standardization committee was to enable communication interoperability among financial institutions, their market infrastructures as well as end-user communities. Within the financial sector a multitude of different and often overlapping standards have already been defined, e.g., Market Definition Language (MDDL) [155], Vendor Reporting Extensible Markup Language (VRXML) [116], Extensible Business Reporting Language (XBRL) [188], and Financial products Markup Language (FpML) [39], just to name a few.

Introducing the Universal Financial Industry Message Scheme

UNIFI aims at a convergence of these different initiatives into one standard in the long term. However, in the short term the different standards need to coexist due to legacy and regulatory reasons. Coexistence of different standards with UNIFI is enabled through a canonical message model, to which the different standard definitions may be mapped to. The canonical model serves as an intermediate format for mapping between different standards. Thus, UNIFI aims at long term convergence while facilitating short term coexistence.

The major advantage of the UNIFI initiative is the reduction of redundant business document standard definitions in the financial domain and the incorporation of distributed concepts into a single standard definition.

Advantages

Nevertheless, a converging standard such as UNIFI also has shortcomings as well. Several industry partners in the domain under consideration might not want to adopt the new single converging standard definition due to various reasons. Apart from criteria such as transition costs it is often stated that a new converged standard definition is simply not needed, because the old implementation is sufficient. Whereas this argument may be true for short-term considerations, an adoption of a converging standard provides strategic advantage in the long-term.

Shortcomings

3 An overview of business document standards

Our survey concludes that converging business document standardization initiatives are of particular importance, given the current abundance of business document standard definitions. Although convergence on a global level towards one single standard definition is still a challenge, there is great potential in industry specific convergence.

3.3 A standard comparison

Focusing on the five most important clusters The key results of our business document standard survey are shown in Table 3.2. We analyzed the identified standard clusters according to (i) business messaging compatibility, (ii) technology features, (iii) potential user groups, and (iv) acceptance. From the originally eight clusters we assess only five clusters, namely top-down approaches, bottom-up approaches, hybrid approaches, integrated approaches, and implementation neutral approaches. We do not further concentrate on early markup adopters, transitioned approaches, and converging approaches, since the standards in these clusters may be associated with one of the other clusters as well, e.g., HL7 is a transitioned standardization approach, but also counts as hybrid standardization approach.

In a first step we examined the *business messaging compatibility* for each standard cluster using four parameters: representation, semantics, business process support, and specified transport protocol.

Representation A business message must have an unambiguous representation format, defined by a syntax (built on a grammar) and a vocabulary. All identified clusters obviously meet this requirement.

Semantics Additionally, the semantics of different data elements and messages must be precisely defined, i.e., all parties must have the same interpretation of the exchanged information, expressed by the business message representation. In principle all standard clusters fulfill this criteria. However, in bottom-up standard definitions and hybrid standard definitions user-specific extensions may be defined. Typically, the agreement on the common semantics of these user-specific-extensions is out of reach of a standardization organization. Thus, bottom-up standards and hybrid standards only partially meet this requirement.

Business processes A business process defines the exact exchange order of

3.3 A standard comparison

	(1)	(2)	(3)	(5)	(7)
Business Messaging Compatibility					
Representation	+	+	+	+	+
Semantics	+	+/-	+/-	+	+
Business Process	-	-	-	+	-
Transport	-	-	-	+	-
Technology features					
Used Syntax	EDI/XML	XML	XML	XML	-
Release iterat.	> 1 p.a.	< 1 p.a.	< 1 p.a.	< 1 p.a.	< 1 p.a.
Implement. compl.	+	+/-	+/-	+/-	+
Delta bet. rel.	+/-	-	+	+/-	+
Backward compat.	-	+	-	-	+
Extensibility	-	+	+	+	+
Cpt. mod. avail.	+	+/-	+/-	+	+
Semant. unambg.	+	-	-	+	+
COTS support	-	+	-	-	-
Standard maturity	+	+/-	+	+	+
Community size	+	-	+	-	+
Adoption	+	+/-	+	-	+
Potential User Groups					
Small entpr	-	+	+/-	-	-
Med-siz. entpr.	-	+	+/-	-	+
Large entpr	+	+	+	+	+
Acceptance					
Indstr. accept.	+	+	+	+/-	+
National accept.	+	+	+	+/-	+
Global accept.	+	-	+	+/-	+

***Table 3.2**
Standard cluster comparison - (1) - top-down approach (2) - bottom-up approach (3) - hybrid approach (5) - integrated approach (7) - implementation neutral approach*

Legend: (+) Fully meets the criteria (+/-) Partly meets the criteria (-) Does not meet the criteria

business documents and ensures that appropriate responses and acknowledgments are sent. However, only integrated approaches such as ebXML [124], OAGIS [131], or RosettaNet [146] consider an integrative approach towards business document standardization, where business processes are considered as well. Thus, we conclude that all other standard clusters only consider the data definition perspective, but do not take business processes into account.

Transport   Furthermore, the participating parties in an electronic business transaction must agree on a transport protocol to interconnect their businesses. In the early days of EDI, Value Added Networks (VAN) were used to interchange business-to-business messages due to the absence of the Internet. With the emergence of the Internet the concept of VANs partly vanished and related technologies such as HTTP (Hypertext Transfer Protocol) and SOAP (Simple Object Access Protocol) became popular for document exchange. However, some VAN providers and their networks still exist today, e.g., EDITEL from GS1 Austria for EDIFACT related messaging.

Today, most standards leave it up to the implementer what protocol to choose for the exchange of a business document. Of all examined standard clusters only integrated approaches specifically recommend a certain technology, e.g., ebXML messaging is built on SOAP. Finally, we conclude that only integrated approaches fulfill the entire needs of business messaging functionality. In fact ebXML is the only representative standard available, covering business messaging in an integrative manner. However, the acceptance of integrated approaches such as ebXML is still very low. This is mainly due to the inherent complexity of these standards and unfortunately also due to low vendor support for compliant interfaces. In the following we elaborate on the *technological features* of each standard cluster.

Used Syntax   As already outlined in the introduction, traditional delimiter-based implementation syntax definitions have been superseded by XML-based standards. Today, XML represents the current state-of-the-art in business document standardization. However, top-down approaches and transitioned approaches still use the EDIFACT syntax. Naturally, implementation neutral standards do not use a specific syn-

3.3 A standard comparison

tax, but are defined on a conceptual model (e.g., using UML models).

Release iterations

In regard to release iterations we identified that top-down standard definitions are the only ones where more than one standard definition is released per year. In particular delimiter-based standards provide new standard releases on a regular basis (e.g., UN/EDIFACT releases new directory versions twice a year). All other standard clusters have longer release cycles. Whether that is of advantage or disadvantage depends on the specific application scenario of the standard. Shorter release cycles enable the inclusion of bug-fixes and new user requirements, but require adaptations of business service interfaces and applications, processing the standard instances. For longer release cycles the situation is vice versa.

Implementation complexity

A critical factor, when choosing a business document standard, is the effort in regard to implementation complexity. In particular top-down and implementation neutral approaches, such as the core component initiative, require considerable implementation effort. This is partly due to the inherent complexity of these standards and partly due to the short release cycles for standard updates. Thus, additional maintenance effort is necessary to be compliant with these updates. For bottom-up, hybrid, and integrated standardization efforts no clear answer in regard to implementation complexity may be given. If tool vendors would keep their promise and provide interfaces, capable of processing these standards in their commercial-of-the-shelf-software (COTS), the implementation complexity would be low. However, the current support in COTS is still very low and therefore considerable implementation effort for a processing of different standards is necessary. In particular SMEs cannot afford to implement complex and costly business service interfaces, since they do not have customizable ERP software available, but rely on COTS.

Delta between releases

Of particular importance in regard to the customization of business service interfaces is the delta between releases of a certain standard. The higher the delta, the higher is the effort for a potential customization of software processing instances of the standard. Our standard evaluation has shown that the delta is the lowest in the cluster of bottom-up standard definitions. Since bottom-up standards are defined as

3 An overview of business document standards

an intersection of requirements, where only the most important elements are considered in the core standard definition, only small changes occur between the different releases. In the cluster of top-down standards the delta is low in regard to delimiter-based standards. These standard families are well tested and maintained and only little changes occur from release to release. However, other non delimiter-based top-down standard definitions may include significant changes from release to release. Hybrid approaches and implementation neutral approaches reflect extensive changes in each release as our examination of UBL and CCTS has shown. In regard to integrated approaches no clear answer may be given, since some parts of, e.g., ebXML remain rather stable (e.g., ebXML messaging) whereas other parts have undergone significant changes (e.g., core components).

Backward compatibility
Another important factor in regard to the adaptation of business document standards is backward compatibility. If backward compatibility is provided, little to no adaptations have to be made to business service interfaces processing instances of a certain business document type. We conclude that only standards from the bottom-up and implementation neutral cluster meet the requirement of high backward compatibility. Since bottom-up standards are specifically focusing on not changing the core standard definition too much, high backward compatibility is provided. We examined that implementation neutral standards such as the Core Components Technical Specification also try not to alter the basic concepts to foster reuse and backward compatibility between different versions. Top-down standards such as EDIFACT, hybrid standards such as UBL, and integrated approaches such as ebXML provide a rather low backward compatibility.

Extensibility
In regard to extensibility, only standards from the top-down cluster do not meet the criteria of user-specific standard extensions. All other standard clusters provide necessary extension concepts for user- or domain-specific standard amendments.

Availability of conceptual models
In particular for the communication between software architects and programmers a conceptual model representation of a business document is useful. We found out that currently only the bottom-up cluster and the hybrid standard cluster are missing a conceptual representation mechanism.

3.3 A standard comparison

Although the core standard definitions of bottom-up standards may well be represented using a conceptual model, currently no appropriate approach for the representation of the different standard extensions exists. The same applies for the different extensions as provided by hybrid standard definitions.

As outlined earlier, semantic ambiguity may occur with bottom-up and hybrid standardization approaches, since their extension mechanisms allow any user-specific amendments. As a countermeasure, a standardization organization may prevent user-specific extensions and provide well defined and standardized extension sets for certain domains (e.g., for the telecom industry).   *Semantically unambiguous*

An important part of our survey was to examine, whether a given standard cluster is supported by commercial-of-the-shelf software (COTS) tools. In particular SMEs cannot afford costly ERP software, but rely on COTS. In fact currently only bottom-up standards are supported by COTS, since all other standard clusters are either too complex or their included standards are not pertinent for SMEs. Unfortunately, support for ebXML in COTS is almost zero, although one of the main goals of ebXML was to support in particular SMEs through standard interfaces integrated in COTS, as well.   *COTS support*

Concerning the maturity of the different standard clusters we found out, that only bottom-up standards still require consolidation and maintenance work. Since bottom-up standards are a rather new concept, several issues are still unresolved. In particular the definition of extension points for domain-specific amendments is still an open research issue in bottom-up standard definitions. We further detail this issue in Chapter 10 of this thesis.   *Standard maturity*

In regard to the user community size of a standard cluster, bottom-up and integrated approaches have the lowest community size. For bottom-up standards this is due to the adolescence of the standard. Integrated approaches such as ebXML unfortunately have never reached a critical mass of users.   *Community size*

Concerning the adoption rate of a standard cluster, only integrated approaches suffer from a low acceptance rate. Taking ebXML as an example, we conclude that although some parts of the standard are accepted and in use in the   *Adoption*

3 An overview of business document standards

industry (e.g., ebXML registry), little to no applications using the full range of ebXML exist. Bottom-up standards, due to their adolescence and partially due to their missing maturity, are also lacking adoption by the industry. In such scenarios interest groups play an important role, as the example of the Austrian Federal Economic Chamber and the bottom-up standard ebInterface has shown.

Potential user groups Considering potential user groups per standard cluster, we evaluated that in particular small and medium-sized enterprises are reluctant to adopt top-down or integrated approaches. Our evaluation has shown that acceptance of a standard by SMEs may only be guaranteed if appropriate tool support for handling document instances is provided. Unfortunately, support by commercial-of-the-shelf (COTS) software is still very low. However, if COTS support increases, bottom-up standard definitions as well as to some extend hybrid standard definitions may be used by SMEs. Naturally, large enterprises are able to handle any of the presented standard clusters due to their ability to dynamically adapt their IT systems.

Acceptance In regard to the acceptance in terms of industry, national, or global level, top-down standards, hybrid approaches, and implementation neutral approaches are equally accepted. Due to their limited inclusion of requirements, bottom-up standards are not well accepted on a global level. Furthermore, standards from the integrated approach cluster lack acceptance on all levels.

3.4 Final assessment

In this Chapter we presented the results of our business document standard survey, conducted during our research work on business document standardization. We have shown how the multitude of different business document standards may be categorized using eight different clusters. For each cluster we examined a representative standard in detail and gave examples for other standards in the respective cluster. The essential result of our survey is the comparison of the different business document clusters in regard to business message compatibility, technology features, potential user groups, and acceptance level of each standard. Based on our survey results, an IT analyst may assess, whether a given

3.4 Final assessment

business document standard meets specific requirements or not.

This survey has given a first overview of current state-of-the-art in business document standardization. Future work must concentrate on extending the current survey by examining additional standards. In particular vendor specific exchange format implementations as used by tool vendors such as SAP or Oracle should be examined to gain insight in the used technology.

A first overview has been given

Currently, the results of the survey are based on our insights acquired by working in various standardization organizations such as UN/CEFACT or the ebInterface consortium. In a follow-up step the scope must be changed from pure desk-research to a field-research oriented approach by conducting surveys in industries and application domains. This is yet to be done.

Extending the scope from desk research to field research

Although several standards exist on the market today, interface heterogeneity between different enterprise systems is still a major obstacle towards seamless integration of ERP systems. Instead of focusing on a single standard solution, enterprises prefer to use mappers to transform instances of standard A to instances of standard B. Thus, interoperability is mostly enabled through mapping middleware such as BizTalk [24] (mapping of HL7, SWIFT, RosettaNet, etc.) or Mirth [112] for mappings in the health care domain.

Standard mappers still prevail

Concerning the provision of a single and global business document standard, the Core Component initiative founded by UN/CEFACT is currently the most promising approach. Unlike other standardization initiatives, UN/CEFACT's members also comprise other standardization organizations such as OAGi and OASIS. Thus, the core component initiative is not yet another industry initiative focusing on a detached and isolated industry sector, but aims at global cross-industry interoperability. Whether the initiative will be successful or not, depends on the willingness of the different stakeholders to accept the new standard definition.

Core components are a possible solution for the current heterogeneity

In regard to existing standard definitions, a market consolidation may be observed. The eighties and nineties of the last century and in particular the dot-com boom have brought a multitude of different and competing B2B standards. Today, almost no new standards are defined any more, but existing definitions are enhanced. Several stan-

Market consolidation may be observed

3 An overview of business document standards

dardization organizations have consolidated their work, e.g., the work of CIDX [19] is now conducted by OAGi and CIDX has ceased to exist as self-contained standardization organization.

The big players dictate Concerning the adaption of a standard, e.g., in a given supply-chain in the industry one single fact remains: Usually the larger company defines the interfaces and used standards and smaller companies have to adapt to these prerequisites.

4 An introduction to Core Components

In the following Chapter we give an introduction to the basic concepts of the Core Components Technical Specification (CCTS) [170]. We outline the history of the core components initiative and introduce the main features of CCTS. Thereby, we abstract from the rather complicated and technical core component standard itself, and introduce the main concepts of the standard, necessary for the further comprehension of the following Chapters. Thus, this Chapter serves as the foundation for the next three consecutive Chapters. The remainder of this Chapter is structured as follows: Section 4.1 gives a short overview of the history of core components. Section 4.2 and 4.3 introduce the basic concepts of core components and business information entities, respectively. Finally, Section 4.4 introduces the concept of a Core Component Library and Section 4.5 concludes the Chapter with a final assessment.

Introducing UN/CEFACT's Core Components

4.1 Introduction and historical background

When the Electronic Business XML (ebXML) [124] initiative started in 1999, one of the architectural cornerstones of the specification was the unambiguous definition of the information, exchanged in an electronic business transaction. The idea was to create reusable building blocks for assembling business documents – core components as part 8 of the ebXML Framework were born. After the final ebXML specification was released in 2001, UN/CEFACT took over the core component development tasks. The first post-ebXML release of the core component specification was the Core Components Technical Specification (CCTS) 2.01 [164], which was released in 2003. Currently, the succeeding

Core Components started as part of the ebXML specification

4 An introduction to Core Components

version 3.0 [170] is being developed and close to completion. All core component concepts presented in this thesis are already based on the newest version CCTS 3.0.

Goal: Achieving semantic interoperability of data
The main goal of the core component initiative was to overcome limitations of other business document standardization approaches. Most of the business document standards have been designed for specific application domains, without considering cross-domain interoperability. Furthermore, as already outlined in Chapter 3, the multitude of different standards impose an additional obstacle towards interoperability. If two arbitrary business partners want to engage in an automated business-to-business interaction, their business document definitions, if defined in isolation by each business partner, will most likely not match. Thereby, mismatches may for instance occur due to different positions of certain elements or due to different semantic meanings of elements, i.e., a *waste movement* may be referred to as *consignment* in standard A, but as *shipment* in standard B.

The Core Component Technical Specification (CCTS) proposes a new approach for the definition of interoperable business documents by defining a common set of semantic building blocks, representing general types of business data in use today. These semantic building blocks are referred to as *core components*. Business partners may retrieve the predefined core components from a common Core Component Library [173] and tailor them to the specific needs of their application domain. Note that a business document modeler may only restrict a given core component, but must never add any attributes or associations to an existing core component. Thus, it is guaranteed that business documents, which are created from the same common core components, share a common semantic basis. Therefore, business partners are able to provide interoperability of business documents, even on a cross-industry level.

Core components are implementation neutral
A major difference of the core component initiative, compared to other business document standardization approaches, is its technical foundation. Core components are defined independent of a specific implementation format. Thus, in principle any implementation format of choice may be chosen to implement core component concepts in applications. In the following Sections we elaborate on two elementary concepts of the core component specification: *core*

4.1 Introduction and historical background

components and *business information entities*. Figure 4.1 gives an overview of the basic concepts of the core component initiative.

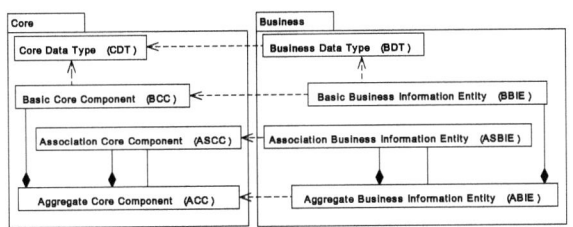

Figure 4.1
Core component architecture

The core component standard distinguishes between a context free part (*core*) and a context specific part (*business*). Generally, we refer to artifacts from the core part as *core components* and to artifacts from the business part as *business information entities*. Core components are standardized building blocks for business documents, independent of a certain business domain. Thus, core components are generic and may be used in any given business domain such as chemical industry, tourism industry, etc. If a core component is used in a certain business scenario, it becomes a *business information entity*. Business information entities are core components, which are tailored to a specific application domain. For the core part of the standard, UN/CEFACT distinguishes between the following artifacts: *aggregate core components (ACC)*, *basic core components (BCC)*, and *association core components (ASCC)*. Data types are referred to as *core data types (CDT)*. For each of the different core artifacts an equivalent counterpart on the business side exists. The respective business information artifacts are *aggregate business information entities (ABIE)*, *basic business information entities (BBIE)*, and *association business information entities (ASBIE)*. Data types on the business side are called *business data types (BDT)*. Each artifact on the business side of the CCTS is based on a respective artifact on the core side of the standard. This underlines the strong relationship between context independent core components and context specific business information entities.

In the following we further examine the basic artifacts from both, the core components and the business information entity domain.

4.2 Core Components

Identifying objects and object properties

As already outlined in the introduction, the main goal of core components is the definition of reusable building blocks. Consequently, a building block must be generic in nature to meet the requirements of any given business scenario or application domain. The basic concept behind defining such a building block is the identification of objects and object properties. Properties are divided into two sub-groups: simple object properties (e.g., name, age) and complex object properties (e.g., references to other objects such as person referencing an address). Table 4.1 gives an overview of the basic property concepts of core components.

*Table 4.1
Core component concepts*

Property type	Core component equivalent
Object type	Aggregate Core Component (ACC)
Simple property	Basic Core Component (BCC)
Simple property data type	Core Data Type (CDT)
Complex property	ASsociation Core Component (ASCC)

Objects are represented using *aggregate core components (ACC)*. An aggregate core component serves as the embracing container for simple object properties. Simple object properties are referred to as *basic core components (BCC)*. Each simple property has an assigned data type known as *core data type (CDT)*, defining the exact value domain of a given basic core component. Dependencies between different objects are depicted using the concept of *association core components (ASCC)*.

Figure 4.2 shows a simple core component example with two aggregate core components `consignment item` and `party`. The `consignment item` has two basic core components, namely `identification` and `net weight`. As indicated by the term *and x other attributes* a real core component has many other basic core components. Each basic core component has an assigned core data type, defining its value domain. The basic core component `identification`, for instance, has the core data type `identifier`.

Furthermore, `consignment item` has exactly two association core components `delivery` and `dispatch`, pointing to the aggregate core component `party`. Thus, it is indicated that a `consignment item` has a `delivery party`, to which the consignment item is delivered and a `dispatch`

4.2 Core Components

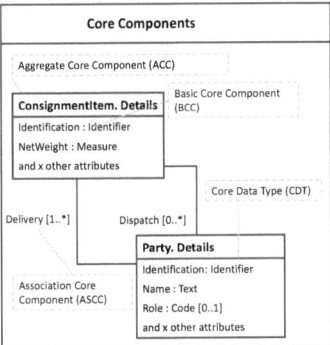

Figure 4.2
Overview of core component concepts

party from which the consignment item is dispatched. Note that the representation format as shown in Figure 4.2 has been arbitrarily chosen by the authors. In principle, any representation format of choice may be used to depict core components. The representation as shown in Table 4.2 may equally serve as a representation format for the core components, introduced in Figure 4.2.

```
ConsignmentItem.Details
ConsignmentItem.Identification.Identifier:1
ConsignmentItem.NetWeight.Measure:1
ConsignmentItem.Delivery.Party:1..*
ConsignmentItem.Dispatch.Party:0..*
Party.Details
Party.Identification.Identifier:1
Party.Name.Text:1
Party.Role.Code:0..1
```

Table 4.2
Text-based representation of core components

However, applying a notation similar to UML class diagrams with classes, attributes, and associations helps to communicate core component structures. In particular in a service oriented environment, where business document definitions have to be communicated between various business partners and other stakeholders, a UML class diagram-based representation format is superior to a pure text-based format. This will be of particular importance in Chapter 5, when we introduce the UML Profile for Core Components. In the following we briefly elaborate on naming conventions of core components.

4.2.1 Aggregate Core Component (ACC)

Aggregate Core Component

As already outlined, an aggregate core component is a collection of related pieces of information that together convey a distinct meaning. An aggregate core component is defined on a context independent level and is identified by its *object class term*, e.g., the caption of the core component consignment item in Figure 4.2 is the *object class term*. Additionally, CCTS mandates that an object class term is followed by a dot, a space character, and the suffix Details. This results in a *dictionary entry name* (DEN), which must be unique for the core component library, the core component is part of. The full dictionary entry name for a consignment item core component is thus: Consignment-Item. Details

4.2.2 Basic Core Component (BCC)

Basic Core Component

A basic core component represents a property of an aggregate core component. Figure 4.3 gives an overview of the naming conventions for basic core components. It shows the aggregate core component consignment item and its basic core components, which were introduced in Figure 4.2.

Figure 4.3 Basic core component naming conventions

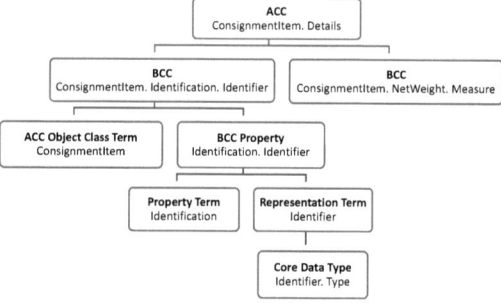

A basic core component consists of a *basic core component property (BCC property)* plus the *object class term* of the parent aggregate core component (ACC). A BCC property itself consists of a *property term* and a *representation term*. A representation term represents the core data type of a basic core component. Note that a basic core component property is reusable across different object classes (e.g., Identification. Identifier). However, once it

4.2 Core Components

has been given the object class of a parent ACC, it becomes a basic core component that is unique to the object class to which it is assigned (e.g., ConsignmentItem. Identification. Identifier). The name of a basic core component must be unique within all basic core components of a given aggregate core component. In data modeling terms, a basic core component is a UML class attribute. In contrast, a core data type is realized as a self-contained class. This class is used to set the type of the class attribute, representing the basic core component.

4.2.3 Association Core Component (ASCC)

Association Core Component

An *association core component (ASCC)* defines an association between one aggregate core component (the associating ACC) and another aggregate core component (the associated ACC). Similar to a basic core component, an association core component consists of an *ASCC property* plus the *object class term* of the parent ACC. Figure 4.4 gives an overview of the naming conventions for association core components. The associated object class term represents a complex data type that defines the value domain of the ASCC. Similar to BCC properties, an ASCC property is reusable across object classes (e.g., Delivery. Party). However, once it has been assigned to a certain ACC object class term, it becomes an association core component (e.g., ConsignmentItem. Delivery. Party). The name of an association core component must be unique within all association core components of a given aggregate core component. In data modeling terms, an association core component is equivalent to a UML association with aggregation kind = shared.

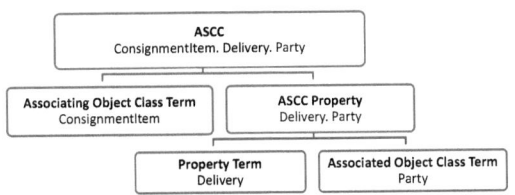

Figure 4.4
Association core component naming conventions

4 An introduction to Core Components

4.2.4 Core Data Types

Core data types We already outlined that *core data types* are used to set the value domain of basic core components (= attributes of an aggregate core component). Data types in the context of the core component standard have a different notion as they have in classic programming languages. The concept of core data types goes beyond simple data types such as double, float, etc. and provides a mechanism divided into actual content and additional meta-information. As shown in Figure 4.5, the core data type identifier has exactly one *content component (CON)* and multiple *supplementary components (SUP)*. In the domain of core data types, a content component holds the actual information (e.g., AT) and supplementary components provide additional meta information (e.g., scheme identifier = 3166-1, scheme version identifier = 1.0, scheme agency identifier = ISO). This indicates that the identifier is a ISO 3166-1 country code identifier.

Figure 4.5
Overview of core data type concepts

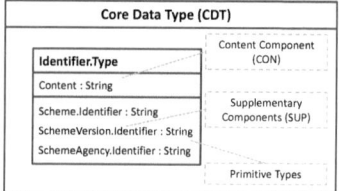

A core data type always has the suffix .Type, to distinguish core components from core data types. Figure 4.6 gives an overview of the naming conventions for core data types.

Figure 4.6
Core data type naming conventions

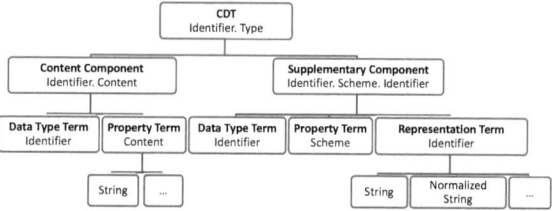

The actual name of a core data type is referred to as *data type term*. As already outlined, a core data type has exactly one content component attribute and zero to many supplementary component attributes. The content component of

4.3 Business Information Entities

a core data type consists of a *data type term* and a *property term*. The data type term is the name of the core data type without the suffix .Type. The property term of a content component must always be named Content and has an allowed value domain defined using primitive types. UN/CEFACT has released a finite set of allowed primitive types in the UN/CEFACT Data Type Catalogue [169], shown in Figure 4.7. A supplementary component consists of a *data type term* plus a *property term* and a *representation term*. The value domain of each representation term is also defined using primitive types.

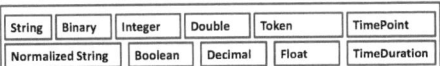

Figure 4.7
Overview of primitive types

A business document modeler may further restrict a primitive type using a *code list* or an *identifier scheme*. A code list represents an enumerated set of values, restricting a certain primitive type. An example for a code list are currency or country codes, restricting either a Token, String or Normalized String primitive type. Thus, code lists provide a finite set of values, which are allowed for a certain content or supplementary component. In contrast to a code list, an identifier scheme prescribes production rules, based on a certain primitive type. An example for an identifier scheme is the European bank account number identifier scheme, prescribing exactly how certain characters must be composed to a String value, to comply with the requirements of a European bank account number. In contrast to a code list, the values of an identifier scheme are typically not enumerated.

In data modeling terms, a core data type is equivalent to a UML class. Content components and supplementary components are realized as class attributes. Likewise, primitive types and identifier schemes are realized as UML classes as well. An enumeration is defined using the UML built-in type enumeration.

4.3 Business Information Entities

If core components are used in a certain business context, they become *business information entities*. The key difference between core components and business information en-

Putting core components in a business context

4 An introduction to Core Components

tities is the concept of a business context. Using a business context, a given core component may be refined according to requirements of a particular data model or business circumstance. Consequently, business information entities are always derived from an underlying core component by restriction. This implies that a business information entity must not contain any attributes or associations, which have not been defined in the underlying core component. Consequently, the structure of core components and business information entities is complementary in many respects.

Similar to the concept of core components, business information entities distinguish between three different elementary types. Table 4.3 gives an overview of the business information entity concepts. An *aggregate business information entity (ABIE)* is used to aggregate simple object properties. Simple object properties are depicted using the concept of *basic business information entities (BBIE)*. The value domain for a given basic business information entity is defined using the concept of *business data types (BDT)*. Dependencies between different business information entities are denoted using the concept of *association business information entities (ASBIE)*.

Table 4.3
Business information entity concepts

Property type	Business information Entity equivalent
Object type	Aggregate Business Information Entity (ABIE)
Simple property	Basic Business Information Entity (ABIE)
Simple property data type	Business Data Type (BDT)
Complex property	ASsociation Business Information Entity (ASBIE)

Figure 4.8 extends the example from Figure 4.2 and shows two aggregate business information entities `waste_ consignment item` and `waste_ party`. Note that the business information entities in Figure 4.8 restrict the underlying core components to the business context of the waste management domain. Business context is indicated by qualifiers. Qualifiers are put in front of the object class term of a business information entity and are separated by underscore characters. In the example, shown in Figure 4.8, the qualifier `waste_` is used.

The aggregate business information entity `waste_ consignment item` has two basic business information entities namely `waste_ identification` and `waste_ net weight`. Each

4.3 Business Information Entities

basic business information entity has an assigned *business data type*, defining its value domain. The basic business information entity `waste_ net weight` has the business data type `waste_ measure`. Note that there is a similar relationship between business data types and core data types, as there is between business information entities and core components. Each business data type must be derived from a core data type by restriction. Thus, a business data type must not contain any content or supplementary components, which have not been defined in the underlying core data type.

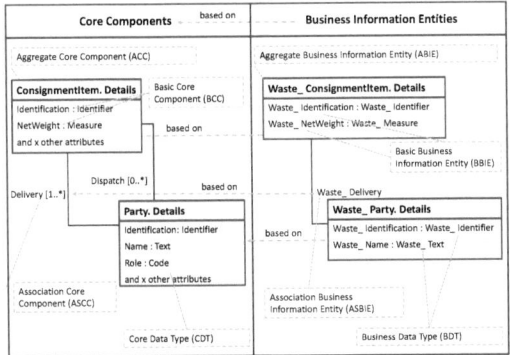

Figure 4.8
Overview of business information entity concepts

Additionally, `waste_ consignment item` has exactly one association business information entity `waste_ delivery`, pointing to the aggregate business information entity `waste_ party`. Thus, it is indicated that a `waste_ consignment item` has a `waste_ delivery party`, to which the consignment is delivered. Note that the association core component `dispatch` is not considered in the aggregate business information entity `waste_ consignment item`.

The strong dependency between business information entities and their underlying core components is emphasized in Figure 4.8. Essentially, a business information entity is always a *specialization* of a core component and every business information entity may be traced back to its underlying core component. As indicated by the *based on* dependencies, an aggregate business information entity is based on an aggregate core component. Consequently, all basic business information entities, contained in an aggregate business information entity, are based on the basic core components,

Dependency between core components and business information entities contained in the aggregate core component, the aggregate business information entity is based on. It follows that, for instance, a `waste_ identifier` is based on an `identifier`, etc. Also shown in Figure 4.8 is the based on dependency between association business information entities and association core components. Implicitly shown in Figure 4.8 is the dependency between core data types and business data types, i.e., the business data type `waste_ identifier` is based on the core data type `identifier`.

In the following we briefly introduce the naming conventions for business information entities.

4.3.1 Aggregate Business Information Entity (ABIE)

Aggregate Business Information Entity   As already outlined before, an *aggregate business information entity* is derived from an *aggregate core component* by restriction. In contrast to an aggregate core component, the aggregate business information entity is defined for a specific context. For this reason, an aggregate business information entity is identified by a *qualifier* and its *object class term* followed by a dot, a space character, and the suffix Details. Consider `Waste_ ConsignmentItem. Details` in Figure 4.8. This rule implies that `waste_` is the *qualifier* and `consignment item` is the *object class term*. Note that an ABIE may be qualified on the object class level and its properties (basic business information entities and association business information entities) may be qualified at the property term level. In data modeling terms, an aggregate business information entity is equivalent to a UML class.

4.3.2 Basic Business Information Entity (BBIE)

Basic Business Information Entity   A *basic business information entity* represents a basic core component, used in a certain business context. Thereby, a basic business information entity serves as a property of an aggregate business information entity. Figure 4.9 gives an overview of the naming conventions for basic business information entities. It shows the aggregate business information entity `waste_ consignment item` and its basic business information entity `waste_ identification`, which were introduced in Figure 4.8.

4.3 Business Information Entities

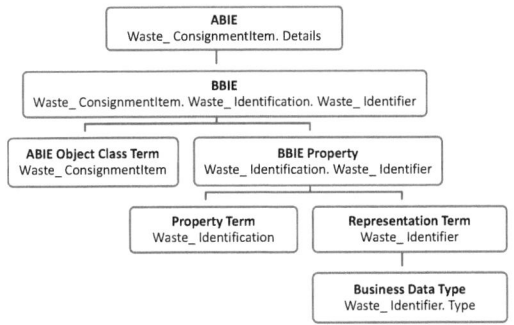

Figure 4.9
Basic business information entity naming conventions

A basic business information entity consists of the *object class term* of the parent ABIE plus a *basic business information entity property (BBIE property)*. The *property term* of the BBIE property may be qualified using a qualifier. The *representation term* of the BBIE property represents the *business data type* of a basic business information entity. Note that like their BCC property counterparts, BBIE properties are reusable across object classes (e.g., waste_ identification. waste_ identifier). However, once they have been given the object class term of a parent ABIE, they become unique BBIEs (e.g., waste_ consignment item. waste_ identification. waste_ identifier). In data modeling terms, a basic business information entity is equivalent to a UML attribute.

4.3.3 Association Business Information Entity (ASBIE)

An *association business information entity* represents a complex property of an aggregate business information entity (*associating ABIE*). Accordingly, the ASBIE represents the structure of another ABIE – the *associated ABIE*. An ASBIE is based on an ASCC, but exists in a certain business context. Figure 4.10 gives an overview of the naming conventions for association business information entities. Similar to the concept of an ASCC, an ASBIE consists of the *object class term* of the parent ABIE plus an *ASBIE property*. An ASBIE property is reusable across different aggregate business information entities (e.g., waste_ delivery. waste_ party). However, once it has been assigned to a cer-

Association Business Information Entity

4 An introduction to Core Components

tain ABIE object class term, it becomes an association business information entity (e.g., waste_ consignment item. waste_ delivery. waste_ party). Similar to a BBIE property, the property term of the ASBIE property may be qualified. In data modeling terms, an association core component is equivalent to a UML association with aggregation kind = composite or aggregation kind = shared. The distinction between the two different aggregation kind types is relevant for the generation of XML Schema artifacts from core component definitions.

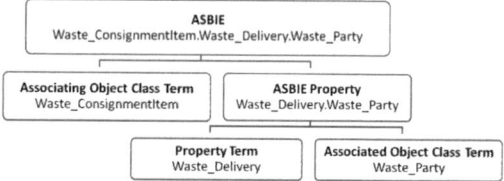

Figure 4.10 Association business information entity naming conventions

It has already been shown that business information entities may impose several restrictions on their underlying core component counterparts. In the following the allowed restrictions are summarized.

4.3.4 From core components to business information entities

Deriving business information entities from core components

We outlined that a business information entity is created from a core component by restriction, but never by extension. An aggregate business information entity may reflect restrictions on the content model of an aggregate core component in several ways. In the following we outline the most important restrictions using the example from Figure 4.8.

❏ Basic business information entities and association business information entities may place restrictions on the cardinality of BCCs and ASCCs. The cardinality of the association core component delivery is [1..*], but the derived association business information entity waste_ delivery has cardinality 1.
❏ Aggregate core components may optionally include ASCC properties and BCC properties. The aggregate core component consignment item has two association core component properties namely delivery and

4.3 Business Information Entities

dispatch. However, the derived aggregate business information entity `waste_ consignment item` only contains one association business information entity property `waste_ delivery`. Additionally, the basic core component `party` contains multiple basic core component properties. The derived `waste_ party`, however, only contains two – `waste_ identification` and `waste_ name`.

❏ Business information entities may use optional qualifiers on their underlying ACCs as well as ASCC properties and BCC properties. All business information entities are qualified using the `waste_` qualifier. This indicates that the business information entities are used in the waste management domain. ASCC properties and BCC properties may have different qualifiers applied. This might result in an ABIE having a greater number of qualified BBIEs than the underlying ACC has unqualified BCCs. However, this is still considered a restriction, since each BBIE represents a restriction to the underlying BCC. Additionally, ASCC properties and BCC properties may have multiple qualifiers applied, resulting in a qualifier hierarchy. Each additional qualifier reflects a further restriction to its less qualified BIE property. E.g., the BBIE `european_ waste_ identification` would be a further restriction of the BBIE `waste_ identification`.

❏ Business information entities may impose restrictions on the content model of an associated ACC for an ASCC. The associated aggregate core component for the association core component `delivery` is `party`. The core component `party` contains multiple attributes. In the derived business information entity, however, `waste_ party` only contains two attributes. Thus, the content model of the association business information entity `waste_ delivery` has changed in comparison to the content model of the underlying association core component `delivery`.

❏ Business data types of a basic business information entity (BBIE) may restrict the core data type of a basic core component (BCC). All basic business information entities use different data types than their underlying

4.3.5 Business Data Types

Business data types

Business data types are used to set the value domain of basic business information entities. For every *core data type*, approved in the UN/CEFACT Core Component Data Type Catalogue [169], an unrestricted *business data type* is created. These default business data types do not have any restrictions on the values of their source CDTs' content and supplementary components. A business document modeler may use the predefined business data types, imposing no restrictions on the underlying core data type, or create his own, restricted business data types. The relationship between core data types and business data types is similar to the relationship between core components and business information entities. A business data type may only be derived from a core data type by restriction. Thus, the restriction represents a qualification of the BDT similar to the qualification of business information entities. As shown in Figure 4.11, the business data type `waste_ identifier` is based on the core data type `identifier`. Note that the business data type does not use all supplementary components of the underlying core data type.

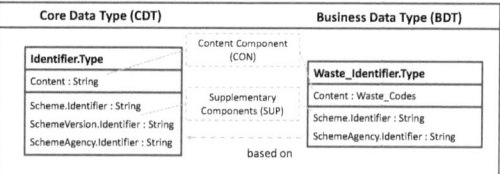

Figure 4.11 Overview of business data type concepts

Similar to core data types, content components and supplementary components also have value domains. For content components and supplementary components this value domain may be expressed using primitive types, code lists, or identifier schemes. The identifier schemes or code lists used for the attributes of a business data type must be a subset of the identifier schemes or code lists, used for the attributes of the core data type, the business data type is based on. E.g., a country code list comprising all country codes in the world may be defined for the content component of a core data type. A business data type, derived from this core component, may now restrict the country code list to European countries only. The same principle applies for identifier schemes and primitive type restrictions.

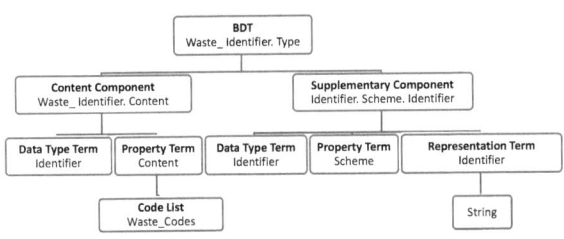

Figure 4.12
Business data type naming conventions

The naming conventions of business data types are very similar to the naming conventions of core data types. Figure 4.12 gives an example for the business data type introduced in Figure 4.11. Note that business data types may be qualified on the data type term level only. In contrast, supplementary components and content components may not be qualified. Furthermore, qualifiers may be applied to identifier schemes and code lists in order to denote restrictions.

4.4 Core Component Library

Based on the technical foundations, defined in the Core Component Technical Specification (CCTS), UN/CEFACT maintains a Core Component Library (CCL) [173]. Based on the core components stored in the core component library, business document modelers may create their own, context specific business information entities. In case a certain core component is missing in the library, a request for inclusion of a new core component may be submitted to UN/CEFACT. A dedicated core component harmonization group within UN/CEFACT examines every core component submission. In case the submission is valid and does not overlap with existing core components, the new core component is included in the UN/CEFACT core component library. Usually UN/CEFACT releases new versions of the core component library twice a year. In general, the core component library serves as the normative reference to every core component modeler, and each business information

Providing a global core component resource

4 An introduction to Core Components

entity created for a specific business context must be based on a respective core component from the library. A business document modeler may still decide to create his own core components. However, in this case the compatibility to the global core component library is lost.

Current issues with the Core Component Library

The Core Component Library of UN/CEFACT is based on the current Core Component Technical Specification 2.01. Since core components based on the 2.01 specification are incompatible with core components based on the 3.0 specification, it follows that all core components defined in the library are incompatible with the CCTS 3.0 specification. The adaption of the current Core Component Library to guarantee compatibility to the latest CCTS release is still an open issue. Additionally, the Core Component Library is maintained using a regular spread sheet. Thus, efficient tool-based lookup and maintenance of the Core Component Library is difficult.

4.5 Final assessment

In this Chapter we gave an overview of the essential concepts of the Core Components Technical Specification (CCTS) 3.0. We outlined the basic building blocks of the standard, represented by core components. Consequently, we elaborated on business information entities, which are core components used in a certain business context.

Implementation neutrality as an obstacle towards broad standard diffusion

We conclude that core components represent one of the most mature approaches towards the definition of business document related data. Since core components are standardized in an implementation neutral manner, they provide a maximum of flexibility. However, this implementation neutrality is also the greatest obstacle towards a broad diffusion of the standard. Only if the core component standard may be employed in an easy manner in every day business life, a broad adoption of the standard is possible. In this thesis we have developed three reference implementations for core components, helping business document modelers to employ core component concepts in real world application scenarios. Figure 4.13 gives an overview of the three reference implementations, we provide for core components.

As shown in Figure 4.13, we transfer the implementation neutral core component technology on three different tech-

4.5 Final assessment

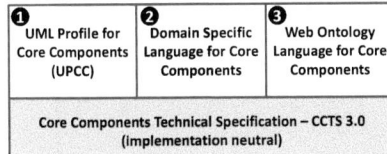

Figure 4.13
Overview of core component implementations

nologies namely (1) the Unified Modeling Language (UML), (2) a Domain-Specific Language (DSL), and (3) Web Ontology Language (OWL). Chapter 5 of this thesis introduces the UML Profile for Core Components and Chapter 6 shows how core components may be used with Domain-Specific Languages. In Chapter 7 we show how core component concepts may be mapped to Semantic Web concepts, using a Web Ontology Language (OWL) reference implementation.

Apart from the implementation neutrality of core components, a missing implementation of an easy to use Core Component Library is another obstacle towards a broad diffusion of the standard. The current spread sheet-based library is difficult to integrate in existing applications. Furthermore, an appropriate versioning of core components in the core component library and the maintenance of company or industry specific subsets of the library are difficult. We further detail these issues and a potential solution in Chapter 9.

Missing Core Component Library implementation

Within the business document standardization community the core component approach is subject to some controversy. Generally, the Core Component Technical Specification (CCTS) provides a sound agreement on a business document meta-model with a broad and flexible focus. However, several critics argue that the CCTS is over-specified and, thus, broad acceptance of the standard may not be achieved. The main reasons for these arguments are the flexible mechanisms in regard to the use of ASCC properties and BCC properties and their business information entity counterparts ASBIE properties and BBIE properties. An ASCC property or BCC property may be used in any ACC, leading to a potentially uncontrolled structure. The argument of the opponents is to abolish the concept of ASCC and BCC properties and use only ASCCs and BCCs instead.

Critical remarks on the core component approach

Furthermore, the necessity of mandatory ASCC properties on which ASBIE properties must be based on, is a

4 An introduction to Core Components

further issue several critics complain about. In particular in the Core Component Library (CCL), ASCCs create quite complex structures. The opponents of ASCCs propose to generally abandon the ASCC concept, and allow for arbitrary associations between different aggregate core components instead.

5 A UML Profile for Core Components

In the previous Chapter we have introduced the basic concepts of the Core Components Technical Specification (CCTS) [170]. We outlined that the implementation neutrality of the specification is one of the greatest obstacles towards a broad diffusion of the standard. To overcome this obstacle, an easy to use implementation format for core components has to be found. Furthermore, efficient tool support is crucial for a broad acceptance of the standard definition.

In this Chapter we introduce the UML Profile for Core Components (UPCC) [172]. The UML Profile maps implementation neutral core component concepts to a formal UML model. As a result, a business document modeler assembles UML-based core component models with any UML modeling tool of choice, which leverages several benefits. Generally, UML-based core component models are easier to communicate between developers, than for instance XML-based document representations. Additionally, a UML-based business document model may also be discussed with non-technical stakeholders. Finally, a UML-based business document model may serve as the basis for the derivation of deployment artifacts, such as XML Schema. The generated XML Schema files are used to configure the business document interfaces of the business partners' IT systems, engaged in a B2B interaction.

Leveraging UML modeling benefits for Core Components

The remainder of this Chapter is structured as follows: Section 5.1 explains the motivation for the UML Profile for Core Components. In Section 5.2 we introduce the conceptual basics of the UML Profile for Core Components and Section 5.3 shows a real world application of the UPCC, using the accompanying waste management example. Section 5.4 concludes the Chapter with a final assessment.

5.1 Introduction

Implementation neutrality is an obstacle towards broad diffusion of core components

Our business document standard survey in Chapter 3 has shown that among all different business document standardization efforts, the Core Components Technical Specification (CCTS) is one of the most promising ones. Currently, core components are standardized using regular spread sheets, thus obstructing integration into modeling tools. To allow for a broad adoption of the standard, we developed the UML Profile for Core Components (UPCC) and consequently submitted it to UN/CEFACT for standardization. The first version, UML Profile for Core Components 1.0 [167], was based on the Core Components Technical Specification 2.01 [164]. When UN/CEFACT started to develop the Core Components Technical Specification 3.0 [170], we decided to update the profile definition accordingly. This resulted in the newest version: UML Profile for Core Components 3.0 [172], on which this Chapter is based on.

Formalizing Core Components using a UML Profile

In principle any representation format of choice may be chosen for core component artifacts. We decided to adapt the Unified Modeling Language (UML) [129] for conceptual core component modeling, due to its broad user community and tool support. In contrast to regular and predefined UML model types, such as class diagrams, activity diagrams, etc., a UML Profile imposes a set of tighter restrictions on the UML meta-model. Thereby, a UML Profile tailors the generic UML meta-model to the specific needs of a certain domain – in our case the domain of core component based business document modeling. Usually, a UML Profile consists of a set of stereotypes, tagged values, and OCL (Object Constraint Language) constraints. As a result, a business document modeler may only use a predefined set of artifacts and associations for modeling – exactly those as defined in the UML Profile.

Ensuring core component model validity with the UPCC

Since the conceptual, UML-based core components models shall be used for the derivation of XML Schema deployment artifacts, it is imperative that each model follows strict constraints. The different stereotypes, tagged values, and OCL constraints as defined in the UML Profile for Core Components, provide the technical foundation for a formal core component model. Based on the constraints in the UML Profile definition, validation routines may be implemented, ensuring model validity against the core compo-

5.1 Introduction

nent standard. Thus, valid models may be provided, which are the basis for the derivation of deployment artifacts, i.e., XML Schema files. Without the UML Profile for Core Components, business document modelers would choose arbitrary representation formats for core components. Even if these representation formats are based on UML, no unique format may be provided. Thus, any transformation to a unique XML Schema representation is very likely to fail. The UML Profile helps to close this gap by ensuring model validity, and enables transformation to unique XML Schema representations. Eventually, these XML Schema representations may be used to configure service interfaces for IT systems in a SOA context.

Additionally, conceptual business document models are easier to communicate between different business partners. In particular in the volatile domain of business-to-business electronic commerce, business partnerships are likely to change. Each new business transaction is preceded by a negotiation process, with the goal to agree upon on a common process choreography and business document format. In general, the negotiation process is easier using conceptual models, depicting requirements in a graphical manner.

Conceptual models are easier to communicate between business partners

In particular when creating business information entities from core components, a business document modeler is confronted with several repetitive tasks. To relieve a business document modeler from these tasks, we have implemented an open-source tool called VIENNA Add-In (Visualizing Inter-ENterprise Network Architectures) [180]. The VIENNA Add-In is an extension of the UML modeling tool Enterprise Architect and supports a business document modeler in creating and validating Core Component models, based on the UML Profile for Core Components. Furthermore, the Add-In provides support for UN/CEFACT's Modeling Methodology (UMM) [174], which we introduce in Chapter 12. In the following we introduce the basic concepts of the UML Profile for Core Components using the accompanying waste management example. Furthermore, we outline where the VIENNA Add-In may be employed to relieve a business document modeler from repetitive modeling tasks.

Introducing the VIENNA Add-In

5.2 UPCC – A UML Profile for Core Components

A unique representation for core components

As indicated in the introduction, core components are standardized independent of any business context or specific syntax, using regular spread sheets. The Core Components Technical Specification (CCTS) defines its own MOF-like (Meta-Object Facility [128]) meta-model as we already outlined in Chapter 4. However, this MOF-like meta-model is entirely independent of the UML meta-model. To overcome these limitations, we have developed a unique and easy to use representation format for core components, which resulted in the UML Profile for Core Component (UPCC) 3.0 standard. Figure 5.1 gives an overview of the different stereotypes used in the UPCC. Since the full names of the stereotypes are quite long, abbreviations have been used. Stereotypes representing modeling artifacts are presented using a black background. In UPCC, modeling artifacts are structured using the concept of packages. In the UPCC meta-model these packages are shown with a white background. In the upper right corner of each stereotype the underlying UML concept is shown, which the stereotype extends, e.g., an `aggregate core component` (ACC) extends Class.

Figure 5.1 UPCC meta-model

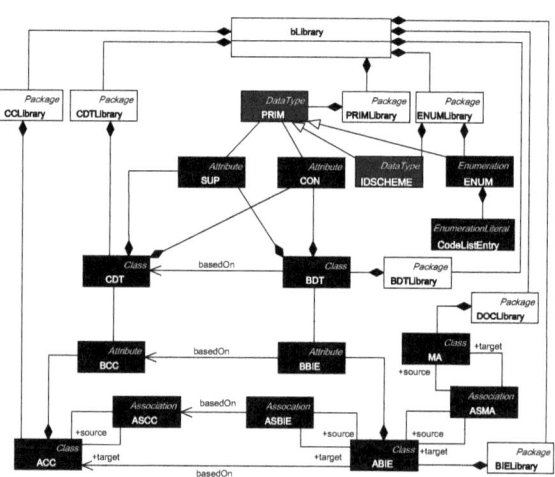

5.2 UPCC – A UML Profile for Core Components

The main goal of the UPCC standard is the precise and unambiguous representation of core components in UML. We built the UML Profile on the naming conventions of the original Core Components Technical Specification. Thus, readers may easily find the necessary associations to the original core component concepts, introduced in Chapter 4.

The very basic stereotype is a *primitive type (PRIM)*. A primitive type is used to express basic types such as String or Integer. The *primitive type* stereotype extends the built-in UML type *DataType*. Currently, the UN/CEFACT Data Type Catalogue [169] defines eleven predefined primitive types. A business document modeler may define restrictions on a primitive type, such as the maximum length of a String or the allowed fractional digits of a decimal type, using the concept of facets. The allowed facets per primitive type are also defined in the Data Type Catalogue and are realized in the UML Profile using tagged values.

Primitive types, codes lists, and identifier schemes

In general the allowed set of values of a *primitive type* may be restricted using two different concepts: *enumeration types* and *identifier scheme types*.

An *enumeration (ENUM)* is used to restrict a primitive type to a specific set of allowed values. Hence, the business document modeler may restrict a primitive type to a specific set of values, e.g., ISO 3166 [76] for valid country codes. In UPCC an *enumeration* is a specialization of a primitive type and is represented using the UML concept of an *enumeration*. Each enumeration contains one to many CodeListEntry attributes.

Enumeration type

In addition to an enumerated restriction, a business document modeler may also chose to define an *identifier scheme (IDSCHEME)* for a primitive type. An identifier scheme defines a set of production rules for a given primitive type. E.g., a String value may be restricted to represent only valid bank account numbers, using a regular expression. Typically, the values generated by an identifier scheme are not enumerated. In UPCC an identifier scheme is represented as a specialization of a primitive type and is based on the built-in UML type *DataType*.

Identifier scheme type

In contrast to *primitive types*, *enumerations*, and *identifier schemes*, a *core data type (CDT)* may express a more meaningful type. Core data types are modeled using UML classes, consisting of multiple attributes. Thereof, exactly

Core Data Types

one attribute is stereotyped as *content component (CON)* and multiple attributes may be stereotyped as *supplementary components (SUP)*. The content component represents an atomic value and supplementary components are used to provide meta information about the content component. An example core data type might for instance be `measure`. The content component contains the decimal number `12.2`. The additional supplementary component `unit code` identifies the unit of measure, e.g., Celsius, Fahrenheit, etc. UML requires that each attribute of a class has a certain type. In case of *content components* and *supplementary components*, the valid types are *primitive type (PRIM)* and its specializations *enumeration type (ENUM)* and *identifier scheme type (IDSCHEME)*. UN/CEFACT defines a finite set of allowed core data types in the UN/CEFACT Data Type Catalogue [169]. For each content component and supplementary component of a CDT, the catalogue defines the allowed primitive types.

Core Components As already outlined in the introduction to core components, *aggregate core components (ACC)* are modeled using UML classes. The attributes of an aggregate core component are stereotyped as *BCC* and are called *basic core components*. A BCC attribute has a certain type called *core data type (CDT)*. For a connection of different aggregate core components it is possible to use the concept of a UML composition stereotyped as *association core component (ASCC)*. By definition, every *ASCC* must have a `source` and a `target`, which is of type *ACC*.

Business Data Types If a core data type is used in a certain business context, it becomes a *business data type (BDT)*. Each business data type must be based on one of the approved core data types, defined by UN/CEFACT. This strong relationship is maintained using a *basedOn* dependency, leading from a business data type to its underlying core data type. Analogous to the concept of a *core data type (CDT)*, a *business data type (BDT)* consists of exactly one *content component (CON)* and multiple *supplementary components (SUP)*, which follow the same purpose as they do in a *core data type*. Similar to a core data type, content components and supplementary components of a BDT are typified using primitive types (PRIM) and its two specializations enumeration (ENUM) and identifier scheme (IDSCHEME). Note that a PRIM,

5.2 UPCC – A UML Profile for Core Components

IDSCHEME, or ENUM of a BDT must be a subset of the respective PRIM, IDSCHEME, or ENUM used to set the content component or supplementary component of the underlying CDT. This is in accordance with the general core component paradigm of restriction.

Similar to the concept of core components, an *aggregate business information entity (ABIE)* is modeled using a UML class. It consists of several attributes, which are stereotyped as *basic business information entities (BBIE)*. Each BBIE has a certain type called *business data type*. Different aggregate business information entities may be assembled to a more complex data representation using UML compositions or UML aggregations, stereotyped as *association business information entities (ASBIE)*. Each ASBIE composition/aggregation must have exactly one ABIE as source and one ABIE as target.

Business information entities

So far the different modeling artifacts have been explained. The UML packages, used to group the artifacts, are shown with a white background in Figure 5.1. Consequently, each package aggregates a certain type of artifact or is itself aggregated by another package. Two packages play a particular role: *business document library (DOCLibrary)* and *business library (bLibrary)*. A *DOCLibrary*, shown on the lower right hand side of Figure 5.1, is used to aggregate different *message assemblies (MA)*. A *message assembly* is used to aggregate different self-contained aggregate business information entities to a business document. In order to connect a message assembly to an aggregate business information entity, or different message assemblies with each other, the concept of an *association message assembly (ASMA)* is used. Each *DOCLibrary* represents exactly one type of business document and thus exactly one *DOCLibrary* is created for each business document.

Grouping artifacts in packages

The different packages of a UPCC model are aggregated in a *bLibrary*. Hence, a business document modeler constructs all necessary business documents of a given business collaboration in exactly one business library, which may be integrated in an inter-organizational business process model. Thereby, the business process model specifies the exact exchange order of the different business documents. We further detail the integration of inter-organizational business process models and business document models in Chapter

12. Having clarified the basic concepts of the UML Profile for Core Components, the following Section introduces the accompanying example from the waste management domain.

5.3 UML Profile for Core Components by example

UPCC example from the waste management domain

In Figure 5.2, the example package structure of a business document model using the UML Profile for Core Components (UPCC) is shown. The presented scenario has been taken from a waste management scenario, which was introduced in Chapter 2. At the bottom of Figure 5.2, four different business documents are shown, stereotyped as *InfEnvelope*: certificate of waste receipt form, waste movement accepted form, waste movement rejected form, and waste movement form envelope.

In the following we outline how the example business document waste movement form envelope is created using the UPCC. The model shown in Figure 5.2 denotes the relevant UPCC packages, already embedded in a business process choreography model, based on UN/CEFACT's Modeling Methodology (UMM). Note the three central views *business requirements view (bRequirementsV)*, *business choreography view (bChoreographyV)*, and *business information view (bInformationV)* on top of Figure 5.2, belonging to the process choreography perspective. We further elaborate on choreography aspects and the integration of business document models therein in Chapter 12. In the following we concentrate on the business document perspective.

We assume that a waste movement form envelope is exchanged between an exporter, export authorities, import authorities, as well as the importer. A *waste movement form envelope* consists of several *waste movement forms*. Waste movement forms contain one to many *consignments*, each representing a waste consignment. Thus, the first task of a business document modeler is to search for an appropriate core component representation of a consignment in the Core Component Library, maintained by UN/CEFACT [173]. There is indeed a core component *consignment*, and we therefore build our following example around this core component.

5.3 UML Profile for Core Components by example

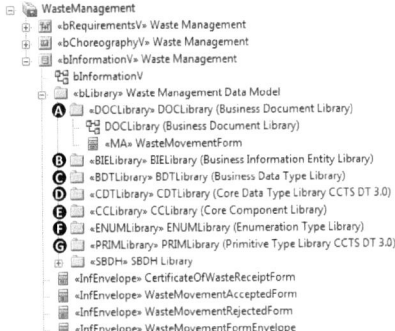

Figure 5.2
UPCC example package structure

Figure 5.3 shows a simplified version of the core component **consignment** with its association core component properties and basic core component properties as defined in the core component library of UN/CEFACT. A **consignment** has zero to many **consignment items**. Every **consignment item** has one or more **importation** and **export countries**, as shown on the right hand side of Figure 5.3. Additionally, zero to many **transit countries** may be specified by the business document modeler. Each **consignment item** has zero or more **physical shipping marks**, identifying the **consignment item**. A **shipping mark** may include either a **bar code**, or a **radio frequency identification (RFID)** tag, or both. Furthermore, each **consignment item** has zero to many **despatch parties** and zero to many **delivery parties**. In the final business document model, core components are aggregated in core component libraries (CCLibrary). Compare mark *A* in Figure 5.2 and 5.3 to find the matching package in the business document model overview.

Introducing the example

As shown in Figure 5.3, *association core components (ACC)* are represented as classes. *Basic core component properties (BCC properties)* are represented by class attributes and the type of the class attribute. Remember that a basic core component property consists of a *property term* and a *representation term*. We take the first attribute from the ACC **consignment item** in Figure 5.3 as example: **identification** = property term, **identifier** = representation term. Together the *property term* and the *representation term* are the *BCC property*. Since the BCC property is

Core components in action

5 A UML Profile for Core Components

Figure 5.3
Core component
library example

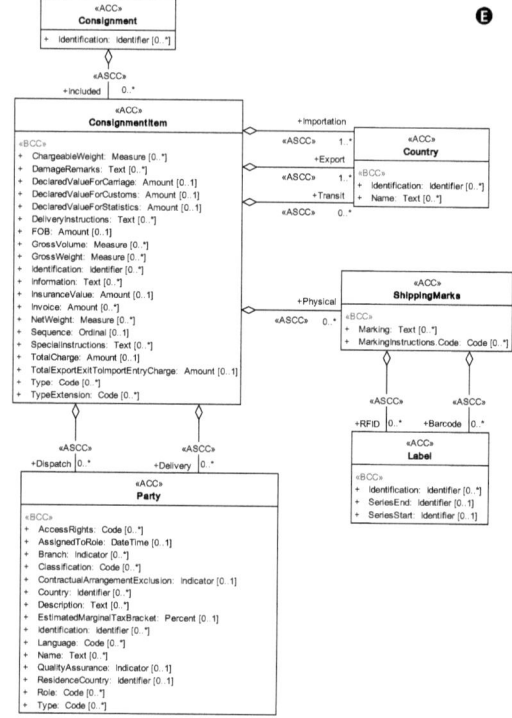

part of the ACC consignment item, it becomes a basic core component (BCC).

BCC properties are not considered in the UPCC

Note that due to the nature of a UML class attribute and the lack of support by the multitude of UML tool vendors, it is difficult to correctly represent BCC properties in a self-contained manner with the UML Profile for Core Components. In most UML modeling tools a class attribute cannot exist without its embracing class. Therefore, a basic core component property often cannot be explicitly modeled. However, we may use tools to extract the attribute definitions from aggregate core components to indicate reusable BCC properties. As a consequence UPCC does not make a distinction between BCC properties and BCCs, but uses only BCCs.

ASCC properties are not considered in the UPCC

Association core component properties (ASCC properties) are represented by association role names and the name

5.3 UML Profile for Core Components by example

of the class, the association is pointing to. Because each association core component property is part of an *aggregate core component (ACC)*, it becomes an *association core component (ASCC)*. We take the first association of the ACC consignment item on the upper right hand side of Figure 5.3 as example: importation = property term, country = associated aggregate core component object class term. Together the *property term* and the *name of the associated aggregate core component* are the *association core component property*. Similar to basic core component properties, we cannot explicitly model association core component properties due to limitations in UML modeling tools, i.e., an association may only exist if there is a source and a target class. Thus, the UPCC does not make a distinction between ASCC properties and ASCCs, but uses only ASCCs. Similar to BCC properties, tools may be used to extract ASCC property definitions from ASCCs.

We already outlined that the *representation term* of a *basic core component* is actually the *core data type* of the basic core component. Remember that core data types are used to set the value domain of a specific basic core component. In the UML Profile for Core Components, core data types are assembled in *core data type libraries (CDTLibrary)*. Figure 5.4 gives an overview of the core data types, which have been used in the different core components in Figure 5.3. The core data types in Figure 5.4 comply with the core data types as defined in the UN/CEFACT Data Type Catalogue [169]. Whereas the Data Type Catalogue only specifies the different data types using a regular text document, the UML representation denoted in Figure 5.4 may be easily exported and imported from different UML tools and reused in different core component models.

Core data types in action

As already outlined, each core data type (CDT) contains exactly one *content component (CON)* and zero to many *supplementary components (SUP)*. The value domains of content and supplementary components are set, using the concept of *primitive types (PRIM), enumeration types (ENUM),* and *identifier schemes (IDSCHEME)*. In the following, we examine the representation of the three different artifacts using the UPCC.

UN/CEFACT also publishes a set of allowed primitive types as part of the Data Type Catalogue. Figure 5.5 shows

Primitive types in action

Figure 5.4
Core data type
library example

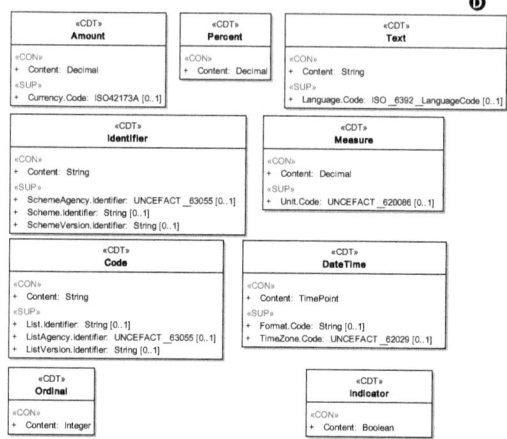

the UML representation from the waste management example for the different primitive types.

Figure 5.5
Primitive type
library example

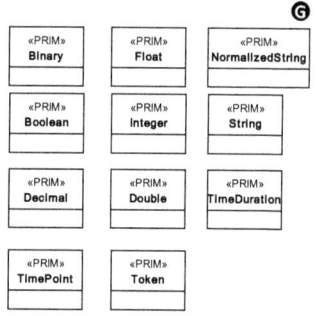

Primitive types are denoted using UML data types. The value domain of a primitive type may be additionally restricted using the concept of facets such as `minimum inclusive`, `maximum inclusive`, etc. Facets are realized using tagged values and are directly attached to the stereotype. Figure 5.6 shows a cut-out from the UPCC meta-model.

A *primitive type* stereotype is defined as an extension of the UML build-in type *DataType*. Note the different tagged values, which are attached to the primitive type definition. Among the different tagged values some are reserved for facet definitions (e.g., `maxLength`, `maxInclusive`, etc.). The

5.3 UML Profile for Core Components by example

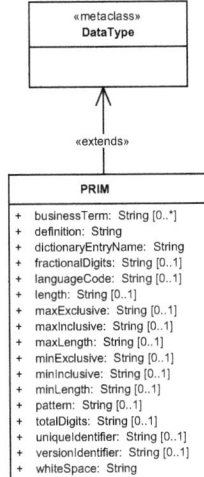

Figure 5.6
UPCC meta-model cut-out

UML Profile for Core Components enforces the correct application of the different tagged values to the different primitive types using OCL constraints. E.g., a `totalDigits` pattern must not be applied to a `String` primitive type. The exact definition, which facet may be applied to which primitive type, is also defined in the Data Type Catalogue of UN/CEFACT. In a UPCC model, a *primitive type library (PRIMLibrary)* covers all primitive types.

Enumerations (ENUM) are used to restrict the allowed values of a primitive type to an enumerated set of values. Typically, enumerations represent code lists, defined by different schema agencies. Using the UML Profile for Core Components, the business document modeler may either define his own code list or refer to a predefined list. Figure 5.7 shows two exemplary enumerations `ISO4217A` and `UN/CEFACT 63055`.

Enumerations in action

The first enumeration is defined by the business document modeler and represents a list of allowed currency codes. The currency code definitions are used for the supplementary component `currency code` in the core data type `amount`, shown on the upper left hand side of Figure 5.4. The decision, whether to use a predefined list of values or to define a new list, depends of the application domain of the enumeration type. In case of the ISO currency code, we may

Figure 5.7
Enumeration type library example

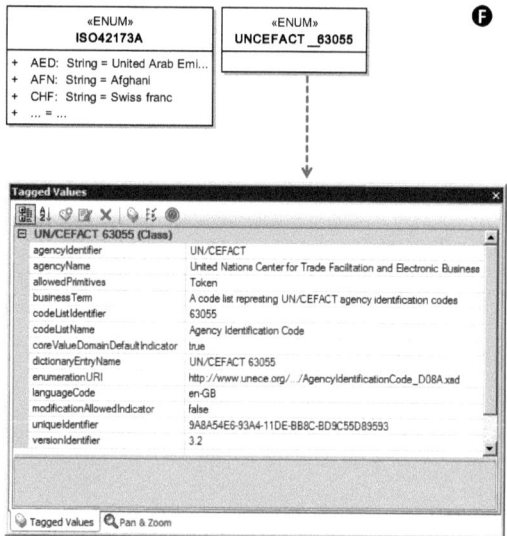

assume a scenario where we would like to have a list of all currency codes, except for those currencies, used in South America. Since such a list is not provided by ISO, a business document modeler has to define a new list as shown by the enumeration ISO42173A in Figure 5.7. Another option, a business document modeler may chose, is to restrict an existing country code list.

Reusing enumerations

In case the business document modeler wants to use a predefined list of values, the UML Profile for Core Components offers the possibility to point to an existing code list. The second enumeration – UN/CEFACT 63055 in Figure 5.7 – represents a list of allowed agency identification codes. Note that the enumeration itself does not contain any user-defined values, but instead points to an existing code list, using the tagged value enumerationURI, shown at the bottom of Figure 5.7. Additionally, UPCC offers the possibility to combine two or more code lists to a new union of code lists. For this purpose UML aggregations are used between different enumeration definitions. Enumerations are defined in *enumeration library (ENUMLibrary)* packages.

Identifier schemes in action

Sometimes the definition of an exact set of restricted values of a primitive type is not desired, but the business document modeler may want primitive types to follow a cer-

5.3 UML Profile for Core Components by example

tain pattern. In such cases *identifier schemes (IDSCHEME)* may be used. Each identifier scheme must be based on one of the predefined primitive types of UN/CEFACT. Using tagged values, regular expressions may be imposed on the primitive type, thus restricting it to a certain scheme. Identifier schemes are aggregated in enumeration library packages as well.

The core component **consignment**, as shown in Figure 5.3, represents the generic concept of a consignment, independent of any application or business domain. However, not all of the association core components and basic core components are needed for our waste management use case. Thus, the generic core component model is tailored to the specific needs of the waste management domain. We already outlined in Chapter 4 that by restricting core components to a certain domain, they become business information entities. In modeling terms, the business document modeler simply takes an existing core component, copies it, and renames it to the correct business information entity terms, including all attributes and associations. The core data types, used to set the value domain of the different basic core components, are becoming business data types. Consequently, it must be ensured that the business data type is always a subset of the underlying core data type. All these tasks may be automatically conducted using the VIENNA Add-In, relieving a business document modeler from repetitive modeling tasks.

From core components to business information entities

The automatically derived business information entities are aggregated in *business information entity libraries (BIELibrary)*. Thus, a BIELibrary contains all necessary building blocks for assembling the final business document. Figure 5.8 gives an overview of the business information entities, which have been derived from the core components in Figure 5.3.

The representation of business information entity concepts is similar to the representation of core component concepts. An *aggregate business information entity (ABIE)* is represented using a UML class. *Basic business information entity properties (BBIE properties)* are represented using UML attributes. Finally, *association business information entity properties (ASBIE properties)* are represented using associations between different ABIEs. In regard to ASBIE properties and BBIE properties, the UPCC follows the same

Business information entities in action

5 A UML Profile for Core Components

Figure 5.8
Business information entity library example

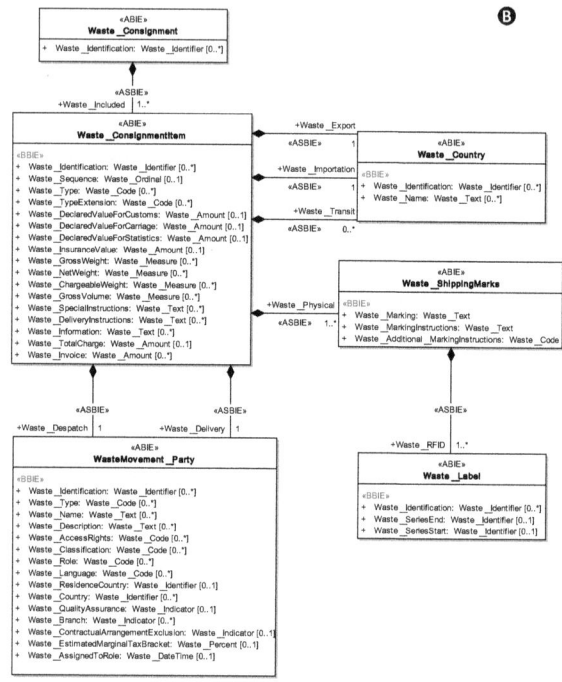

concept as for ASCC properties and BCC properties. Since UML tools do not support attributes without an embracing class, and associations without source and target elements, the UPCC does not consider ASBIE properties and BBIE properties, but uses ASBIEs and BBIEs only. However, a business document modeler may still use tools to extract the attribute definitions from aggregate core components to indicate reusable BBIE and ASBIE properties.

Note that for all three artifact types the qualifier waste_ has been used, to indicate the waste management domain. Thereby, business information entities restrict their underlying core components by putting them in the waste management context. We outline the restriction mechanism using the ABIE waste_ consignment item, which is based on the underlying core component consignment item, shown in Figure 5.3. From the basic core components of the underlying ACC, the ABIE waste_ consignment item omits FOB (free on board), damage remarks and total export exit

5.3 UML Profile for Core Components by example

to import entry charge. Another restriction is applied to the number of association core components of the ACC shipping marks. The derived aggregate business information entity waste_ shipping marks has only one association business information entity waste_ RFID and omits bar code. Note that all basic business information entities in Figure 5.8 have their own designated business data type.

We already outlined that *business data types* are derived from *core data types* by restriction. Similar to the relation between a business information entity and a core component, a business data type is based on a core data type. Figure 5.9 shows the business data types used for the business information entities in Figure 5.8. Note that business data types are put into a certain context using qualifiers. All business data types in Figure 5.9 use the qualifier waste_ to indicate the waste management context. Content components and supplementary components, however, must not be qualified.

From core data types to business data types

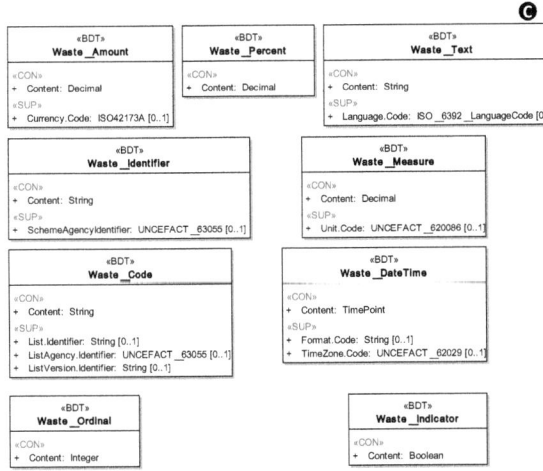

Figure 5.9
Business data type library example

The business data type waste_ identifier restricts the underlying core data type identifier by omitting two of its supplementary components. Additionally, a business data type may also restrict the value domain of content components and supplementary components using facets such as *MinimumInclusive*, *MaximumInclusive*, etc. Business data

5 A UML Profile for Core Components

types are aggregated in *business data type libraries (BDTLibrary)*

Assembling the final business document
After the business document modeler has created all necessary business information entities and business data types, the final business document may be assembled. Business documents are assembled in *business document libraries (DOCLibrary)* (cf. Figure 5.10). In the final phase of the business document modeling process, a business document modeler may encounter one major issue when assembling business information entities to a final business document. It is not allowed to draw arbitrary *association business information entities* between different *aggregate business information entities*. Recall that every *business information entity* must be based on a respective underlying *core component* concept. Thus, *association business information entities* may only be used if there is an *association core component* specified on the core component level. However, even if the core components defined in the core component library are very generic and aim at meeting as many requirements as possible, it cannot be guaranteed that the correct *association core component* may be found. Nevertheless, in some use cases the business document modeler may want to assemble existing *aggregate business information entities* to a new business document, even if there exists no predefined association between the aggregate business information entities.

To meet these requirements, the UML Profile for Core Components introduces two new stereotypes for the document library: *message assembly (MA)* and *association message assembly (ASMA)*. A *message assembly* is used to aggregate different *aggregate business information entities*, without the prerequisite of having a respective core component construct underneath. Thereby, *association message assemblies* are used to associate a *message assembly* to an *aggregate business information entity*. Figure 5.10 shows the final waste movement form business document.

On the upper left hand side of Figure 5.10 the message assembly waste movement form is shown. Using an association message assembly, a waste movement form aggregates one to many attached waste_ consignments. Note that a waste movement form *message assembly* may aggregate even more *aggregate business information entities*.

5.3 UML Profile for Core Components by example

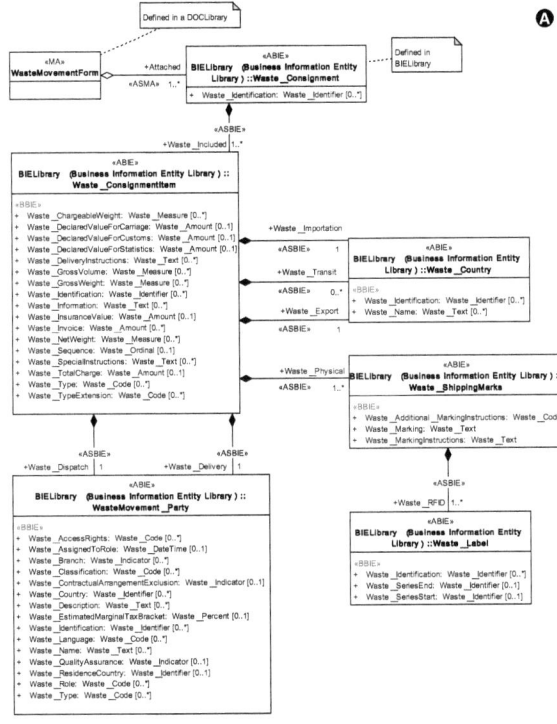

Figure 5.10
Business document library example

Thus, complex business document definitions may be built, based on reusable business information entity building blocks. With the finalization of the business document library artifacts, the conceptual business document modeling part is completed.

To ensure that the finalized UPCC model is fully compliant to the UPCC specification, a business document modeler must carefully respect all necessary constraints, as defined in the UML Profile for Core Components. However, even the precisest modeler may forget to define a mandatory tagged value or accidentally delete a mandatory *basedOn* dependency between a core component and a business information entity. Both of the mentioned actions would invalidate a core component model and a further error-free processing of the model cannot be guaranteed. To relieve a business document modeler from this burden, the VIENNA Add-In provides a core component validator module. The core com-

Checking model validity

ponent validator incrementally checks a UPCC model and validates whether all constraints as defined in the UPCC specification are fully met. In case an error is detected the business document modeler is presented with a detailed error message, specifying the erroneous element and the violated constraint.

With the final and validated core component model all necessary business document requirements are captured in an unambiguous manner. The finalized UML-based core component model may now serve as input for the generation of further deployment artifacts such as XML Schema.

5.4 Final assessment

Conceptual model for core components

In this Chapter we have introduced the UML Profile for Core Components (UPCC) as a means of applying UN/CEFACT's Core Components Technical Specification (CCTS) to UML. We have shown how implementation neutral core component concepts may be uniquely represented using a formal UML representation. Consequently, we introduced the UML Profile, tailoring the UML meta-model to the specific needs of business document modeling and guaranteeing an unambiguous UML representation of core components. Thereby, we provided the foundation for a two-layered approach for core component modeling. In a first step, core component-based business documents are assembled on a conceptual level, which may be achieved with the UML Profile for Core Components. In a consecutive second step, the conceptual core component model serves as input for further processing such as the derivation of XML Schema deployment artifacts.

Enable broad adoption of the CCTS using the UPCC

With the UML Profile for Core Components, the business document modeler is given an easy to use method to create core component compliant models. Conceptual business document models help to facilitate the reconciliation process between different stakeholders in an inter-organizational business process. Thereby, a major benefit is that non-technical people are also able to read and understand the UML representation of core components. With the opensource implementation VIENNA Add-In even an inexperienced business document modeler may start to build core component models from scratch. Using the core component

5.4 Final assessment

validator, which is part of the VIENNA Add-In, a business document modeler may easily check the validity of his model at any time. The formal correctness of a UPCC model is of crucial importance, if the model is the basis for the derivation of deployment artifacts. We further investigate the derivation of deployment artifacts in Chapter 8.

Even if the UML Profile for Core Components is a significant enhancement in regard to the applicability of implementation neutral core components, several shortcomings remain. A UML profile aims at tailoring the general purpose language UML to the specific needs of business document modeling. Due to meta-model restrictions of the UML, not all concepts of the CCTS may be fully represented in UML, without impeding an efficient UML-based modeling workflow. If we would for instance follow the strict CCTS approach of distinguishing between BCC properties and BCCs, every attribute of an ACC would have to be modeled as a self contained class and be connected to the parent ACC using an association. This would be necessary, since every BCC property is a self-contained entity in the CCTS. However, a UML attribute may not exist without its parent class – thus our current UPCC approach does not meet the requirement of self contained BCC properties. If we would follow the BCC property approach with the UPCC, this would unnecessarily blow up a UPCC model and thus an efficient modeling would not be possible any more. However, a business document modeler may still ensure an ASCC and BCC property mechanism using pertinent tools. We conclude that the UPCC does not provide a mapping of all CCTS artifacts, but accepts limitations for the sake of facilitating modeling.

Limitations of the UML

In the following Chapter we examine an alternative approach for modeling core component compliant artifacts, using a Domain-Specific Language (DSL) approach. Domain-Specific Languages are a promising approach for conceptual modeling and are able to overcome limitations of the UML.

6 A DSL for Core Components

In the previous Section we have introduced the UML Profile for Core Components (UPCC), mapping implementation neutral core component concepts to the Unified Modeling Language (UML). Another solution would be to define a dedicated core component modeling language in the first place, without tailoring an existing general purpose language. A promising approach for such a solution are Domain-Specific Languages (DSL). Using a Domain-Specific Language, it is possible to build a dedicated and streamlined modeling language for any given application scenario and context. Restrictions, as for example with UML, typically do not apply to DSLs. The DSL approach abstracts from irrelevant features, unnecessary for core component modeling. Thus, a business document modeler is provided with an easy to use modeling language, which is fully core component compliant. Similar to the approach based on UML, a core component DSL may be used to define business documents on a conceptual level. In a consecutive step the conceptual document models may be used to derive logical level XML artifacts.

Moving beyond the Unified Modeling Language

The remainder of this Chapter is structured as follows: The basic concepts of Domain-Specific Languages are introduced in Section 6.1. In Section 6.2 we elaborate on the concepts of our Domain-Specific Language for Core Components together with an accompanying example. The major advantages of a DSL, compared to UML-based approaches are outlined in Section 6.4. Finally, Section 6.5 concludes the Chapter with a final assessment.

6.1 Introduction

A Domain-Specific Language (DSL) is a language tailored to a specific domain, for solving a specific set of problems. In general, we distinguish between textual and graphical

6 A DSL for Core Components

Overcoming limitations of the Unified Modeling Language

DSLs. A textual DSL represents domain-specific characteristics and relationships between the different characteristics in a textual manner. Compared to a general purpose language such as C or Java, addressing problems of a wide area, a textual DSL focuses on a well defined problem area. Since textual DSLs are not well suited for graphical modeling, we do not consider them in our approach. Compared to a textual DSL, a graphical DSL provides an intuitive and error insusceptible approach to create valid concepts of the domain. A DSL model typically captures entities of a certain domain and relationships between entities. DSL models may further be used to derive machine processable artifacts, including program code or descriptive definitions for service oriented architectures, such as Web Service Definition Language (WSDL) or XML Schema files.

The graphical DSL used in our solution, is based on Microsoft Visual Studio DSL Tools [22], which have been introduced in version 2005 of Microsoft Visual Studio. Visual Studio DSL Tools enable the graphical definition of a DSL directly in Microsoft Visual Studio. Figure 6.1 gives an overview of the technical foundations of our DSL approach for core components.

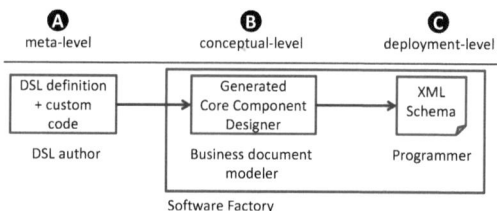

Figure 6.1 Technical foundations of the DSL approach

Building a dedicated core component designer

First, a modeler creates the DSL definition together with custom code on the meta level (cf. A in Figure 6.1). In case of our core component approach the custom code includes definitions, necessary for the validation of the core component model. In a second step, the DSL definition from the meta-level is used to generate a core component designer (cf. B in Figure 6.1). Since the core component designer has been generated out of the Domain-Specific Language, it contains only modeling elements, necessary for the assembly of a business document model. A business document modeler uses the core component designer to model core component compliant business document models. The built-in template

6.1 Introduction

mechanism of the Microsoft DSL is employed to transform the DSL-based core component model to XML Schema artifacts for the deployment level (cf. C in Figure 6.1). Thus, the DSL approach perfectly fits our requirements to define a business document model on a conceptual level and use the conceptual model to derive XML Schema artifacts for a service oriented environment.

Furthermore, Software Factories may leverage the use of DSLs, whereby a Software Factory provides a guidance for the business document modeler during the entire modeling process from creating the model to generating the artifacts. Software Factories aggregate different DSLs and may also include smart wizards, assisting the business document modeler and helping to automate repetitive tasks. Wizards may for example be used to derive a business information entity from a core component definition. Additionally, the validation component allows to check the correctness of a model, making the approach suitable for inexperienced business document modelers as well.

Leveraging DSL benefits together with Software Factories

In the following we briefly introduce the meta-modeling environment for creating a Domain-Specific Language in Visual Studio (meta-level in Figure 6.1). The conceptual level, where the actual core component models are assembled using the DSL generated core component designer, is introduced in Section 6.2. As seen in Figure 6.2, the DSL Tool's meta-modeling canvas consists of two swimlanes: *classes and relationships* and *diagram elements*. Using a simple drag-and-drop mechanism, a DSL designer may easily assemble a new Domain-Specific Language in a graphical manner. The entire model, shown in Figure 6.2, is referred to as *domain model* and defines the logical structure of the DSL. A domain model, among other artifacts, consists of *domain classes* (round-cornered squares) and *domain relationships* (squares).

A meta-modeling environment for creating a DSL

In a nutshell, domain classes define the classes of elements which may occur in an instance of the DSL. Domain classes have attributes, called *domain properties*. Domain properties consist of a name and a data type. Relationships among domain classes are defined using the concept of domain relationships. A domain relationship may either be an *embedding relationship* (shown as a solid line) or a *reference relationship* (shown as a dashed line). Embedding relation-

Defining the allowed elements in a DSL

6 A DSL for Core Components

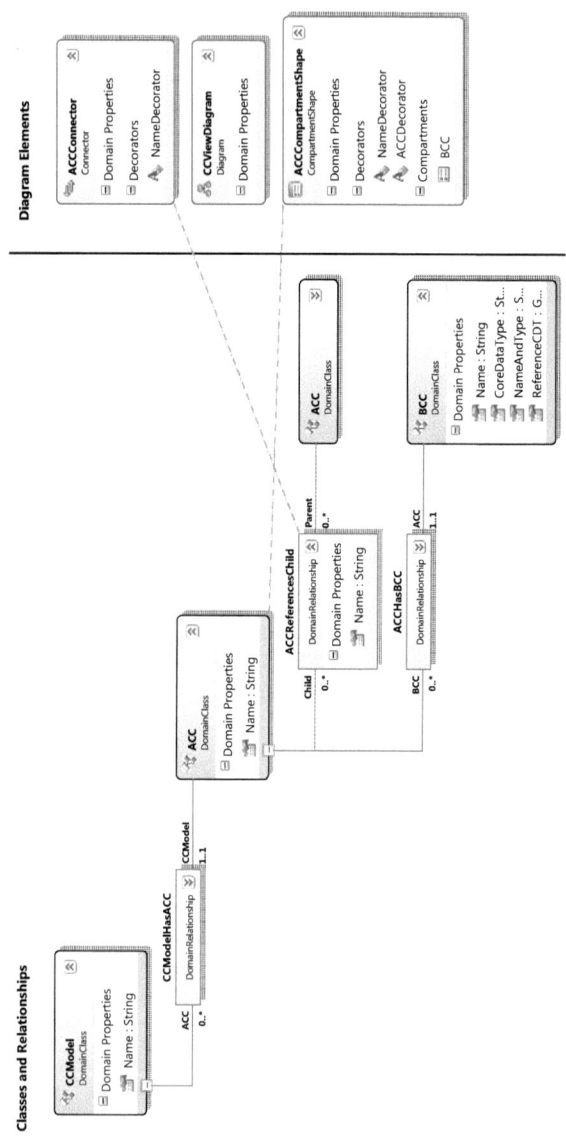

Figure 6.2
Domain model for core components

ships embed the element of the target domain class into the elements of the source domain class. Thus, if the source element is deleted, the embedded target elements are deleted as well. In contrary, reference relationships do not delete referenced elements, if the source element is deleted. The domain class CCModel, shown on the upper left hand side of Figure 6.2, is the root class of the DSL. There may be at most one root class in a given DSL. In the instance model the root class will represent the parent element for all other classes and their instances.

On the right hand side of Figure 6.2, different *diagram elements* of the DSL are shown. Diagram elements are used to define the shape of domain classes and domain relationships in the model instance, which will be generated out of the DSL definition. Thus, any shape of choice may be assigned to an arbitrary domain class or domain relationship. Hence, a DSL-based approach goes beyond classical modeling approaches such as the Unified Modeling Language (UML), where the modeler is bound to a confined set of elements and their assigned shapes.

Defining the appearance of DSL elements

6.2 The Core Component DSL

The Core Component DSL approach consists of six DSLs for core components (CC), business information entities (BIE), core data types (CDT), business data types (BDT), primitive types (PRIM), and a single DSL for enumerations (ENUM) and identifier schemes (IDSCHEME) (cf. A in Figure 6.1). All six DSLs are aggregated to a single Core Component Software Factory, providing a business document modeler with all necessary core component modeling concepts. After examining the meta-model of the Core Component DSL, we provide an example DSL instance, representing a cut-out from our accompanying waste movement form example. The required steps for creating a core component model and deriving a business information entity model from it are explained. Furthermore, we elaborate on the technical realization of important features, such as model transformation, artifact generation, validation, and serialization.

Six dedicated Domain-Specific Languages for Core Component modeling

The Visual Studio DSL Tools provide a graphical interface to conveniently assemble a specific DSL. Figure 6.2 shows the DSL meta-model for core components. The element CCModel represents the root of the model, including a name property. CCModel may have any number of ag-

Defining core component dependencies

6 A DSL for Core Components

gregate core component (ACC) elements, defined through the `CCModelHasACC` domain relationship. Any ACC may reference other ACCs through association core components (ASCC), defined by a `ACCReferencesChild` domain relationship. Furthermore, an ACC element may contain multiple basic core component (BCC) elements, defined through the `ACCHasBCC` domain relationship. A BCC element has four distinctive properties: *Name, CoreDataType, NameAndType*, and *ReferenceCDT*. *Name* defines the name of the BCC and *CoreDataType* is the name of the associated core data type. The *ReferenceCDT* property of a BCC contains the Globally Unique Identifier (GUID) of the core data type, setting the value domain of the BCC. Since the DSL Tools in the current version do not support cross-model references natively, we decided to use GUIDs to make cross-model references as described in [22]. The property *NameAndType* is for presentation purposes only, and contains the name of the basic core component together with the name of its associated core data type.

Defining the core component layout

As shown on the right hand side of Figure 6.2, there are three diagram elements in the core component DSL: `ACCConnector`, `CCViewDiagram`, and `ACCCompartmentShape`. An `ACCConnector` is mapped to the `ACCReferencesChild` domain relationship. Thereby, the connector shape associates two `ACCCompartmentShapes`. The shape prescribes that the source side of the connector must be represented as a diamond, and the target side of the connector is simply represented as a solid line. Additionally, the target side is annotated with the name of the association core component (ASCC), represented by the `NameDecorator` property in `ACCConnector`, shown on the upper right hand side of Figure 6.2. The `CCViewDiagram` element represents the diagram, which on the instance level holds the different core components and their relationships. Additionally, the `ACCCompartmentShape` is mapped to the `ACC` domain class. An `ACCCompartmentShape` consists of two decorators, namely (`NameDecorator` and `ACCDecorator`) and one compartment. The name decorator displays the name of the ACC and the ACC decorator simply shows the static text <<ACC>>. The BCC compartment of the `ACCCompartmentShape` may contain multiple BCCs. For convenience reasons, the business document modeler may optionally choose to expand

6.2 The Core Component DSL

or collapse the BCC compartment to enhance readability of the core component model.

In the following we dwell on how to use the developed DSL concepts to model core component compliant documents, by building on our accompanying example from the waste management domain. We start with a core component model instance for a `consignment`, which is part of the embracing `waste movement form`. Figure 6.3 shows the example `consignment` core component model. Each ACC has at least one basic core component (BCC). Based on our example, we explain a typical core component modeling workflow, and how the DSL representation helps to overcome repetitive modeling tasks. A business document modeler usually retrieves an existing core component definition from the UN/CEFACT Core Component Library. The generic core component is then tailored to the specific needs of the business domain. In the rare case that the business document modeler does not find a pertinent core component in the library, core components may also be created from scratch. Note that these core components are not aligned with the core components of UN/CEFACT and thus no interoperability guarantee of any kind may be given. However, in certain scenarios user-created core components are useful – e.g., if interoperability is only desired in an intra-organizational context. Thus, we distinguish between two different tasks: creating a core component definition from scratch and using an existing core component definition.

Creating a new DSL-based core component model

To create a new core component definition from scratch, a business document modeler may use the Core Component Software Factory for core components, which guides towards a valid core component definition. Among other components, such as code generators and wizards, the Software Factory for core components also contains the business document modeling environment, which has been generated out of the core component DSL. Using the DSL, a business document modeler may drag and drop aggregate core components (ACC) from the toolbox onto the modeling canvas. Additionally, basic core components (BCC) may be added to ACCs and data types of basic core components may be set. A business document modeler is automatically presented with a set of core data types, which he may assign to a basic core component. By default, all core data

Creating a core component from scratch

6 A DSL for Core Components

Figure 6.3
Consignment item core component DSL instance

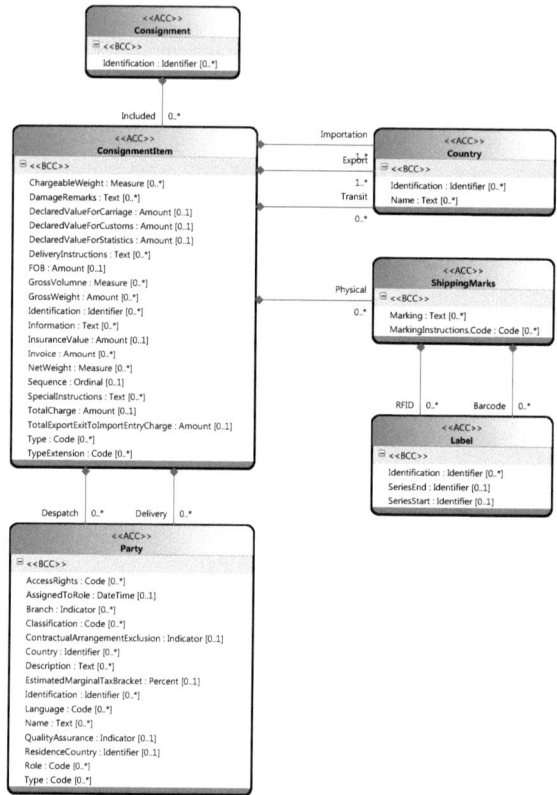

types as defined in the Core Component Data Type Catalogue of UN/CEFACT are available. In case no pertinent core data type (CDT) is present, a business document modeler may use the core data type DSL and create a new CDT definition. Using the concept of a connector, an existing ACC may be associated with another ACC to represent an association core component (ASCC).

Reusing a core component from the core component library

In case an existing core component definition is present in the UN/CEFACT registry, a business document modeler may retrieve the core component definition from the registry. To allow seamless access to core component definitions in the UN/CEFACT Core Component Library, two possible scenarios are possible. The first scenarios requires

6.2 The Core Component DSL

a full implementation of the UN/CEFACT library in terms of a registry solution, accessible over the Internet. Using a registry interface, a business document modeler may directly search and retrieve core component definitions out of the DSL-based core component designer. By 2009 such a solution still does not exist. We present the theoretical foundation for such a registry in Chapter 9. The second option requires that the spread sheet-based Core Component Library is transformed to an XML representation of DSL-based core components, which may be imported into the DSL core component designer. In the following we assume the latter scenario.

Utilizing the *Get BIE from CC* wizard, which is part of the Core Component Software Factory, a business information entity (BIE) may be derived from an existing core component definition. A business document modeler may restrict the existing core component definition and is able to automatically generate a business information entity from it. The wizard ensures that the created business information entity is compliant to the underlying core component. Figure 6.4 shows the resulting business information entity `waste_ consignment`, which has been generated out of the core component in Figure 6.3.

From core components to business information entities

Note that the core component DSL is very similar to the representation as defined by the UML Profile for Core Components. Since the UML Profile for Core Components has become a popular mechanism to represent core components, a switch in the representation mechanism would have brought potential confusion to business document modelers. However, in principle any representation format of choice could have been chosen with the DSL approach.

In regard to presentation features, DSL-based solutions offer a set of interesting options. In particular in the domain of core component modeling large scale models are becoming hard to read and perceive for business document modelers. A DSL-based solution allows to expand and collapse aggregate business information entities as well as their attributes and associations. This guarantees a better overview in particular if models are quite large. Figure 6.5 shows an example for a document library. The document library contains a message assembly `waste movement form` and an association message assembly pointing to the ABIE `waste_`

6 A DSL for Core Components

Figure 6.4
Consignment item business information entity DSL instance

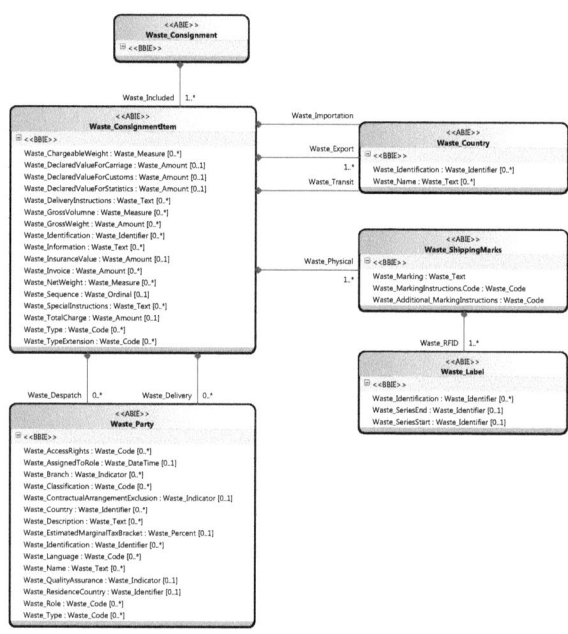

consignment. Note that only the root aggregate business information entity `waste_ consignment` is shown. All other business information entities are collapsed and are thus not visible.

Figure 6.5
Waste movement form DSL instance

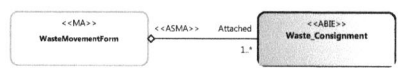

Using the business information entity DSL, a business document modeler may assemble different business information entities to represent a business document. Eventually, the business document model may be used to generate XML Schema artifacts. These XML Schema artifacts can be used to represent message definitions in a service oriented architecture. Having examined the theoretical background of the DSL, using our waste management example, we now briefly examine technical considerations of a DSL.

6.3 Technical considerations of a DSL

The in-memory representation of DSL models in the DSL Tools is provided by a *store*, providing the ability to modify models. Hence, the developer is able to load DSL models and iterate through them or search for specific model elements in it. As shown in Listing 6.1, each modification in the store has to occur in a transaction (line 1). First, a collection of all aggregate core components is retrieved in line 2. In the next step the collection is iterated, and for every ACC an appropriate aggregate business information entity (ABIE) is created and added to a collection (line 8 in Listing 6.1). Outside of the scope of Listing 6.1, we additionally have to transform BCCs to BBIEs and ASCCs to ASBIEs. Instead of using the store to generate one model out of another, it could also be used to automatically generate artifacts such as XML Schema out of an model.

Automating core component modeling tasks

```
1 using (Transaction transaction = store.TransactionManager.
        BeginTransaction("Generate BIEModel", true)){
2       ReadOnlyCollection<ModelElement> foundaccs = store.
        ElementDirectory.FindElements(ACC.DomainClassId);
3       if (foundaccs.Count > 0){
4           curbiev = new BIEModel(mystore);
5           foreach (ACC acc in foundaccs){
6               ABIE abie = new ABIE(mystore);
7               abie.Name = acc.Name;
8               curbiev.ABIE.Add(abie);
9           }
10      }
11 }
```

*Listing 6.1
Model transformation through store*

Another approach to derive artifacts, is with the help of the Text Template Transformation Toolkit (T4), which is a template-based code generation engine developed by Microsoft. The T4 templates are defined by processing directives, text blocks, and code blocks. Code blocks may be written in C# or Visual Basic .NET. Since the business document modeler may either use the built-in T4 template language or native C# for the manipulation of the DSL store, good performance results may be achieved. In particular if larger models are transformed or analyzed, a DSL-based solution works more efficient than a UML-based solutions. In most UML tools, third-party add-ons must be provided through vendor specific APIs, to access modeling artifacts. Typically, these third-party add-ons never reach the same performance as direct operations on the DSL store.

Using T4 templates

Faster than UML-based manipulations

Validating DSL-based core component models

An important prerequisite for the successful generation of code artifacts from a conceptual model, is the validity of the model. Validation of a DSL is either done by specifying soft constraints or hard constraints. Soft constraints are validated at specific tasks, such as opening a file, saving a file, or starting the validation through a menu item, and do not constantly provide a correct model throughout the modeling process. For example, a business document modeler may assemble an aggregate core component without any basic core components or association core components, which violates a constraint defined in the Core Component Technical Specification. However, if the business document modeler tries to save the model, a validation error message arises. On the other hand, hard constraints assure the correctness of the model at any time. For example, a business document modeler is not able to add a string value in a numeric field at any time.

DSL tools provide different approaches to enable soft and hard constraints. Soft constraints may either be assigned by adding validation methods to the model class or to the elements class. Hard constraints are directly wired into the DSL definition. There are already some hard constraints embedded within each DSL: maximum multiplicities, type constraints on role players, and type constraints on property values. Nevertheless, the developer is also able to add his own hard constraints. For example, in our core component DSL a hard constraint is used to validate that a basic core component (BCC) references a core data type (CDT), which exists in a CDT model.

Persisting DSL-based core component definitions Of particular importance for our core component DSL is the possibility to serialize core component definitions, to allow for storage and retrieval. As outlined at the beginning, a core component library, holding reusable core component definitions, is the central basis for all context specific business information entities. DSL Tools automatically create methods for saving and loading DSLs to/from files, when compiling the DSL meta-model. XML is used as the standard file format to save DSL specific model information, whereby a business document modeler may specify which information is saved, e.g., whether for each element type a GUID (Globally Unique Identifier) is saved or not. In our solution this is important, since we use the GUIDs to cross-reference between models. For each saved model there are two files created. One for the model data itself and the other one for the appearance of the diagram data. Still an open issue is a core component serializer, allowing to save a core component in a central core component registry. This is partly due to the still missing implementation of a central core component registry, where all core components from the UN/CEFACT Core Component Library are stored.

Having specified the most important aspects of our DSL-based approach towards a core component compliant implementation, we outline the most important advantages a DSL has compared to a UML-based approach.

6.4 Advantages of the DSL compared to UML

Since its inception in the mid-nineties of the last century, the Unified Modeling Language (UML) has gained considerable attention in particular in the model driven development community. As outlined in the previous Chapter, we have adopted UML to transfer implementation independent core component concepts on an easy to use platform. As a result, the UML Profile for Core Components (UPCC) specification has been developed and consequently been submitted to UN/CEFACT for standardization. In particular in regard to core component modeling a DSL has a set of advantages, compared to a solution based on UML. Table 6.1 shows the most important differences between UML and a DSL.

	UML	DSL
Dedicated	+/-	+
Extensible	+/-	+
Restrictable	+/-	+
Shape adaptable	-	+
Processable	+/-	+
Integrative	+/-	+

Table 6.1
UML vs. DSL

Legend: (+) Fully meets the criteria (+/-) Partly meets the criteria (-) Does not meet the criteria

Dedicated

DSLs and UML are both used for modeling, but aim at different problem areas and application domains. UML may in principle be used to depict any problem scenario in regard to application structure, behavior, architecture, as well as business processes, and data structures. In contrast, a DSL leaves out unnecessary aspects and focuses entirely on a specific problem domain, e.g., business document modeling. Thus, DSL-based solutions are streamlined and less complex than their UML equivalent.

Extensible   The UML is defined on the meta-model layer (M2) according to the Meta Object Facility [128]. Consequently, the concepts defined in the UML meta-model [129] are used to build UML models on the model layer (M1). In principle anybody may adapt the UML meta-model using the concept of UML profiles to customize the generic UML meta-model to a specific application domain. However, UML profiles are still limited in their expressiveness, because they must adhere to the UML meta-model specification. Apart from limitations in the UML profile mechanism, many UML modeling tools offer only a limited functionality in regard to UML Profile definitions. In contrast, a DSL defines its own meta-model and must not consider any predefined meta-model restrictions. As a result more powerful domain-specific solutions are feasible.

Restrictable   As part of its profile mechanism, UML provides the Object Constraint Language (OCL), allowing to restrict the UML meta-model in a formalized manner. However, most of the currently available UML modeling tools cannot interpret OCL. If extension mechanisms of the UML modeling tool are available, OCL interpreters or validators, checking the OCL constraints against a UML model, must be implemented manually. However, such an approach requires considerable coding effort. In contrast, DSL definitions allow to define customized code, specifically restricting a DSL. These code fragments, checking the consistency of a DSL-based model, are relatively easy to implement. Using the built-in validation feature of the DSL, a business document modeler is for instance prevented of nesting core components recursively.

Shape adaptable   In regard to the graphical representation of a UML model, a UML modeler is limited to a well defined set of shapes, representing classes, packages, etc. Although the UML meta-model would in principle allow to use different shapes, e.g., for classes, some UML modeling tools restrict the set of allowed shapes. Although this may be regarded as a benefit, since all modelers have a common understanding of elements by visually recognizing their purpose, domain-

6.4 Advantages of the DSL compared to UML

specific amendments are not possible. In contrast a DSL, using the built-in shape mechanism, allows any visual representation of choice for classes and for connections between classes. Thus, any domain-specific realization in regard to visual representation of concepts is possible.

The overall goal of a model-driven approach is the generation of code artifacts (e.g., XML Schema) from platform independent models (e.g., from a conceptual core component model, based on UML). For a transformation of a UML-based core component model to XML Schema artifacts, the Naming and Design Rules [170] of UN/CEFACT must be reflected. Thereby, XML Schema generators are built on top of UML tools, which is an expensive and complex task. Some UML case tools do not even allow direct access to the tool-internal representation format of the UML model. In contrast, a DSL store may be easily accessed using a programming language. With the T4 template mechanism an additional powerful transformation feature is provided by Microsoft.

Processable

An integrative model-driven development approach requires a set of different features such as transformation mechanism between different model types (e.g., between platform independent models and platform specific models). Additionally, the transformation of model representations to code representations, such as XML Schema, must be realized. Although all these features are in principle possible with UML, considerable coding effort and the integration of different tools for the specific tasks is necessary. In a DSL environment Software Factories may be used, which typically comprise code generators, different Domain-Specific Languages, as well as wizards, guiding a modeler through transformation tasks. Thus, the modeler is provided with an integrative solution approach for a domain-specific problem.

Integrative

We conclude that in general a DSL helps to overcome limitations of UML, which are either inherent to the UML meta-model or which are caused by a UML modeling tool. E.g., in most UML tools an attribute may not exist without its parent class – a limitation which does not exist in a DSL environment. Thus, in principle we could implement BCC properties, ASCC properties, BBIE properties, and ASBIE properties in a DSL. Nevertheless, one major goal of our DSL design was to closely follow the same notation

Overcoming limitations of the UML

using classes, attributes, and associations as used by the UML Profile for Core Components (UPCC). Thus, we do not consider properties in a DSL either, although it would in principle be possible.

6.5 Final assessment

Providing a dedicated modeling environment In this Chapter we introduced a new approach, based on Domain-Specific Languages (DSL), aiming to overcome limitations of the UML. Domain-Specific Languages provide the foundation for a dedicated modeling environment, focusing on a specific application domain. In the case of the Core Component DSLs and the Core Component Software Factory, a business document modeler has all necessary concepts for core component modeling at hand. All other unnecessary concepts are not reflected in the DSLs. Thus, workarounds as necessary in UML modeling tools are not required. Additionally, the performance of code generation from a DSL is faster than code generation from a UML representation. Validation and serialization for core components may also be easily implemented on top of a DSL. In regard to the core component representation format in a DSL, we closely followed the approach pursued by the UML Profile for Core Components, since the class diagram-based notation of the UPCC has become the de facto standard for the representation of core components.

Provide a conceptual core component model The overall goal of the Domain-Specific Language for Core Components is the same as the goal of the UML Profile for Core Components. Provide methods and tools for the definition of core component models on a conceptual and platform independent level. Consequently, the platform independent representation may be used to derive XML Schema code artifacts for a Service Oriented Architecture (SOA). Using our model-driven approach for the definition of SOA interfaces, changing requirements may be reflected in a more flexible manner.

Open issues Although the core component DSL provides a sound foundation for the definition of core components, some open issues still remain. A registry connector, built into the DSL tools, is still missing. Using the registry connector, core component definitions may easily be searched and retrieved from a central core component registry. However, the imple-

6.5 Final assessment

mentation of a registry connector is still blocked, because no appropriate core component registry implementation exists as of today. Furthermore, the serialization of core component definitions out of a DSL-based representation into another, e.g., UML-based representation is still an open issue. Both, the DSL-based representation and the UML-based representation, use different serialization formats, which are not interoperable.

Similar to the UML Profile for Core Components, the Domain-Specific Language for Core Components does not consider all CCTS characteristics in order to enable straightforward core component modeling. The DSL for Core Components does for instance not consider BCC property and ASCC property mechanisms, as well as their business information entities counterparts. However, BCC properties and ASCC properties may be reflected using additional custom code added to the Core Component DSL. This custom code could be realized using the GUID (Globally Unique Identifier) mechanism of the Microsoft DSL.

Non-considered CCTS characteristics

7 Building a global reference ontology with OWL

In this Chapter we abstract from a conceptual core component representation, based on UML or a DSL, and examine the leverage effects of Semantic Web Technologies for Core Components.

To allow for a processing of core component concepts with Semantic Web technologies, we propose a formalized ontological representation for core components. Consequently, we introduce a Web Ontology Language (OWL) [183] representation for core component concepts. In a first step, the basic core component concepts, as defined in the Core Component Technical Specification, are represented using OWL. In a second step we show how standardized core components from the Core Component Library (CCL) may be transformed to an OWL representation and serve as a common business document model. Different business document standard definitions, based on OWL, may further be mapped to the common business document model, which serves as the interchange format between business document standards.

Using semantic technologies for representing a common business document ontology

The remainder of this Chapter is structured as follows: in Section 7.1 be briefly motivate why ontological representations for business document formats are beneficial. Section 7.2 introduces the basic concepts of the reference ontology, based on core components. In Section 7.3 we elaborate on the specifics of the core component part of the ontology, and Section 7.4 shows how different OWL representations of business document standards may be mapped to the reference ontology. Finally, Section 7.5 concludes the Chapter with a final assessment.

7 Building a global reference ontology with OWL

7.1 Introduction

Conquering heterogeneous business document standard definitions

In the field of business document standardization several different approaches and standards have emerged over the past few years (cf. Chapter 3). Most of these standardization approaches focus on the definition of a common syntax for business documents and business information. Thereby, XML Schema has established itself as the de facto standard for the definition of business documents. However, even if business document standards are based on the same XML syntax, they are mostly incompatible, since every standard defines its own XML Schema. Thus, in case two business partners want to engage in an automated B2B interaction, they either have to support the same business document standard or they have to implement a costly syntactical mapping mechanism from one standard to the other standard. Assuming n different business partners, where each business partner uses a different business document standard x_j out of a set of available business document standards X, whereby $X := \{x_1, x_2, ..., x_n\}$, leads to a quadratic growth of $\frac{n(n-1)}{2}$ mappers, as shown in Figure 7.1.

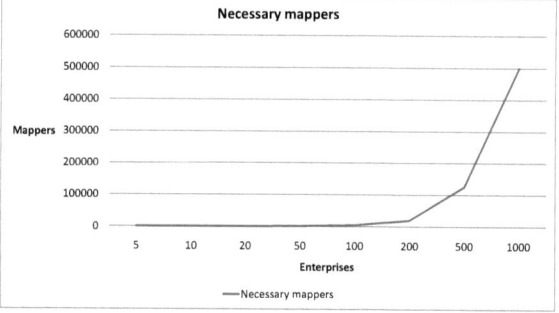

Figure 7.1 Necessary mappers for business document formats

As an alternative, a single business document standard format y may be introduced, to which each of the different business document formats, defined in X, may be mapped to. As a result, only one mapper must be implemented for each business document standard x_j, mapping from the single business document standard format y to the business document standard x_j and vice versa. This approach reduces the amount of necessary mappers to a linear growth of n.

7.1 Introduction

However, the definition of a common standard format y and the mapping of a different format x_j to it, imposes several challenges:

Challenges for a common business document standard

- Different business document standards do not necessarily have to follow the same encoding standard. E.g., EDIFACT messages use a different encoding than XML-based standards.
- Even if both standards use the same encoding such as XML, elements may be structured in a different way, e.g., there is no guarantee, that the first element in an *address* is always *street*.
- Two elements may be aggregated to one element in standard A, but may be two separate elements in standard B. E.g., *street* and *street number* – compare:
   - <street>Favoritenstrasse 9-11/188</street>
   - <street>Favoritenstrasse</street>
     <streetnumber>9-11/188</streetnumber>
- The semantic meaning of elements in different standards may be the same, even if the naming conventions are different. A *consignment* may be named *consignment* in standard A, but may be referred to as *shipment* in standard B.
- Even if two elements have the same semantics in standard A and standard B, they may still use different data types or other restrictions such as facets.
- Typically, different business document standards have different coverage areas. Thus, an element (e.g., *consignment*) which is considered in standard A, might not occur in standard B. Thus, mapping heuristics have to be applied. We further investigate mapping heuristics in Chapter 11 of this thesis.
- The common document format, to which each business partner maps his business document standard, must be defined in a globally unique manner. Thus, an international support for the common business document format must be provided; otherwise a globally accepted common document format is not feasible.

As a consequence, we propose to implement the common standard format based on UN/CEFACT's Core Components. By using core components for the definition of a common

Leveraging the benefits of Core Components

7 Building a global reference ontology with OWL

business document ontology, a maximum level of international acceptance may be guaranteed.

Interoperability scenarios In the field of semantic business document interoperability, we identify two important use case scenarios. On the one hand, business documents are defined in a top-down manner. As shown on the left hand side of Figure 7.2, a common reference ontology is defined, from which the local ontologies of business partner A and business partner B are derived. Thus, any local ontologies, derived from the common reference ontology, are compatible to each other (via the common reference ontology) and both business partners have a common understanding of what they actually exchange in a business transaction. This approach is for instance pursued by the core components initiative. UN/CEFACT defines a set of reusable core components in the Core Component Library. Consequently, business partners may take the reusable core components, tailor them to their specific needs, and create context specific business information entities.

Figure 7.2 Top-down vs. bottom-up standardization

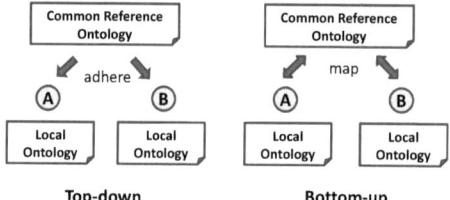

Mapping existing document ontologies to a common reference ontology On the other hand, business partners might already have their own business document standards and ontology definitions, independent of any common ontology. In such a bottom-up scenario, as shown on the right hand side of Figure 7.2, business partner A and business partner B map their existing local ontologies to the common reference ontology. Based on the ontological mapping definitions, which both business partners define once, any instances of a business document standard may unambiguously be mapped to the common reference ontology. As such, the common reference ontology serves as an interchange format between different standard definitions.

Since both business partners have a compliant exchange format, based on the common reference ontology, an automated business document exchange between the two business partners is possible. In a real world application, bottom-up scenarios occur more often than top-down scenarios, since most business partners already have their well established business document standards and ontologies. In both cases, the provision of a common reference ontology is important to achieve a common interoperability basis.

7.2 Reference ontology

Since core components are agreed upon by a broad industry and other standardization organizations as well as interest groups, they provide the ideal basis for a reference ontology. However, a formalized representation of core components is needed to allow for core components to represent a common reference ontology. In this Chapter we formalize the Core Components Technical Specification using the Web Ontology Language (OWL).

Building a reference ontology with OWL

Figure 7.3 gives an overview of the common reference ontology. In terms of the Meta-Object Facility (MOF) [128], the common reference ontology is defined on the M2 layer. The top class of the ontology is `owl:Thing`, serving as the superclass for all other classes. For a better legibility Figure 7.3 has been divided into three compartments, embracing core component, business information entity, and data type specific artifacts respectively. As namespace for core component specific classes, properties, etc. http://www.umm-dev.org/owl/ccts3# with the prefix cc has been chosen. According to the usual conventions the entire ontology definition may also be retrieved from this URL by the interested reader.

The upper left compartment of Figure 7.3 represents all core component specific artifacts of the common reference ontology. The superclass of every core component artifact is `cc:CC`, which has seven `owl:AnnotationProperty` values, representing specific core component properties. `cc:businessTerm` is a term under which the core component is commonly known and used in business and `cc:definition` is used to store the unique semantic meaning of the core component. If core components are stored and retrieved from business registries, they require a unique name. This name is represented by `cc:dictionaryEntryName`. To support multilingualism, `cc:languageCode` defines the language used for the core component. `cc:usageRule` specifies con-

Representing core component concepts using an ontology

straints on the usage of core components in free-form text. `cc:uniqueIdentifier` and `cc:versionIdentifier` are additional meta-information fields, required for registry storage and retrieval.

`cc:CC` has two sub-classes namely `cc:ACC`, representing aggregate core components, and `cc:ACCProperty`, which is a newly introduced superclass for basic core components and association core components. Both, association core components and basic core components, are represented by their respective *owl:Classes* `cc:ASCC` and `cc:BCC`. The annotation property `cc:sequencingKey` in `cc:ACCProperty` is used to assign an arbitrary order to an `cc:ACCProperty`.

Mapping business information entity concepts to the ontology

Similar to the core component concepts, the elements in the compartment on the right hand side of Figure 7.3 represent the business information entity specific artifacts of the ontology. The superclass of all business information entities is `cc:BIE`. Since business information entities are based on core components and traceability between these two artifacts must be guaranteed at any time, a `cc:isBasedOn` object property is defined between `cc:CC` and `cc:BIE`. Similar to a core component, a business information entity also has a set of annotation properties such as `cc:businessTerm`, etc. Their meaning is the same as the meaning of the properties of a `cc:CC`.

`cc:BIE` has two sub-classes, namely `cc:ABIE`, representing an aggregate business information entity, and `cc:ABIEProperty`, which is the superclass for basic business information entities and association business information entities. For both, association business information entities and basic business information entities, the respective *owl:Class* elements `cc:ASBIE` and `cc:BBIE` are defined. Similar to a `cc:ACCProperty`, a `cc:ABIEProperty` has an annotation property `cc:sequencingKey`, to specify an arbitrary sequencing order. Note the different `cc:basedOn` object properties between artifacts from the core component and business information entity compartments in Figure 7.3. These object properties help to trace business information entity artifacts back to the core component artifacts, on which they are based on.

Mapping data type concepts to the ontology

The lower compartment in Figure 7.3 shows the data type specific elements of our reference ontology. As outlined before, the value domain of basic core components

7.2 Reference ontology 125

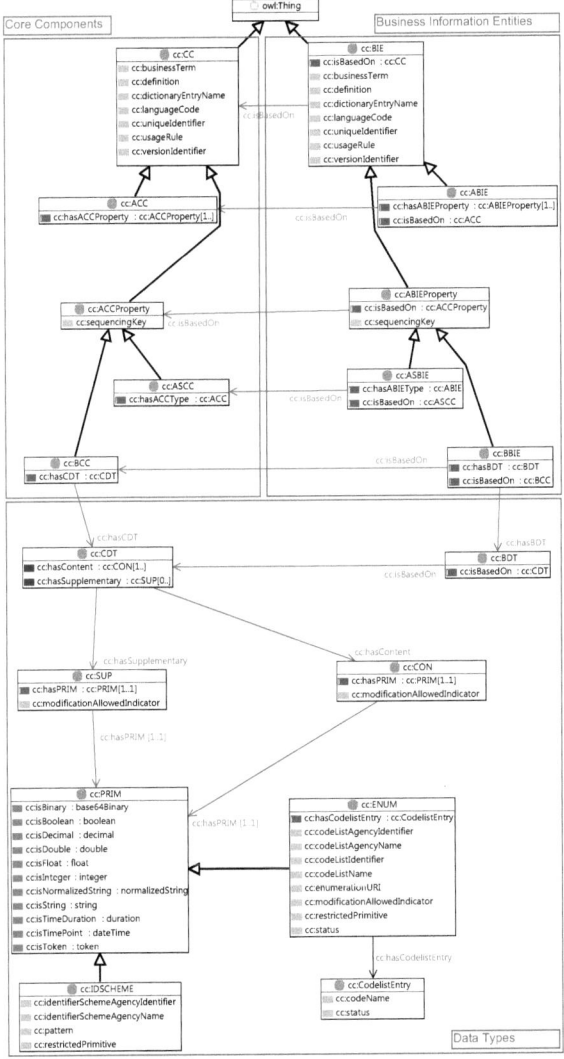

Figure 7.3
Overview of the common reference ontology

is set by core data types (CDT) and the value domain of basic business information entities is set by business data types (BDT). Consequently, each business data type must be based on exactly one core data type. This relationship is reflected in the ontology as well and a cc:isBasedOn object property is defined between a cc:BDT and a cc:CDT. Both, a core data type and a business data type, always consist of exactly one content component and zero to many supplementary components. Accordingly, cc:hasSupplementary and cc:hasContent object properties are defined in the reference ontology. Note that these two properties are not shown for cc:BDT on the lower hand side of Figure 7.3. Since a cc:BDT is based on a cc:CDT, these dependency properties are implicitly given.

Mapping primitive types Finally, the concept of a primitive type is reflected by cc:PRIM. As outlined on the lower side of Figure 7.3, a primitive type has eleven data type properties. Each data type property has a predefined data type, defined as *rdfs:range*, e.g., cc:isTimeDuration has *rdfs:range* xsd:duration.

Mapping enumerations and identifier schemes Specializations of a primitive type are represented by enumeration types (cc:ENUM) and identifier scheme types (cc:IDSCHEME). Enumerations consist of code list entries, represented by cc:CodelistEntry. The different annotation properties of cc:IDSCHEME, cc:ENUM, and cc:Codelist-Entry are used to provide meta-information about the different data types.

In the following, we elaborate on the context free part of the ontology – the core component ontology. The business information entity part of the ontology is constructed analogously, since business information entities are based on core components and in principle share the same concepts (with the exception of context neutrality).

7.3 Core component ontology

Core component concepts in detail Figure 7.4 shows the core component ontology in detail. The top core component class cc:CC is shown on the right hand side of Figure 7.4. It serves as the superclass for the two direct sub-classes cc:ACC and cc:ACCProperty. In turn, an cc:ACCProperty is the super-class of cc:BCC and cc:ASCC, representing basic core components and association core components, respectively. The dependency between a cc:ACC and its ACC properties is defined by the two object properties in the upper left corner of Figure 7.4. The object property cc:hasACCProperty indicates that an ACC has ACC properties. Additionally, the cardinality of the object property is set to 1. Thus, there cannot be an ACC

7.4 Mapping instances to the core component ontology

without ACC properties. The allowed values for the object property are restricted to `cc:ACC` and `cc:ACCProperty` using *rdfs:range* and *rdfs:domain*, respectively.

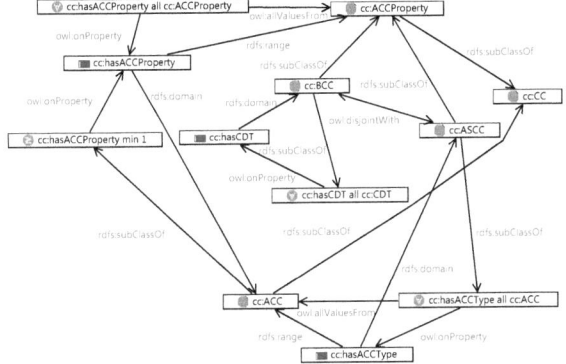

Figure 7.4
Core component ontology in detail

A basic core component has an assigned core data type, which is reflected by the object property `cc:hasCDT` in the center of Figure 7.4. Allowed values of `cc:hasCDT` are restricted to `cc:CDT` and `cc:BCC`, using *rdfs:range* and *rdfs:domain*, respectively. A `cc:hasACCType` object property defines that an association core component points to an aggregate core component. Using the `cc:hasACCType`, each `cc:ASCC` may be assigned with the appropriate `cc:ACC`. As with all other object properties, the allowed domain and range is restricted as well. An ACC property must be either a `cc:BCC` or an `cc:ASCC`. Thus, an `owl:disjointWith` property exists between the two classes.

The remaining parts of the reference ontology cover aspects of business information entities and data types in the same manner as explained above for the core component part of the ontology. Having defined the basic concepts, we further elaborate on how to map specific document instances to the reference ontology in the following Chapter.

7.4 Mapping instances to the core component ontology

Our common business document reference ontology is the starting point for integrating heterogeneous business docu-

7 Building a global reference ontology with OWL

Exemplary mapping from UBL to OAGi

ment standards. As shown in Figure 7.5, we distinguish between three different levels in regard to business document interoperability, according to the first three Meta-Object-Facility (MOF) layers [128]. For the accompanying mapping example we assume a UBL [121] and an OAGi [131] business document instance.

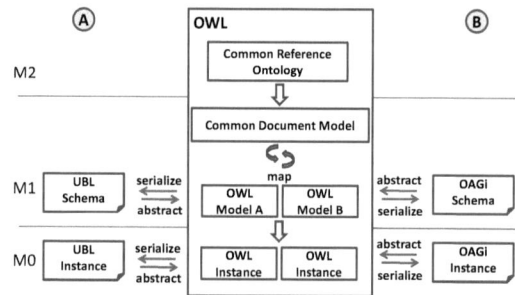

Figure 7.5 Overview of ontology mapping principles

In a typical interoperability scenario, partner A and partner B exchange business document instances as shown on the M0 level in Figure 7.5. We first transform platform independent core component concepts to OWL and define the common reference ontology on the M2 layer. This common reference ontology has been thoroughly introduced in Figure 7.3. Based on the concepts defined on the M2 level, a common document model may be created on the M1 level. For this reason, implementation neutral core components as defined in the core component library [173] are transferred to an OWL model, according to the definitions specified in the common reference ontology. Business document standards, such as UBL or OAGi, are transformed to a OWL representation on the M1 layer as well, resulting in OWL Model A and OWL Model B in Figure 7.5. This task has to be realized by the respective standardization organizations. Consequently, the OWL representation of different standards may be mapped to the common document model. The mapping of the OWL models to the common document model must be described using OWL mappings. Based on these OWL mappings, a set of transformation rules must be specified in a transformation language, uniquely defining a transformation process from standard A to standard B and vice versa. Since the mappings between two standards are now uniquely described on the M1 layer, transformation

7.4 Mapping instances to the core component ontology

rules for the M0 layer may be derived. The definition of a transformation language and the automated derivation of mappings on the instance level are still subject to research.

However, we are already able (i) to abstract business document standards from their XML representations and represent them in OWL and (ii) to align these OWL representations with a common business document model which is (iii) based on a common reference ontology, using core component concepts.

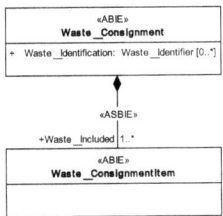

Figure 7.6
Simplified core component example

As accompanying example we map two instances of UBL and OAGi to a common business document model, defined using the common reference ontology. Figure 7.6 shows a simplified version of the accompanying waste movement form. For presentation purposes we reduced the model to exactly two aggregate business information entities (`waste_ consignment` and `waste_ consignment item`), one basic business information entity (`waste_ identification`), and one association core component (`waste_ included`). Furthermore, we do not consider data types in the mapping example.

Introducing the mapping example

As an example, Figure 7.7 shows how the common business document on the M1 level is based on the common reference ontology on the M2 level. Implementation neutral core components from the core component library are defined using OWL on the M1 level. We show three different core components namely `abie:Waste_Included` (ASBIE), `abie:Waste_Identification` (BBIE), and `abie:Waste_ - Consignment` (ABIE) as an example. Note the dependency between the different artifacts on the M1 and the M2 layer, guaranteeing the unique semantic meaning of each artifact on the M1 layer. The OWL representation of the OAGi and UBL artifacts are mapped to the common business document model on the M1 layer, e.g., `oagi:ShipmentUnitItem`

7 Building a global reference ontology with OWL

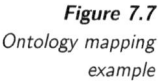

Figure 7.7
Ontology mapping
example

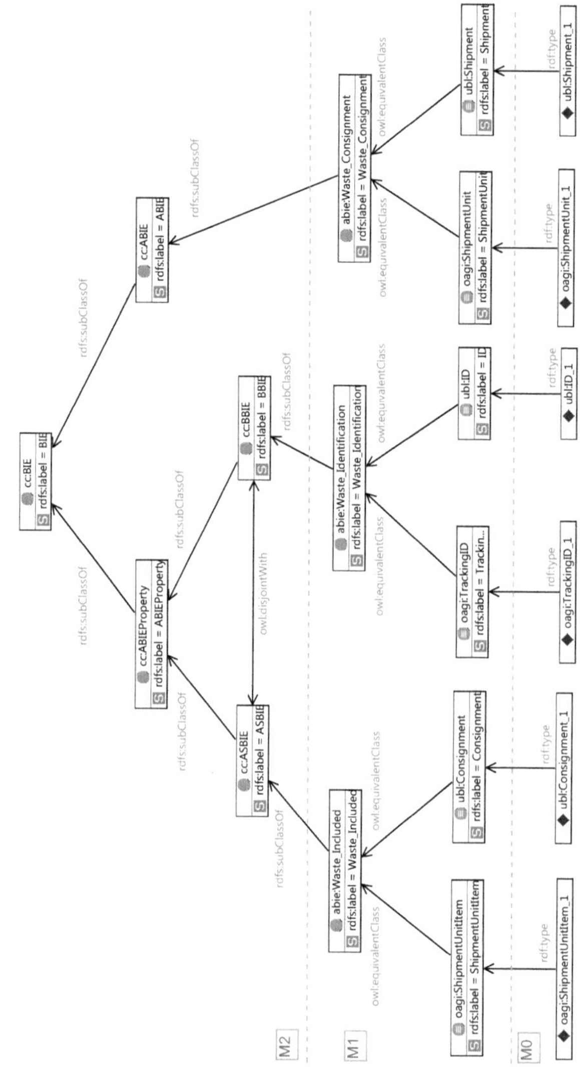

and ubl:ConsignmentItem both map to the ASBIE abie:-
Waste_Included. The different namespaces of all OAGi and
UBL artifacts indicate that the respective elements belong
to a different ontology defined in a different namespace. Fi-

nally, OAGi and UBL instances on the M0 layer are aligned to their conceptual definitions on the M1 layer.

In the example described above, the common business document model on the M1 layer serves as the interchange format between different business document standards. Since we base our mappings on the Web Ontology Language, we may leverage benefits from semantic technologies.

7.5 Final assessment

In this Chapter we introduced a two-fold approach for the transformation of implementation neutral core component concepts to a Web Ontology Language (OWL) representation. First, the basic core component concepts are represented using OWL, resulting in a common reference ontology. Based on the basic concepts of the common reference ontology, implementation neutral core components from the core component library are transformed to an OWL representation. This results in a common business document model, to which any arbitrary business document standard may be mapped to.

Provide an implementation format for core components

The approach, present in this Chapter, is in particular useful if two or more existing business document definitions are to be mapped to a common core component basis. In principle two business document standards could be mapped on a syntactical level only, using regular XSLT mappings. However, the mapping of two business document standards to a common core component model guarantees that both standards have the same semantic mapping basis and thus no semantic heterogeneities occur during the mapping. In contrast, the UML and DSL-based solutions presented in the previous Chapters follow a top-down approach, where a common core component model is created and respective deployment artifacts such as XML Schema are derived from the common business document model. We conclude that it depends entirely on the application scenario, whether a UML, DSL, or OWL-based solution should be chosen.

Difference to UML and DSL-based solutions

Since we base our common business document model on the Web Ontology Language, Semantic Web technologies may be leveraged for the mapping of different business document standards. In particular in regard to the development of a transformation language – transforming instances

Leverage the advantage of Semantic Web technologies

of two different business document standards, based on the defined mappings on the schema level – semantic technologies such as reasoners may be used.

Open issues   The definition of transformation rules, allowing for an automated mapping of instances on the M0 layer, based on mapping definitions on the M1 layer, is still an open research issue. Thereby, the automated derivation of a transformation rules, based on the formalized ontology mappings, remains the main research issue.

8 Deriving XML Schema from Core Components

In the previous Chapters we have introduced three representation formats for implementation neutral core components: the UML Profile for Core Components, the Core Component DSL, and an OWL representation for Core Components. With the first two approaches, a business document modeler may easily assemble core component compliant business document definitions on a conceptual level. In particular in environments, where a multitude of different stakeholders work on a common business document definition, a conceptual document representation provides several benefits. In contrary, an OWL-based solution is useful if two or more business document standards are to be mapped to a common core component model. In the following we concentrate on the derivation of XML Schema artifacts from conceptual UML or DSL-based core component models. Note that in principle even an OWL representation of core components may serve as the input for XML Schema generation purposes. As an example we use the UML-based core component representation, although all concepts introduced in this Chapter may also be applied to a DSL or OWL-based representation.

For a technical implementation in IT systems, however, conceptual models cannot be directly used. In particular in a service oriented environment, XML document representation are currently state of the art. Business service interface definitions on each business partner's side are defined using XML Schema, unambiguously prescribing which XML instance documents are accepted for a specific service invocation. Thus, a solution is needed where the advantages of both worlds, conceptual business document definitions and XML Schema representations, may be used. In this Chapter we propose a solution based on the Naming and Design Rules [171] of UN/CEFACT. In this Chapter

From conceptual business document models to XML Schema

8 Deriving XML Schema from Core Components

we present the theoretical foundations for the derivation of XML Schema artifacts from core component models, defined with the UML Profile for Core Components (UPCC) and the Core Component DSL. Thus, this Chapter is closely related to Chapter 5 and 6 and reuses the introduced UPCC examples, to show the basic concepts of the Naming and Design Rules.

The remainder of this Chapter is structured as follows: Section 8.1 explains the theoretical foundations of the transformation mechanism, based on the Open-edi reference model. Section 8.2 introduces the transformation concepts of the XML derivation from core components, using the accompanying waste management example. Finally Section 8.3 concludes the Chapter with a final assessment.

8.1 Introduction

From conceptual models to deployment artifacts

Since XML was introduced in 1996 [184], its popularity has constantly increased due to its versatility, flexibility, and easy applicability. An additional boost has been brought by the introduction of Web Services and their related technologies such as Web Service Definition Language (WSDL) [187], Simple Object Access Protocol (SOAP) [186], and Universal Description Discovery and Integration (UDDI) [118]. In particular in the context of Web Services, the clear and precise definition of a business document is important. Usually, interfaces defined by WSDL import the appropriate XML Schema, defining the type of business document the interface accepts.

Introducing the Open-edi reference model

With the implementation of the UML Profile for Core Components (UPCC) and the Domain-Specific Language for Core Components, we follow the idea of the Open-edi reference model [78]. Figure 8.1 gives an overview of the basic concepts of the Open-edi reference model.

Figure 8.1 Open-edi reference model

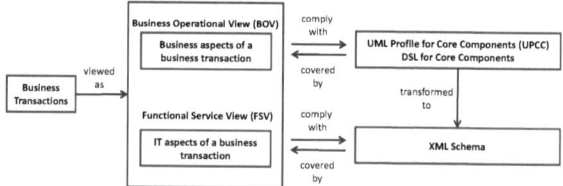

In the context of the Open-edi, a business transaction is viewed from a two-fold perspective: from a *Business Operational View perspective (BOV)* and from a *Functional Service View perspective (FSV)*. The Business Operational View of a business transaction abstracts from technical implementation details and focuses on business aspects, such as business information, business conventions, agreements, and rules among organizations. Thus, non-technical people may also be involved in the definition of BOV related artifacts. In core component terms, artifacts created by the UML Profile for Core Components and the Domain-Specific Language for Core Components belong to the BOV.

Business Operational View

In a consecutive step, the created artifacts from the Business Operational View are transformed to artifacts for the Functional Service View (FSV). In contrast to the Business Operational View, these artifacts are technical ones, and may be used for deployment in IT systems. In terms of core component modeling, XML Schema artifacts are derived from the conceptual core component models, created in the business operational view. To allow for a unique transformation of BOV artifacts to FSV artifacts, specific rules and guidelines are needed. We further elaborate on the basic transformation concepts in the following Section.

Functional Service View

8.2 Transformation concepts

This Section outlines, how a conceptual core component model may be used to derive XML Schema artifacts. XML artifacts form the logical level business document model, to which every document instance, exchanged between two B2B systems, must comply to. UN/CEFACT suggests the use of Naming and Design Rules (NDR) [171], defining a unique representation of core components in XML. Along with each new release of the Core Components Technical Specification and its UML Profile, UN/CEFACT delivers pertaining Naming and Design Rules. An overview of the basic NDR concepts is given in Figure 8.2.

Thereby, Figure 8.2 describes rules for the transformation of business information entity concepts, including business data types (BDT), basic business information entities (BBIE), aggregate business information entities (ABIE), as well as association business information entities (ASBIE).

Transformation rules guarantee unambiguous XML documents

8 Deriving XML Schema from Core Components

Figure 8.2
Transformation concepts of UPCC to XML Schema components

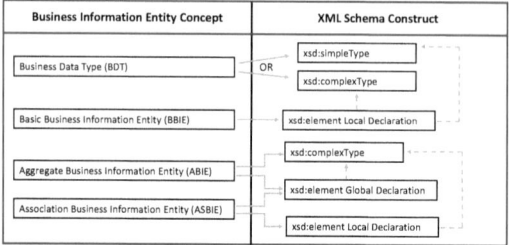

The concept of a BDT is represented through the XML Schema construct `simpleType` or `complexType`. In case a BDT contains only a content component, it is represented by a `simpleType`. Otherwise, if it contains supplementary components as well, it is represented using a `complexType`. An ABIE is represented by the XML Schema construct `complexType`. Within the complex type definition for an ABIE, local element declarations are defined, representing the BBIEs of the particular ABIE. BBIEs are either typified by a `simpleType` or a `complexType`, representing a particular BDT. In addition to the complex type definition, a global element declaration is created for each ABIE. For representing ASBIEs, which are used for defining associations between ABIEs, either local or global element declarations are used. In case the association is of type shared, a global element is defined for the ASBIE. The globally declared element is then referenced from within the complex type definition of the ABIE. Otherwise, in case the association is of type composite, the ASBIE is declared as a local element within the complex type definition of the ABIE.

Structure of the generated schemas

Another aspect of generating XML Schemas from conceptual models is the structure of the resulting XML Schemas. Core component artifacts are, as introduced earlier, organized in different libraries. The libraries relevant in respect of BDTs, ABIEs, BBIEs, ASBIEs, as well as business document definitions, are the packages named `BDTLibrary`, `BIELibrary`, and `DOCLibrary`. According to the package structure and following the Naming and Design Rules (NDR), the generated XML Schema representations are organized into three separate XML Schema files. An overview of the generated deployment artifacts is provided in Figure 8.3,

8.2 Transformation concepts

showing that a separate XML Schema file is generated for each library.

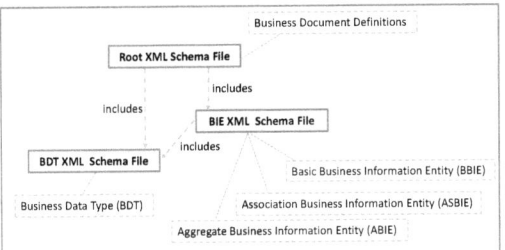

Figure 8.3
XML Schema deployment artifacts

Since business documents are defined using business information entities, the different rules defined in the Naming and Design rules apply to business information entity artifacts only. However, an important aspect when generating deployment artifacts for business information entities, is maintaining the basedOn dependency between a business information entity and the underlying core component. To perpetuate these dependencies, the NDRs specify that the names of the business information entities must contain the name of the core component, from which they are derived from. Therefore, when generating an XML Schema for business information entities, all generated artifacts contain the name of the core component that they are based on. Through this name matching, the conceptual basedOn dependency between a business information entity and the underlying core component is maintained on the XML Schema level as well.

To allow for an efficient transformation workflow of conceptual business document models to their XML Schema equivalents, transformation routines must be implemented. We have already introduced our open-source tool VIENNA Add-In (Visualizing Inter ENterprise Network Architectures) [180] in Chapter 5. The VIENNA Add-In does not only help a business document modeler in creating valid UML-based core component models, but also provides an XML generator, which fully conforms to the Naming and Design Rules of UN/CEFACT.

As already outlined, a core component model is defined using different packages, following a rigid structure. Using the XML generator, the business document modeler sim-

Employing generation tools

Creating a root schema for the business document

8 Deriving XML Schema from Core Components

ply clicks on a package and initiates the transformation of core components to the appropriate XML Schema representation. The XML Schema generator automatically detects dependencies in the core component model and generates additional XML Schema files, containing data type definitions, code list definitions, etc. The XML Schema in Listing 8.1 shows the root schema, generated from the business document library (cf. Figure 5.10 in Chapter 5). The root schema serves as a container for all the other defined schemas and their elements and represents exactly one business document. First, the necessary namespaces are defined in line 12 of Listing 8.1. Consequently, other schema definitions, required by the root schema, are imported (lines 13-15). In line 14 the business data type scheme is imported and line 15 imports the schema with the business information entity definitions, generated from the *BIELibrary*.

The schema contains exactly one root element for the *message assembly (MA)* artifact waste movement form, shown in line 16. For each *message assembly (MA)* a dedicated complexType is created as shown in line 18. The complexType waste movement form type consists of a sequence (shown in line 31), containing exactly one element attached waste_ consignment. This element represents the *association message assembly (ASMA)*, connecting the message assembly waste movement form and the aggregate core component waste_ consignment. Since an association message assembly is always of type shared, the resulting element is first declared globally (line 17) and then referenced from within the complexType definition (line 32).

Using predefined annotation schemes   Note the different annotations for each complexType (line 19-30 and line 33-48 in Listing 8.1). The annotation structure is predefined by UN/CEFACT's Naming and Design rules and imported into the root schema (line 13). The content of the annotations is taken from the model artifacts in the conceptual core component model and automatically transferred into the correct XML annotation by the XML Schema generator.

Listing 8.1
Waste movement form XML Schema

```
12<xsd:schema xmlns:edn='http://www.eudin.org/doc' xmlns:ccts='
    urn:un:unece:uncefact:documentation:standard:XMLNDRDocumentation:3
    ' xmlns:bdt='http://www.eudin.org/doc' xmlns:bie='http://www.
    eudin.org/doc' xmlns:xsd='http://www.w3.org/2001/XMLSchema'
    targetNamespace='http://www.eudin.org/doc' elementFormDefault='
    qualified' attributeFormDefault='unqualified' version='1.0'>
13 <xsd:import namespace='
    urn:un:unece:uncefact:documentation:standard:XMLNDRDocumentation:3
    ' schemaLocation='documentation/standard/
    XMLNDR_Documentation_3p0.xsd'/>
```

8.2 Transformation concepts

```
14 <xsd:include schemaLocation='BusinessDataType_1.0.xsd'/>
15 <xsd:include schemaLocation='BusinessInformationEntity_1.0.xsd'/>
16 <xsd:element name="WasteMovementForm" type="
      edn:WasteMovementFormType"/>
17 <xsd:element name="AttachedWaste_Consignment" type='
      bie:Waste_ConsignmentType'>
18 <xsd:complexType name="WasteMovementFormType">
19   <xsd:annotation>
20     <xsd:documentation xml:lang='en'>
21       <ccts:UniqueID>9B3530F2-9721-11DE-BDC8-0E7455D89593</
            ccts:UniqueID>
22       <ccts:VersionID>1.0</ccts:VersionID>
23       <ccts:ObjectClassQualifierName>WasteMovementForm</
            ccts:ObjectClassQualifierName>
24       <ccts:ObjectClassTermName>WasteMovementForm</
            ccts:ObjectClassTermName>
25       <ccts:DictionaryEntryName>WasteMovementForm. Details</
            ccts:DictionaryEntryName>
26       <ccts:Definition>Waste Movement Form</ccts:Definition>
27       <ccts:BusinessTermName>Representing an accompanying document for
            a waste transport</ccts:BusinessTermName>
28       <ccts:AcronymCode>ABIE</ccts:AcronymCode>
29     </xsd:documentation>
30   </xsd:annotation>
31   <xsd:sequence>
32     <xsd:element ref='edn:AttachedWaste_Consignment'>
33       <xsd:annotation>
34         <xsd:documentation xml:lang='en'>
35           <ccts:UniqueID>B1A885B4-9721-11DE-ABE8-977455D89593</
                ccts:UniqueID>
36           <ccts:VersionID>1.0</ccts:VersionID>
37           <ccts:Cardinality>1..*</ccts:Cardinality>
38           <ccts:SequencingKey>1</ccts:SequencingKey>
39           <ccts:DictionaryEntryName>WasteMovementForm. Attached.
                Waste_Consignment</ccts:DictionaryEntryName>
40           <ccts:Definition>The consignment of the waste movement form</
                ccts:Definition>
41           <ccts:BusinessTermName>Representing a consignment</
                ccts:BusinessTermName>
42           <ccts:AssociationType>Composite</ccts:AssociationType>
43           <ccts:PropertyTermName>Waste_Attached</ccts:PropertyTermName>
44           <ccts:PropertyQualifierName>Waste</ccts:PropertyQualifierName>
45           <ccts:AssociatedObjectClassTermName>Waste_Consignment</
                ccts:AssociatedObjectClassTermName>
46           <ccts:AcronymCode>ASBIE</ccts:AcronymCode>
47         </xsd:documentation>
48       </xsd:annotation>
49     </xsd:element>
50   </xsd:sequence>
51 </xsd:complexType>
52</xsd:schema>
```

For each business information entity library (BIELibrary), a dedicated XML Schema file is created. We already outlined that business information entities are used to assemble business documents. In XML Schema terms, the necessary business information entity schemas are imported in the final root schema (line 15 in Listing 8.1).

Creating a schema for business information entities

Listing 8.2 shows a cutout from the XML Schema, created for the BIELibrary of the waste movement form example (cf. Figure 5.8 in Chapter 5). Line 53 defines necessary namespaces and in line 54 the business data type schema, used to set the value domains of basic business information entities, is imported. In line 55 the complex type for the business information entity `waste_ consignment` is shown. Note that this complex type is used in the root schema (Listing 8.1, line 17), to set the type of the association message assembly `attached waste_ consignment`. The complex type `waste_ consignment` defines a sequence

8 Deriving XML Schema from Core Components

of exactly one basic business information entity (BBIE) and one association business information entity (ASBIE). Line 69 of Listing 8.2 shows the BBIE and line 85 the ASBIE.

Listing 8.2
Business
Information Entity
XML Schema

```
53 <xsd:schema xmlns:edn='http://www.eudin.org/doc' xmlns:ccts='
     urn:un:unece:uncefact:documentation:standard:XMLNDRDocumentation:3
     ' xmlns:bdt='http://www.eudin.org/doc' xmlns:tns='http://www.
     eudin.org/doc' xmlns:xsd='http://www.w3.org/2001/XMLSchema'
     targetNamespace='http://www.eudin.org/doc' elementFormDefault='
     qualified' attributeFormDefault='unqualified' version='1.0'>
54 <xsd:include schemaLocation='BusinessDataType_1.0.xsd'/>
55 <xsd:complexType name='Waste_ConsignmentType'>
56   <xsd:annotation>
57     <xsd:documentation xml:lang='en'>
58       <ccts:UniqueID/>
59       <ccts:VersionID/>
60       <ccts:ObjectClassQualifierName>Waste</
             ccts:ObjectClassQualifierName>
61       <ccts:ObjectClassTermName>Consignment</ccts:ObjectClassTermName>
62       <ccts:DictionaryEntryName>Waste_Consignment. Details</
             ccts:DictionaryEntryName>
63       <ccts:Definition/>
64       <ccts:BusinessTermName/>
65       <ccts:AcronymCode>ABIE</ccts:AcronymCode>
66     </xsd:documentation>
67   </xsd:annotation>
68   <xsd:sequence>
69     <xsd:element name='Waste_IdentificationWaste_Identifier' type='
           bdt:Waste_IdentifierStringType' minOccurs='0' maxOccurs='
           unbounded'>
70       <xsd:annotation>
71         <xsd:documentation xml:lang='en'>
72           <ccts:UniqueID/>
73           <ccts:VersionID/>
74           <ccts:Cardinality>0..*</ccts:Cardinality>
75           <ccts:SequencingKey/>
76           <ccts:DictionaryEntryName/>
77           <ccts:Definition/>
78           <ccts:BusinessTermName/>
79           <ccts:PropertyTermName>Waste_Identification</
                 ccts:PropertyTermName>
80           <ccts:RepresentationTermName>Waste_Identifier</
                 ccts:RepresentationTermName>
81           <ccts:AcronymCode>BBIE</ccts:AcronymCode>
82         </xsd:documentation>
83       </xsd:annotation>
84     </xsd:element>
85     <xsd:element name='Waste_IncludedWaste_ConsignmentItem' type='
           tns:Waste_ConsignmentItemType'>
86       <xsd:annotation>
87         <xsd:documentation xml:lang='en'>
88           <ccts:UniqueID/>
89           <ccts:VersionID/>
90           <ccts:Cardinality>1..*</ccts:Cardinality>
91           <ccts:SequencingKey/>
92           <ccts:DictionaryEntryName/>
93           <ccts:Definition/>
94           <ccts:BusinessTermName/>
95           <ccts:AssociationType>Composite</ccts:AssociationType>
96           <ccts:PropertyTermName>Waste_Included</ccts:PropertyTermName>
97           <ccts:PropertyQualifierName/>
98           <ccts:AssociatedObjectClassTermName>Waste_ConsignmentItem</
                 ccts:AssociatedObjectClassTermName>
99           <ccts:AcronymCode>ASBIE</ccts:AcronymCode>
100        </xsd:documentation>
101      </xsd:annotation>
102    </xsd:element>
103  </xsd:sequence>
104 </xsd:complexType>
105 ...
106</xsd:schema>
```

Creating a schema for business data types

The value domain of each basic business information entity (BBIE) is set, using the concept of business data types (BDT). Both, the root schema and every business information entity schema include the necessary business data type schemas to set the type of the respective BBIE elements. The root schema of the waste movement form, shown in List-

8.2 Transformation concepts

ing 8.1, includes the business data type schema in line 14. The business information entity schema, shown in Listing 8.2, imports the necessary data types in line 54. Recall, that each business data type consists of exactly one content component and multiple optional supplementary components. Listing 8.3 shows a cut-out of the XML Schema created for the business data type library of the waste movement form example (cf. Figure 5.9 in Chapter 5). The XML equivalent for the business data type waste_ identifier is shown in line 110. The content component of a `waste_ identifier` is of type `string`. In XML this is denoted by a `simpleContent`, with the data type of the content component as the extension base (line 123 and 124 in Listing 8.3). For each supplementary component of a business data type an attribute is created. The business data type `waste_ identifier` has exactly one supplementary component shown in line 125 of Listing 8.3.

Listing 8.3 Business Data Type XML Schema

```
107 <xsd:schema xmlns:edn='http://www.eudin.org/doc' xmlns:ccts='
        urn:un:unece:uncefact:documentation:standard:XMLNDRDocumentation:3
        ' xmlns:xsd='http://www.w3.org/2001/XMLSchema' xmlns:clm63055='
        urn:un:unece:uncefact:codelist:standard:6:3055:D05A'
        targetNamespace='http://www.eudin.org/doc' version='1.0'>
108  <xsd:import namespace='
        urn:un:unece:uncefact:codelist:standard:6:3055:D05A'
        schemaLocation='codelist/standard/
        UNECE_AgencyIdentificationCode_D05A.xsd'/>
109  ...
110  <xsd:complexType name='Waste_IdentifierStringType'>
111   <xsd:annotation>
112    <xsd:documentation xml:lang='en'>
113     <ccts:UniqueID>9bece510-ea80-11dd-ba2f-0800200c9a66</
             ccts:UniqueID>
114     <ccts:VersionID>CCL08A</ccts:VersionID>
115     <ccts:DictionaryEntryName>Identifier.Type</
             ccts:DictionaryEntryName>
116     <ccts:Definition>Identifier is a character string used to
             identify and distinguish uniquely, one instance of an object
             in an identification scheme from all other objects within
             the same scheme.</ccts:Definition>
117     <ccts:BusinessTermName>Identifier for things.</
             ccts:BusinessTermName>
118     <ccts:PropertyTermName>Waste_Identifier</ccts:PropertyTermName>
119     <ccts:LanguageCode>en-GB</ccts:LanguageCode>
120     <ccts:AcronymCode>BDT</ccts:AcronymCode>
121    </xsd:documentation>
122   </xsd:annotation>
123   <xsd:simpleContent>
124    <xsd:extension base='xsd:string'>
125     <xsd:attribute name='SchemeAgencyIdentifierUNCEFACT_63055' type='
             enum1:AgencyIdentificationCodeContentType'>
126      <xsd:annotation>
127       <xsd:documentation xml:lang='en'>
128        <ccts:PropertyTermName>SchemeAgencyIdentifier</
                ccts:PropertyTermName>
129        <ccts:RepresentationTermName>UNCEFACT_63055</
                ccts:RepresentationTermName>
130        <ccts:PrimitiveTypeName>UNCEFACT_63055</ccts:PrimitiveTypeName
                >
131        <ccts:DataTypeName>Waste_Identifier</ccts:DataTypeName>
132        <ccts:DictionaryEntryName>Waste_Identifier.
                SchemeAgencyIdentifier. UNCEFACT_63055</
                ccts:DictionaryEntryName>
133        <ccts:ModificationAllowedIndicator>true</
                ccts:ModificationAllowedIndicator>
134        <ccts:AcronymCode>SUP</ccts:AcronymCode>
135       </xsd:documentation>
136      </xsd:annotation>
137     </xsd:attribute>
138    </xsd:extension>
```

8 Deriving XML Schema from Core Components

```
139   </xsd:simpleContent>
140   </xsd:complexType>
141   ...
142</xsd:schema>
```

Setting the value domain of a supplementary component

Note that the supplementary component is of type `agency identification code content type` (line 125 in Listing 8.3), a predefined code list named `agency identification code` from UN/CEFACT. The code list is a common code list, universally defined for all contexts and imported into the target business data type XML Schema, as shown in line 108 of Listing 8.3. Listing 8.4 shows a cut-out of the corresponding code list XML Schema, which is imported in line 108 of Listing 8.3.

Code list schemas

Generally, we distinguish between two different types of code lists: *common code lists* and *business code lists*. On a conceptual level, code lists are referred to as *enumerations* and the distinction between *common code lists* and *business code lists* is enforced by the business document modeler. We already mentioned that common code lists are standardized independent of a certain business context. Business code lists are always created from a common code list by restriction. However, the XML representation of a common code list and a business code list is the same. The example shown in Listing 8.4 shows a cut-out for the enumeration `UN/CEFACT 63055` (cf. Figure 5.7 in Chapter 5). The enumeration represents a predefined common code list, defined by UN/CEFACT.

Listing 8.4 Common code list

```
143<xsd:schema xmlns:xsd='http://www.w3.org/2001/XMLSchema'
    xmlns:clm63055='
    urn:un:unecе:uncefact:codelist:standard:6:3055:D05A' xmlns:ccts=
    'urn:un:unecе:uncefact:documentation:standard:CoreComponents-\\
    TechnicalSpecification:2' targetNamespace='
    urn:un:unecе:uncefact:codelist:standard:6:3055:D05A'
    elementFormDefault='qualified' attributeFormDefault='unqualified
    ' version='2.0'>
144 ...
145 <xsd:simpleType name='AgencyIdentificationCodeContentType'>
146   <xsd:restriction base='xsd:token'>
147     <xsd:minLength value='1'/>
148     <xsd:maxLength value='3'/>
149     <xsd:enumeration value='1'>
150       <xsd:annotation>
151         <xsd:documentation>
152           <ccts:Name>CCC (Customs Co-operation Council)</ccts:Name>
153           <ccts:Definition>Customs Co-operation Council (now World
                              CustomsOrganization).</ccts:Definition>
154         </xsd:documentation>
155       </xsd:annotation>
156     </xsd:enumeration>
157     <xsd:enumeration value='2'>
158       <xsd:annotation>
159         <xsd:documentation>
160           <ccts:Name>CEC (Commission of the European Communities)</
                        ccts:Name>
161           <ccts:Definition>Generic: see also 140, 141, 142, 162.</
                        ccts:Definition>
162         </xsd:documentation>
163       </xsd:annotation>
164     </xsd:enumeration>
165     ...
166   </xsd:restriction>
```

```
167 </xsd:simpleType>
168</xsd:schema>
```

In addition to code lists, UN/CEFACT also supports the concept of identifier schemes. Identifier schemes are different to code lists in regard to their concept and purpose. A code list is an enumerated set of values, based on a certain primitive type. In contrast, an identifier scheme defines a certain pattern, based on a primitive type. The pattern unambiguously defines, how different values of the primitive type may be constructed. Thus, an identifier scheme may be thought of as some sort of production rule for a certain primitive type. Values, generated according to an identifier scheme, are typically not enumerated, e.g., bank account numbers. Similar to common code lists and business code lists, we distinguish between common identifier schemes and business identifier schemes. An example for a common identifier scheme is shown in Listing 8.5. The `simpleType` in line 171 of Listing 8.5 defines a pattern for a UN/CEFACT Data Type identifier. On an XML level no distinction between a business identifier and a common identifier is made and both follow the same pattern as shown in Listing 8.5.

Identifier schemes

```
169<xsd:schema xmlns:ism6ccts5='
     urn:un:unece:uncefact:identificationscheme:standard:6:CCTS5:08B'
     xmlns:ccts='
     urn:un:unece:uncefact:documentation:standard:CoreComponentsTechnical
     -\\Specification:2' xmlns:xsd='http://www.w3.org/2001/XMLSchema'
     targetNamespace='
     urn:un:unece:uncefact:identificationscheme:standard:6:CCTS5:08B'
     elementFormDefault='qualified' attributeFormDefault='
     unqualified' version='3.0'>
170  <xsd:element name='DataTypeUniqueIdentificationScheme' type='
       ism6ccts5:DataTypeUniqueIdentificationSchemeContentType'/>
171  <xsd:simpleType name='DataTypeUniqueIdentificationSchemeContentType
       '>
172    <xsd:restriction base='xsd:token'>
173      <xsd:pattern value='UNDT[0-9]{6}\-[0-9]{3}'/>
174    </xsd:restriction>
175  </xsd:simpleType>
176</xsd:schema>
```

Listing 8.5
Common identifier scheme

For the definition of primitive types, the built-in data types of the XML Schema specification are used. For each primitive type a named `xsd:simpleType` is created. Note that the facets defined by the primitive type directly map to the facets of the XSD built-in type.

Primitive types

8.3 Final assessment

In this Chapter we outlined a model-driven approach for the definition of XML Schema artifacts. Based on the principles of the Open-edi reference model, business document

Model-driven approach for XML Schema definitions

8 Deriving XML Schema from Core Components

models are first defined on a conceptual basis, using either the UML Profile for Core Components, the Domain-Specific Language for Core Components, or the Web Ontology Language (OWL) for Core Components. In a consecutive step and using the Naming and Design Rules (NDR) of UN/CEFACT, core component models may unambiguously be transformed to an XML Schema representation. Thereby, the Naming and Design Rules of UN/CEFACT represent the link between the Business Operational View and the Functional Service View of the Open-edi reference model.

Note that in principle any representation of choice may be chosen for the Business Operational View, since the NDRs do not mandate a specific input format for a transformation, but describe the necessary mapping rules from a neutral perspective. Furthermore, we outlined how tool supported transformation mechanisms may help a business document modeler to quickly generate XML Schema artifacts from conceptual document models.

Flexibility to changing requirements   In particular in a service oriented context, the flexibility to exchange one business partner with another business partner, or to add a new business partner without the need to rigorously redesign the entire system, is one of the key qualities. IT systems are reconfigured using declarative XML-based business process and business document definitions instead of being re-implemented using considerable coding effort. However, negotiations in regard to process choreographies and exchanged business documents must be conducted in an efficient manner to allow for a quick reconfiguration of the respective IT system. Using the model-driven core component approach for the definition of business documents, the necessary level of flexibility required by a modern SOA environment, is provided.

Open issues   In this Chapter we have introduced the Naming and Design Rules of UN/CEFACT based on a UML model according to the UML Profile for Core Components (UPCC). However, the Naming and Design Rules of UN/CEFACT are not bound to a specific core component implementation format and, thus, may also be applied to a DSL or OWL-based representation of core components.

9 A registry for Core Components

In regard to every day use of core components, a major shortcoming still remains. To make existing core component definitions, as defined in the Core Component Library (CCL) [173] of UN/CEFACT, available to a large user community, an easy to use implementation of a common core component registry is necessary. Since core component models are used to define business documents schemas, which in turn define the type of document a service interface accepts, they must be available to any interested business partner in an easy manner.

In this Chapter we introduce an approach for the definition of a common core component registry, based on the ebXML Registry Information Model (ebRIM) [119]. We outline how the registry serves as the storage, search, and retrieval point for both, conceptual service interface definitions based on UML and XML Schema artifacts, respectively. We also stress the importance of a registry federation concept, to allow for different levels of core component interoperability. Note that the concepts introduced in this Chapter may also be applied to a DSL-based or OWL-based representation of core components.

Introducing a core component registry model

The remainder of this Chapter is structured as follows: Section 9.1 motivates the necessity of a common core component registry and Section 9.2 introduces the basic concepts of the ebXML registry specification. Based on the ebXML Registry Information Model, we introduce the core component registry model in Section 9.3 and exemplarily show how to map conceptual and logical level business document definitions to the registry model. Finally, Section 9.4 introduces the concept of a federated registry for core components and Section 9.5 concludes the Chapter with a final assessment.

9 A registry for Core Components

9.1 Introduction

In most SOA based scenarios, XML Schemas are used to define the interface of each business partner. Thus, it are the business document definitions, represented using XML Schema, which essentially define what type of XML instances a service interface accepts. We already introduced a promising approach for the collaborative definition of service interfaces, using the core components technology and its three reference implementations using the Unified Modeling Language (cf. Chapter 5), Domain-Specific Languages (cf. Chapter 6), and Web Ontology Language (cf. Chapter 7).

Missing core component registry

However, what is still missing is an access point, where business partners may easily retrieve predefined core component and business information entity definitions from a registry. In a nutshell, business partners should be able to store their existing business document definitions for a service interface in a publicly accessible registry to share them with other business partners. Since in our scenario each business document is assembled using business information entities, their underlying core components must be available using a registry as well. We conclude that for a seamless interoperability scenario, using the core component technology, a publicly available registry for core component and business information entity artifacts must be provided. Figure 9.1 gives an overview of our motivating business scenario.

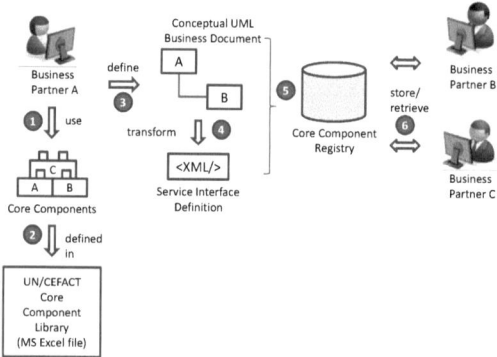

Figure 9.1 Motivating business scenario for a registry

Business partner A uses predefined core components (1) to assemble a conceptual business document definition (3).

9.1 Introduction

These core components are standardized by the United Nations Center for Trade Facilitation and Electronic Business (UN/CEFACT) and may be retrieved from the Core Component Library (CCL) [173] (2). Using the core component concepts, business documents are built in a semantically unambiguous manner, following a globally defined standard. However, core components are standardized in an implementation neutral manner, making integration into modeling tools and machine processing difficult. Thus, we introduced the UML Profile for Core Components (UPCC) [172] and consequently submitted it to UN/CEFACT for standardization (cf. Chapter 5). The UML Profile may be used to assemble business document definitions on a conceptual, UML-based level (3). Based on the UML Profile for Core Components, implementation neutral core components as defined in the Core Component Library may also be transformed to a UML representation. Thus, our introduced registry approach serves for core components and business information entities and all other related artifacts such as data types, likewise.

Providing document models to potential business partners

A conceptual UML-based business document definition is easy to communicate between different developers and IT architects. However, service interfaces are defined using XML Schema artifacts. Conceptual service interface definitions ease the communication between developers and IT architects, but cannot be used directly for interface definitions in IT systems. XML-based service interface definitions are difficult to communicate between different developers, but may be directly used in IT systems. Thus, we argue that it is necessary to store both – the conceptual and the XML-based representation of a service interface in a registry (5). Other business partners may search the registry for pertinent service interface definitions and retrieve both, the UML-based and XML-based business document definitions (6).

Leveraging benefits from UML and XML Schema-based business document definitions

A core component registry, which is able to store UML-based and XML-based core component definitions, is still missing. In the following we outline the basic technical foundations of the ebXML registry specification on which we built our registry information model.

9.2 Introduction to the ebXML registry specification

Registry vs. repository
In terms of a registry we distinguish between two elementary concepts: a registry and a repository. In general, a repository is responsible for storing the actual artifacts such as XML files, media files, etc. An efficient search and retrieval requires that the different artifacts are annotated with metadata. Thus, for artifacts stored in a repository a meta-model is needed, unambiguously defining which metadata definition belongs to which artifact type. Furthermore, the different artifact types in a registry may be related to each other, forming some sort of taxonomy or ontology. These interdependencies must also be specified in a meta-model. Thus, in addition to a repository a registry is defined, storing the different metadata about repository artifacts. If a business document modeler wants to retrieve an artifact from the repository, he first queries the registry. Based on the metadata in the registry the business document modeler is able to find the given artifact and retrieve it from the repository.

ebXML registry
The ebXML registry specification is also based on these two pillars and provides an integrated registry/repository [119]. An ebXML registry may be thought of as a service oriented architecture registry as well as repository and comprises the following functions:

- Providing a classification template mechanism of any type of information.
- Managing the relationships between the different artifacts using taxonomies and ontologies.
- Providing an environment for hosting, browsing, and validation of the stored artifacts.
- Providing a file and folder organization principle for information.

Extending the ebRIM
The ebXML registry specification comprises two main parts, namely the ebXML Registry Information Model (ebRIM), defining what metadata and content may be stored in the registry, and the ebXML Registry Services and Protocols, defining the services and service interfaces provided by the registry.

In the following Section we provide an extension to the ebXML registry information model, allowing for a seamless integration of core component concepts in the ebXML registry specification. We do not further elaborate on technical implementation details as provided in the ebXML Registry Services and Protocols standard.

9.3 The Core Component Registry Model

In the following we discuss how both, conceptual core component artifacts based on UML and core component artifacts, based on XML Schema, are managed in a registry. For this purpose we provide a registry meta-model, based on the ebXML registry information model [119], which supports the specifics of the conceptual and logical layer. The registry meta-model has the purpose to define which artifacts are maintained in the registry and how the different artifacts are related to each other. An ebXML registry stores artifacts as *extrinsic objects*, which are XMI (XML Metadata Interchange) and XML artifacts in our case, but may in principle be any data format of choice. Note that the content of an extrinsic object is encapsulated – this means a query to the registry does not access the content of an extrinsic object directly. It follows, that an extrinsic object must be annotated with pertinent metadata, to allow for an effective search. Additionally, the different artifacts and their metadata have dependencies on each other. Our registry meta-model defines the required links between the extrinsic objects of the different artifacts and also between their metadata if required.

Introducing the core component registry model

We built our registry meta-model for core components based on the foundations of the UML Profile for Core Components (UPCC). Figure 9.2 summarizes the basic concepts of the UPCC (cf. Chapter 5).

Recall, that each of the artifacts shown with a white background in Figure 9.2 are packages, where artifacts of a certain type are aggregated. Artifacts shown with a black background are elements and attributes, used to assemble core components, business information entities, and data types, respectively. The registry meta-model must ensure that all necessary dependencies as defined by the UPCC are

Preserving UPCC dependencies

9 A registry for Core Components

Figure 9.2
UPCC
meta-model

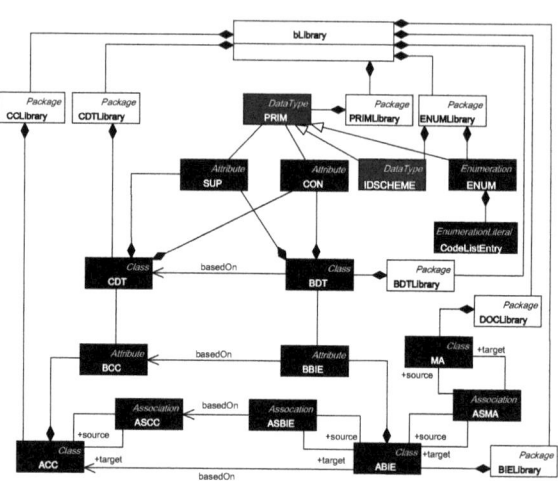

preserved in the registry as well. Additionally, each package as shown in Figure 9.2 results in exactly one XML Schema artifact, e.g., a CCLibrary on the conceptual UML-based level becomes exactly one XML Schema file, when transformed to an XML representation. Thus, these dependencies must be preserved in the registry as well.

Introducing the registry meta-model

Figure 9.3 shows the resulting meta-model of our core component registry. We do not show the entire meta-model, but limit our discussion to the business information entity part of the meta-model. Other meta-model parts, covering core component and data types specific artifacts, are to be read accordingly. Extrinsic objects are denoted with a thick border. Classes, referring to logical level artifacts, are denoted with a gray background. Each class of our core component registry is based on an existing meta-class of the ebRIM. The meta-class is denoted in the upper-right corner of each class.

As shown in Figure 9.3, our meta-model cut-out contains four extrinsic objects for the conceptual layer, namely ABIE (aggregate business information entity), BBIE (basic business information entity), ASBIE (association business information entity), and BDT (business data type). Each of the mentioned extrinsic objects has several associated *slots* and *classifications*. The concept of *slots* and *classifications* is

9.3 The Core Component Registry Model

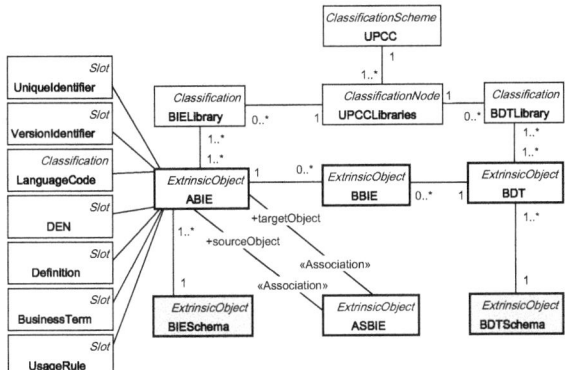

Figure 9.3
Cut-out: core component registry meta-model

used to annotate an extrinsic object with metadata information, to allow for search and retrieval of the artifact. To keep it short, we only show the slots and classifications for the extrinsic object ABIE in detail, which however also apply to BBIE, ASBIE, and BDT artifacts. For the logical level layer we define exactly two extrinsic objects, namely BIESchema and BDTSchema. The extrinsic objects ABIE and BDT are associated with the *classification* artifacts BIELibrary and BDTLibrary, respectively. *Classification scheme* and *classification node* are concepts built into the ebRIM and are used for defining taxonomies of metadata.

Having defined the registry meta-model, we may implement the core component extension of the ebRIM. Consequently, conceptual and logical level core component artifacts may be stored in the repository with the appropriate metadata being maintained in the registry.

9.3.1 Registering conceptual core component models

As outlined before, business document modelers prefer to use the UML Profile for Core Components, the Domain-Specific Language for Core Components, or the Web Ontology Language for Core Components to integrate the implementation neutral core component concepts in their modeling environments. In our proposed scenario, introduced in this Chapter, a conceptual core component model based on the UML syntax is used. The graphical UML syntax may

9 A registry for Core Components

also be represented in XMI (XML Metadata Interchange), which we use to store a core component model as an extrinsic object in the registry.

Introducing the accompanying example

The mapping of conceptual and logical level core component artifacts to our registry meta-model is illustrated using our accompanying *waste movement form* example. Figure 9.4 shows a simplified version of the waste movement form example, consisting of two aggregate business information entities waste_ consignment and waste_ consignment - item. For simplification purposes not all association business information entities and basic business information entities are used.

Figure 9.4 Sample business information entity model

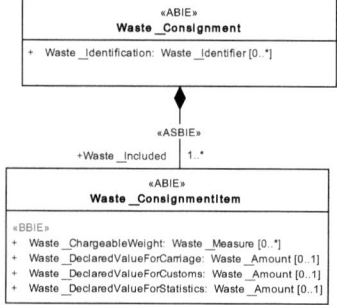

Storing core component artifacts

Figure 9.5 gives an overview of how the business information entity artifacts, shown in Figure 9.4, are stored in the core component registry. We denote *classification* and *slot* artifacts using a dark background to foster distinction from *extrinsic objects*. In most use cases a business document modeler may want to retrieve or store a single business information entity artifact from the registry. In case an aggregate business information entity, such as waste_ consignment, is stored in the registry, its XMI representation is stored in the extrinsic object ABIE. The basic business information entity waste_ identification is stored in the respective extrinsic object BBIE. The same applies for the association business information entity waste_ included, which is stored in the extrinsic object ASBIE. Business data types, defining the value domain of basic business information entities are stored in their respective extrinsic object BDT. The classification of BIELibrary and BDTLibrary is

9.3 The Core Component Registry Model

used to indicate, to which library a given aggregate business information entity or business data type belongs.

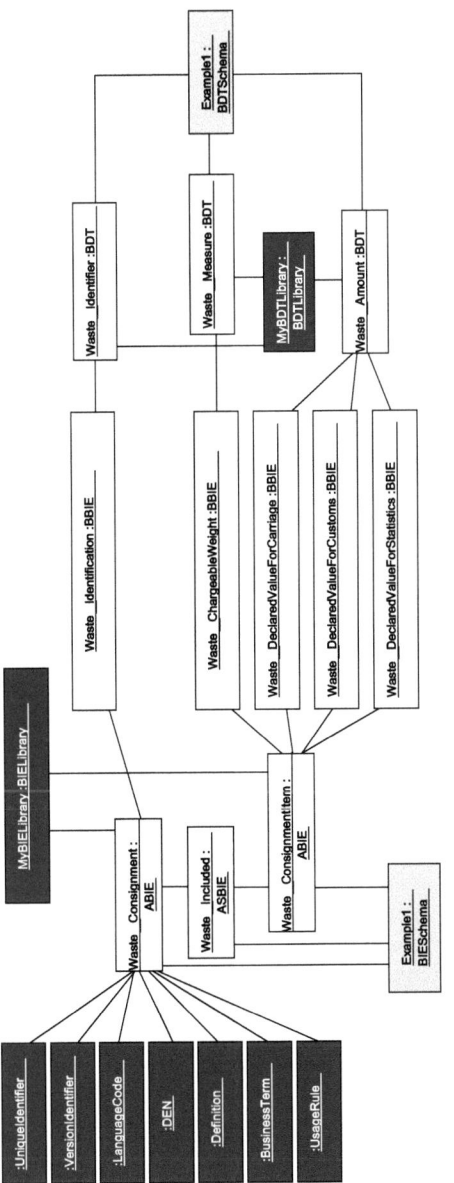

Figure 9.5
Core component registry example

Storing metadata for extrinsic objects

Note that the different slots such as `UniqueIdentifier` or `VersionIdentifier` are only shown for the extrinsic object `ABIE` due to space limitations. However, in a real world example the different slots also apply to all other extrinsic objects, i.e., `BBIE`, `ASBIE` and `BDT` artifacts also have a `UniqueIdentifier`, `VersionIdentifier`, etc. In case an entire business information entity model is stored in the registry, the same steps as for storing a single business information entity are applied. However, the registry has to check whether a given business information entity already exists in the registry, before inserting a new definition. For this purpose the unique identifier slot is used.

The same principles, as shown for business information entities in Figure 9.5, are also applied if core components are stored in the registry. Of particular importance is the establishment of the correct dependencies between core components and business information entities in the registry. Business information entity must, for example, not be inserted into the registry if no connection to an underlying core component definition exists, since that would violate the principles as specified by the Core Components Technical Specification.

9.3.2 Registering logical level core component artifacts

Linking conceptual models and XML Schema artifacts

In the previous Section we showed how conceptual core component artifacts are stored in the registry. Consequently, we outline how to map deployment XML Schema artifacts to the core component registry model and link them to business information entity artifacts. In general, a business document modeler defines a core component model using the UML Profile for Core Components by retrieving ready-to-use core component artifacts from the core component registry and tailoring them to the specific needs of a certain business context. Thereby, context free core components become context specific business information entities. Alternatively, a business document modeler may also retrieve predefined business information entities from the registry. In a consecutive step transformers such as our freely available VIENNA Add-In [180] are used to derive XML Schema definitions from the UML-based business information entity models.

9.3 The Core Component Registry Model

However, in certain cases a business document modeler may want to avoid the creation of XML Schema artifacts from business information entity models, but uses predefined and ready-to-use XML Schema artifacts instead. We already outlined that a single library of business information entities results in exactly one XML Schema file. Consequently, the business data types, used for the business information entities, also result in a single XML Schema file. Thus, in case a business document modeler submits an entire business information entity library to the registry, the accompanying XML Schema files may be stored together with the conceptual definitions. In case a business information entity library is stored in the registry, it is recommended to submit the underlying XML Schema files as well. This guarantees that a business document modeler may retrieve the necessary XML Schema definitions for a given business information entity library at any time. As shown in Figure 9.5, we use the two extrinsic objects `BIESchema` and `BDTSchema` to store business information entity schema files and business data type schema files, respectively. Both extrinsic objects are associated with the business information entity artifacts and business data type artifacts they belong to.

Storing XML Schema artifacts

In case the business document modeler submits a single conceptual business entity definition, the association with an XML Schema file is not as straightforward. If no existing XML Schema file with the definition of the business information entity exists in the registry, the file is simply stored and associated as it would be done when submitting an entire business information entity library. However, in case an XML Schema already exists in the library, either an association to the existing XML Schema file is made or a new XML Schema file is stored, as described in the former case. In either case, the registry must ensure that both artifacts are aligned in regard to version, included basic business information entities, association business information entities, etc.

Dealing with existing XML Schema definitions

Since business document modelers are able to store XML Schema files together with the conceptual definition, an easy search and retrieval of XML Schema artifacts using the definitions on the conceptual level such as the slots `UniqueIdentifier`, `Definition`, etc. is possible. However, business document modelers may also search for business

Retrieving XML Schema definitions

information entities by retrieving all business information entities from a certain business information entity library using the classification `BIELibrary`. In either case, the business document modeler is able to retrieve the right business information entities from the registry together with their XML Schema equivalent.

Even if the core component registry provides several benefits to a business document modeler, our presented approach might raise issues due to its centralized nature. In the following we introduce strategies on how to align multiple core component registries in a decentralized and federated manner.

9.4 Registry Federation

Shortcomings of a single global core component registry

The provision of a single global core component registry has a set of shortcomings. The core component definitions in the global core component registry are quite generic, since they aim at global interoperability. However, in certain cases an enterprise does not require such complex core components, but may be satisfied with a sub-set of the global core components, tailored to a specific industry domain. Furthermore, certain industry domains may define their own core component definitions, which are exclusively used in the respective industry domain and are not aligned with the core component definitions of UN/CEFACT.

Introducing federation concepts

In this thesis we propose a federated registry approach, to overcome these shortcomings. Figure 9.6 gives an overview of our approach. Core components are standardized and harmonized by UN/CEFACT, serving as the single entity shown on top of Figure 9.6. Different interest groups such as SWIFT (Society for Worldwide Interbank Financial Telecommunication) [160] or CIDX (Chemical Industry Data Exchange Standard) [19] and entire industry sectors (Automotive industry) represent the needs of their involved companies and stakeholders. Each interest group maintains its own core component library, which is aligned to the UN/CEFACT library. Companies such as Shell or BP retrieve their core component definitions directly from their interest group registry (CIDX), instead of the generic UN/CEFACT library. Additionally, industry sector specific libraries such as for the automotive industry are created. This ensures core component compatibility for sub-groups of the industry domain such as AIAG (North American car industry) [3] and ODETTE (European car industry) [130].

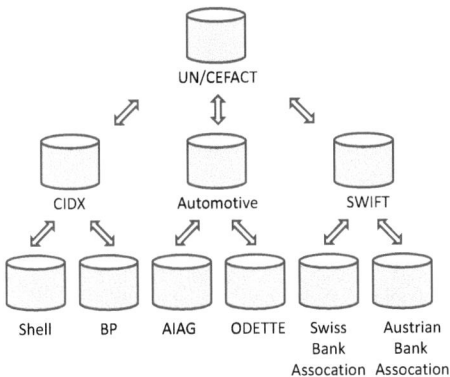

Figure 9.6
Federated registry approach

The advantages of such a federated approach are apparent. Companies do not need to use generic and overloaded core component definitions, but may use core component definitions which are already tailored to their specific industry domain. If industry groups such as CIDX align their industry specific registries to the generic UN/CEFACT core component library, business document definitions may easily be mapped between different industries, e.g., between SWIFT and CIDX as shown in Figure 9.6. However, an alignment of industry specific libraries towards the generic UN/CEFACT library is not imperative. In certain scenarios industries may choose to create their own core components. An automotive industry representation such as AIAG may choose to create its own core component for the automotive supply chain, because alignment of these core components to the financial industry may be considered unnecessary. However, in such a case interoperability of core components at a cross-industry level is not feasible any more. Nevertheless, core components from the upper level (UN/CEFACT) may still be used if interoperability to other industries is required.

Finally, each enterprise may choose to implement its own core component definitions in a dedicated enterprise-wide registry. As shown at the bottom of Figure 9.6, Shell may for instance choose to implement its own core component definitions, which are valid for the whole enterprise. Such a step ensures interoperability between different company departments and sub-groups, e.g., between Shell Asia and Shell Europe.

9.5 Final assessment

Registry implementation is crucial for broad acceptance of the registry

As outlined in this Chapter, the availability of a federated registry for storage and retrieval of core component artifacts is crucial for a broad acceptance of the core component standard. The introduced registry model serves a two-fold purpose. First, it may be used to make core components, predefined by UN/CEFACT and standardized in the Core Component Library, available to a broad user community. Benefits of a registry, such as tool-based access through well defined interfaces, may be used to find and retrieve core components. Second, the registry may be used to make already contextualized business information entities available to other interested business document modelers and stakeholders. Based on our approach, core component definitions and business information entity definitions are made available to a broad user community through a central registry. The theoretical foundations provided in this Chapter may serve as a guideline for the implementation of a core component registry.

Implementation of multiple connectors and registry clients

A real-world core component registry must provide different connectors, allowing to retrieve core component definitions in different formats. Since for instance not all UML modeling tools support the same XMI format, the registry must be able to provide core component and business information entity definitions in different XMI dialects (e.g., for Enterprise Architect, Magic Draw, etc.). In addition, the registry must be able to provide core component definitions in other formats than UML, such as Domain-Specific Language for Core Components (cf. Chapter 6) or Web Ontology Language (cf. Chapter 7). We conclude that a broad adoption of the registry may only be ensured if appropriate clients, based on the different core component tools are provided. Apart from the technical foundations, the *network effect* is crucial for a broad registry acceptance, i.e., the more companies are using core components, the higher is the value of core component to each companies.

10 Extensions for bottom-up standard approaches

In the previous Chapters we have thoroughly examined a promising top-down business document standardization approach – UN/CEFACT's Core Components. Top-down approaches represent a superset of all requirements of the involved stakeholders and are thus often extensive and complex. In particular, small-and-medium sized enterprise and even some large enterprises often do not require fine grained business document standards, including a multitude of different elements and attributes. In contrast, bottom-up standard definitions tackle the interoperability issue of business document standards from a different perspective. Instead of meeting all requirements of the involved stakeholders, a bottom-up standard aims at the definition of a sub-set of the most important requirements of all involved stakeholders. This results in a core standard definition, focusing on the most important requirements. However, in certain cases domain-specific extensions of a standard are still needed. Thus, appropriate extensions mechanisms must be found to support domain-specific amendments for a standard without altering the core standard definition.

Introducing bottom-up standard definitions

In this Chapter we examine extension mechanisms for XML-based bottom-up standard definitions, using the Austrian e-Invoice standard *ebInterface* as an accompanying example. The remainder of this Chapter is structured as follows: Section 10.1 introduces the core idea for bottom-up extensions and Section 10.2 explains the main concepts of the ebInterface standard. In Section 10.3 we introduce the different extension mechanisms for bottom-up standards and Section 10.4 concludes with a final assessment.

10 Extensions for bottom-up standard approaches

10.1 Introduction

Top-down standards are still predominant

Most of the business document standards, developed over the last 30 years, follow a top-down approach (cf. Chapter 3). Typically, large enterprises are able to implement their own software or at least to customize their existing software to handle these kind of business document standards. However, most of the SMEs do not have this flexibility, but rely on low cost commercial-of-the-shelf-software (COTS). In order for SMEs to participate in B2B scenarios, the COTS systems should also allow the seamless import and export of business documents. Therefore, vendors of COTS have to provide appropriate import/export interfaces. However, they cannot foresee and implement partner specific requirements. Thus, they require a business document standard, covering only those elements that are common to all industries. If numerous COTS vendors provide interfaces for such a core business document standard, the operators of COTS systems may exchange business documents on the fly. However, the core standard cannot consider specific elements, required by a certain industry. To overcome this restriction, a flexible extension mechanism for controlled domain-specific amendments is required. Depending on the target customer base, a COTS vendor may choose to implement certain domain-specific extensions, but not necessarily all.

Providing extensions for the ebInterface standard

We followed the idea of defining a core business document standard plus domain-specific extensions, when starting the ebInterface initiative [8] for the Austrian Chamber of Commerce. The goal of ebInterface is to define an unambiguous e-Invoicing standard for the Austrian market. In the current status an agreement between twelve COTS vendors on the core elements has been established. However, an extension mechanism for domain-specific amendments (e.g., telecom industry) is still missing. In this Chapter we introduce different XML extension mechanisms for defining domain-specific extensions in a bottom-up business document standard. The goal is to define a plug-in based solution to add industry and partner specific extensions, without altering the core of a bottom-up standard. Thus, interoperability of the core specification is provided at any time with any given partner. We specifically focus on the strengths and weaknesses of each extension mechanism and evaluate the applicability of each extension approach using the ebInterface standard. Thereby, we evaluate every approach in regard to four criteria: i) core schema integrity ii) core schema compatibility iii) extension control, and iv) guarantee of validity. A successful bottom-up standard extension approach must meet all of the four criteria.

10.2 ebInterface – the core

In the following we introduce the XML-based standard ebInterface and provide an accompanying example from the telecom industry. We use the example throughout the article to evaluate the applicability of the introduced XML Schema extension mechanisms.

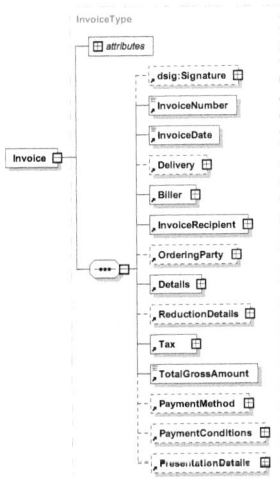

Figure 10.1
A cut-out of the ebInterface standard

Figure 10.1 illustrates the main structure specified by the ebInterface standard, including elements such as `InvoiceDate`, `Biller`, and `Details`. A more detailed view of the element `Details` is given in Figure 10.2. The element `Details` may be used to represent items typically listed in an invoice – hence it is designed to contain one or more elements named `LineItem`. Each `LineItem` contains further elements such as `PositionNumber` and `UnitPrice`. An excerpt of the ebInterface XML Schema, representing an element `LineItem`, which is the target of extensions in the following Sections, is provided in Listing 10.1. All other elements of the stan-

10 Extensions for bottom-up standard approaches

dard are not discussed any further, but may be found in the ebInterface specification [8].

Figure 10.2
The details section of ebInterface

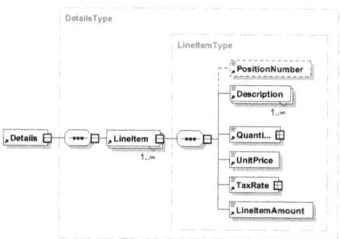

The ebInterface standard is illustrated using the following example, based on invoices for telephone customers. Consequently, we examine how domain-specific extensions for the telecom domain may be defined for the ebInterface standard.

Figures 10.3 and 10.4 illustrate excerpts from a real world telephone bill.

Figure 10.3
Excerpt from example invoice

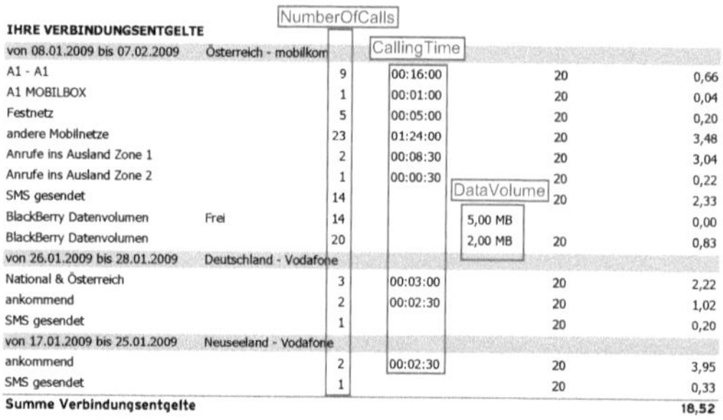

The first excerpt illustrated in Figure 10.3, shows different line items such as "A1 - A1" and "Festnetz". The line item "Festnetz", for instance, represents a summary of all calls made to land line phones. In the ebInterface standard, line items are typically represented using the element `LineItem` (cf. Figure 10.2 or Listing 10.1). However, the elements of `LineItem` are not sufficient to fully represent all information of a line item in the telephone bill. In fact, the number of calls, calling time, and data volume (cf. Figure 10.3) cannot be represented using the element `LineItem`.

The second excerpt, illustrated in Figure 10.4, shows a detailed view of the call charges, listing every single call

10.3 Alternative strategies for a bottom-up approach

made, including certain details such as the date or duration of the call. The detailed view is from now on referred to as *itemized phone bill*. Representing the itemized phone bill, using the ebInterface standard is currently not possible, since the standard neither provides suitable elements nor any mechanism to extend the standard itself. In the following we elaborate on different strategies for an extension of a bottom-up standard.

```
177<xs:complexType name='LineItemType'>
178  <xs:sequence>
179    <xs:element ref='PositionNumber' minOccurs='0'/>
180    <xs:element ref='Description' maxOccurs='unbounded'/>
181    <xs:element ref='Quantity'/>
182    <xs:element ref='UnitPrice'/>
183    <xs:element ref='TaxRate'/>
184    <xs:element ref='LineItemAmount'/>
185  </xs:sequence>
186</xs:complexType>
```

Listing 10.1
Line Item XML syntax

Figure 10.4
Excerpt from itemized bill

10.3 Alternative strategies for a bottom-up approach

In the following we evaluate how different extension mechanisms may be used in a real-world environment, to extend an existing business document definition. We demonstrate the different extension mechanisms by means of the ebInterface standard. However, it should be noted that the proposed extensions are valid in any given bottom-up business document standard approach.

10.3.1 Custom section

The first approach to meet the requirements of different stakeholders, i.e., storing customized information, is achieved by introducing a so-called custom section in the ebInterface XML Schema. The definition of the custom section is shown in Listing 10.2. The XML Schema element xs:any, used for the definition of the custom section, is discussed in the following.

The wildcard xs:any may be used in an XML Schema for defining placeholders, enabling stakeholders to store ad-

10 Extensions for bottom-up standard approaches

ditional, custom information in the actual XML document instances. The `xs:any` element contains two attributes, namely `namespace` and `processContents`.

Listing 10.2
Custom section
```
187<xs:group name='Custom'>
188  <xs:sequence>
189    <xs:any namespace='##other' processContents='strict'/>
190  </xs:sequence>
191</xs:group>
192 ...
193<xs:complexType name='InvoiceType'>
194  <xs:sequence>
195    ...
196    <xs:group ref='Custom' minOccurs='0'/>
197  </xs:sequence>
198</xs:complexType>
```

The attribute `namespace` is used for specifying the namespace that the content in the instance document must comply with. Allowed values of the attribute include `##any`, `##local`, `##other`, `##targetNamespace`, and a particular namespace. Assigning the attribute `namespace` the value `##any` determines that the content may be any well-formed XML from any namespace. Using `##local` defines that the content may be any well-formed and unqualified XML. `##other` specifies that the content may be any well-formed XML from any namespace, other than the current target namespace. `##targetNamespace` defines that the content may be any well-formed XML as long as it belongs to the `##targetNamespace`. The fifth option is to list one or more namespaces such as `http://www.ebinterface.at/ext/telecom` in the attribute `namespaces`. Listing one or more namespaces restricts the placeholder the strongest, and defines that the content may be any well-formed XML and that it must belong to any of the namespaces listed.

Validity of the custom section
The attribute `processContents` provides instructions, regarding the validation of the custom section in the instance document and may have one out of the three following values: `strict`, `lax`, and `skip`. The attribute value `strict` specifies that content stored in the custom section must be qualified through a namespace. Second, the value `lax` expresses that content in the custom section may be validated in case the backing XML Schema is available. Otherwise, in case the backing XML Schema is not present, the validation of the instance document is skipped and validation succeeds. The third attribute value `skip` specifies that content in the custom section in the instance document is not validated at all. Depending on the values used for the attributes `namespace` and `processContents`, the resulting namespace design may be *heterogeneous namespace*

10.3 Alternative strategies for a bottom-up approach

design, *homogeneous namespace design*, or *chameleon namespace design*. In the following, three different approaches for defining single and multiple custom sections are explained.

xs:any and any namespace

Listing 10.2 illustrates the definition of the custom section, used to extend the ebInterface standard. As shown in line 189 of Listing 10.2, the content of the custom section must be well-formed XML, defined in a namespace other than the current target namespace. Furthermore, the value of the attribute `processContents`, also illustrated in line 189 of Listing 10.2, is set to `strict`, specifying that any content stored in the custom section must be backed by an XML Schema.

xs:any and any namespace

Adding custom information requires to define a custom XML Schema, specifying the content of the custom section. The XML Schema, used in this example, is illustrated in Listing 10.3. The schema describes an itemized phone bill, containing a detailed list of all calls made and a summary of the duration and cost of all calls made (cf. Figure 10.4).

```
199 <xs:schema xmlns:xs='http://www.w3.org/2001/XMLSchema' xmlns='http://
    www.ebinterface.at/ext/telecom' targetNamespace='http://www.
    ebinterface.at/ext/telecom' elementFormDefault='qualified'
    attributeFormDefault='unqualified'>
200   <xs:complexType name='ItemTelephonyType'>
201     <xs:sequence>
202       <xs:element name='Date' type='xs:date' />
203       <xs:element name='Begin' type='xs:time'/>
204       <xs:element name='Service' type='xs:string' />
205       <xs:element name='Duration' type='xs:time' />
206       <xs:element name='Type' type='xs:string' />
207       <xs:element name='NumberCalled' type='xs:string' />
208       <xs:element name='Amount' type='xs:decimal' />
209     </xs:sequence>
210   </xs:complexType>
211   <xs:complexType name='SummaryTelephonyType'>
212     <xs:sequence>
213       <xs:element name='TotalDuration' type='xs:time' />
214       <xs:element name='TotalAmount' type='xs:decimal' />
215     </xs:sequence>
216   </xs:complexType>
217   <xs:element name='ItemizedBillTelephony'>
218     <xs:complexType>
219       <xs:sequence>
220         <xs:element name='ItemTelephony' type='ItemTelephonyType'
                maxOccurs='unbounded'/>
221         <xs:element name='SummaryTelephony' type='SummaryTelephonyType'/>
222       </xs:sequence>
223     </xs:complexType>
224   </xs:element>
225 </xs:schema>
```

Listing 10.3
Domain-specific extension: XML Schema

Listing 10.4 illustrates an excerpt of an XML document instance, representing the custom section of the updated ebInterface XML Schema in combination with the XML Schema defined in Listing 10.3.

Extending the standard through adding a custom section adds great flexibility to the ebInterface standard. Further-

10 Extensions for bottom-up standard approaches

more, the implementer is forced to define an XML Schema, describing the structure of the information, stored in the custom section. The latter is achieved through the attribute `processContents`. The attribute's value is set to `strict`, instructing any parser performing validation of an ebInterface XML document that, in case a custom section is present, a corresponding XML Schema must exist. Alternatively, the `processContents` attribute's value could be set to `lax`. If set to `lax`, an XML Schema which is present will be used for validation. However, the presence of an XML Schema is then optional.

Listing 10.4
Domain-specific extension: XML instance

```
226 <eb:Invoice xmlns:eb="http://www.ebinterface.at/schema/3p0/"
        xmlns:tco="http://www.ebinterface.at/ext/telecom"   xmlns:xsi="
        http://www.w3.org/2001/XMLSchema-instance" xsi:schemaLocation="
        http://www.ebinterface.at/schema/3p0/ Invoice.xsd http://www.
        ebinterface.at/ext/telecom Telecom.xsd">
227    ...
228    </eb:PresentationDetails>
229
230    <tco:ItemizedBillTelephony>
231      <tco:ItemTelephony>
232        <tco:Date>2009-01-01</tco:Date>
233        <tco:Begin>10:25:43</tco:Begin>
234        <tco:Service>TEL</tco:Service>
235        <tco:Duration>00:00:35</tco:Duration>
236        <tco:Type>Anrufe ins Ausland Zone 1</tco:Type>
237        <tco:NumberCalled>002337774335</tco:NumberCalled>
238        <tco:Amount>0.3583</tco:Amount>
239      </tco:ItemTelephony>
240
241      <tco:ItemTelephony>
242        <tco:Date>2008-12-31</tco:Date>
243        <tco:Begin>22:31:03</tco:Begin>
244        <tco:Service>SMS</tco:Service>
245        <tco:Duration>00:00:00</tco:Duration>
246        <tco:Type>SMS gesendet</tco:Type>
247        <tco:NumberCalled>01235681295</tco:NumberCalled>
248        <tco:Amount>0.1666</tco:Amount>
249      </tco:ItemTelephony>
250
251      <tco:SummaryTelephony>
252        <tco:TotalDuration>00:00:35</tco:TotalDuration>
253        <tco:TotalAmount>0.5249</tco:TotalAmount>
254      </tco:SummaryTelephony>
255    </tco:ItemizedBillTelephony>
256 </eb:Invoice>
```

The great flexibility also implies that the standards body creating the standard may not be able to control the content, stored in custom sections. Theoretically, implementers of the standard may store information completely disconnected from the context of an electronic invoice. Moreover, it is necessary to modify the original ebInterface XML Schema. Thus, the approach is not desirable for defining a core schema with domain-specific extensions.

xs:any and defined set of namespaces

xs:any and defined set of namespaces

As outlined in Section 10.3.1, the attribute `namespace` of the element `xs:any` allows to define a set of namespaces containing one or more namespaces. If namespaces are defined,

10.3 Alternative strategies for a bottom-up approach

it is required that the content, stored in the instance document, must be backed by an XML Schema whose namespace is listed in the `namespace` attribute. Therefore, it is necessary to modify the definition of the custom section (cf. Listing 10.2) and specify a set of allowed namespaces. In the current example, the namespace `http://www.ebinterface.at/ext/telecom` is specified, as illustrated in Listing 10.5. Note that the namespace refers to the XML Schema, defined in Listing 10.3.

```
257<xs:group name='Custom'>
258  <xs:sequence>
259    <xs:any namespace='http://www.ebinterface.at/ext/telecom'
           processContents='strict'/>
260  </xs:sequence>
261</xs:group>
262 ...
263<xs:complexType name='InvoiceType'>
264  <xs:sequence>
265    ...
266    <xs:group ref='Custom' minOccurs='0'/>
267  </xs:sequence>
268</xs:complexType>
```

Listing 10.5
Single custom section XML syntax

Thus, the elements in the custom section must correspond to the structure, defined in the domain-specific extension XML Schema, identified through the namespace `http://www.ebinterface.at/ext/telecom` (cf. Listing 10.3). One of the major advantages, resulting from utilizing the `xs:any` attribute `namespaces`, is the ability to restrict the content of the custom section through listing a set of namespaces. On the contrary, to list a set of namespaces it is also required to modify the original ebInterface XML Schema. Hence, using `xs:any` is not a desired extension mechanism.

Multiple custom sections

Another possibility for utilizing the custom section is the use of references. Recall, that the example used throughout the article assumes that the ebInterface instance document represents a telephone bill of a single telephone customer. The element `LineItem`, specified by the element `LineItemType`, is used to represent the different call charges. In addition, an itemized phone bill was represented in the custom section of the ebInterface XML document instance (cf. Listing 10.4).

Using multiple custom sections

The example is further extended by assuming that the telephone bill represents the bill for two customers (e.g., in case of a partner tariff). Following the idea for a single customer, the element `LineItem` may be used to represent call charges (cf. Figure 10.3) for both customers and the cus-

10 Extensions for bottom-up standard approaches

tom section may be used to store the itemized phone bill (cf. Figure 10.4) for both customers as well. However, it is not possible anymore to determine which itemized phone bill belongs to a particular call charge summary. Thus, it is desirable to create appropriate references between call charges and itemized phone bills. One option to create references is to modify the element `LineItemType` and add an additional element, containing a unique identifier. Also, each section stored within the custom section must provide an element for storing references, used in the call charge summaries. By utilizing the reference mechanism it would be possible to assign each call charge summary particular itemized phone bills.

Extensive use of references
As shown by the example it is a quite sophisticated process to use references to properly represent information. If it is desired to use references, it is also necessary to modify the `LineItemType` of the ebInterface schema, which again is not a desired method to extend the ebInterface standard. An alternative approach to using references may be achieved by introducing more than one custom section in the ebInterface XML Schema. The definition of a custom section would still be the same as shown in Listing 10.5.

A resulting advantage would be that the quite complex use of references may be avoided. Instead, custom sections may be added where appropriate. On the other hand, through a number of custom sections within an XML Schema, implementers may store customized information in any of the custom sections available. Hence, it is not possible to distinguish which customized section is used to store which kind of information.

10.3.2 Redefine

Applying redefine elements
A `redefine` element has a dual functionality. First, it implicitly includes the referenced schema file and enables access to all of the elements of the referenced schema. Second, it enables the business document modeler to redefine zero or more of the components of the referenced schema. Using a redefine statement, the business document modeler may extend or restrict an existing component. The redefine mechanism may only be applied if both schemas have the same target namespace or the included (redefined) schema has no target namespace.

10.3 Alternative strategies for a bottom-up approach

```
269<xs:schema xmlns='http://www.ebinterface.at/schema/3p0/' xmlns:xs='
       http://www.w3.org/2001/XMLSchema' targetNamespace='http://www.
       ebinterface.at/schema/3p0/' elementFormDefault='qualified'
       attributeFormDefault='unqualified'>
270  <xs:redefine schemaLocation='Invoice.xsd'>
271   <xs:complexType name='LineItemType'>
272    <xs:complexContent>
273     <xs:extension base='LineItemType'>
274      <xs:sequence>
275       <xs:element name='NumberOfCalls' type='xs:integer' minOccurs='0
              '/>
276       <xs:element name='CallingTime' type='xs:integer' minOccurs='0'/
              >
277       <xs:element name='DataVolume' type='xs:decimal' minOccurs='0'/>
278      </xs:sequence>
279     </xs:extension>
280    </xs:complexContent>
281   </xs:complexType>
282  </xs:redefine>
283</xs:schema>
```

Listing 10.6
Redefine XML Schema

As shown in line 270 of Listing 10.6, the redefine statement includes the main ebInterface schema and redefines the complex type `LineItemType` (line 271 to 281). The redefined `LineItemType` extends the original `sequence` and adds three elements: `NumberOfCalls`, `CallingTime`, and `DataVolume`. Note that the namespace of the redefined schema is the same as the namespace of the original ebInterface schema (line 269).

In the instance document, shown in Listing 10.7, all elements of the `LineItem` element have the same namespace, since the redefined schema does not apply a different namespace, but uses the original ebInterface namespace `http://www.ebinterface.at/schema/3p0/`. A different namespace prefix `tco` has been used to underline, that although the namespace `http://www.ebinterface.at/schema/3p0` is still the same, the elements have telecom industry specific extensions. Using the redefine approach a new invoice definition is created for every domain-specific extension. The included elements from the original schema may be used, as if they have been defined in the same schema. Furthermore, multiple namespaces are avoided, since all elements share the same `targetNamespace`.

```
284<tco:Details>
285  <tco:LineItem>
286   <tco:PositionNumber>1</tco:PositionNumber>
287   <tco:Description>Calls to other providers</tco:Description>
288   <tco:Quantity tco:Unit='Units'>60.00</tco:Quantity>
289   <tco:UnitPrice>0.1</tco:UnitPrice>
290   <tco:TaxRate>20.00</tco:TaxRate>
291   <tco:LineItemAmount>6.00</tco:LineItemAmount>
292   <tco:NumberOfCalls>43</tco:NumberOfCalls>
293   <tco:CallingTime>1800</tco:CallingTime>
294  </tco:LineItem>
295</tco:Details>
```

Listing 10.7
Redefine XML instance document

Although easy to implement, the redefine approach has a set of drawbacks. The redefined schema overwrites the element definitions of the original schema, thus making backward compatibility to the original ebInterface schema impossible. This means for example, that a system being capable of processing ebInterface schema X is not able to process schema X', which is a redefined version of X. Furthermore, the possibility to redefine arbitrary X' schemas with domain-specific extensions leads to a multitude of different and incompatible business documents definitions.

10.3.3 Substitution group

Using substitution groups

The concept of substitution groups allows the substitution of an existing element (called head element) using another element from a defined group of elements (substitution group). First, the business document modeler declares a head element and then defines which elements may be used to substitute the head element (substitutable elements). The head element and the substitutable elements must be declared globally. The substitutable elements must have the same type as the head element or must have an extended or restricted type of the head element's type. This rule ensures, that the substituted elements make sense, if used in place of the head element. Note that the existence of a substitution group does not imply that the use of the elements in the substitution group is mandatory nor does a substitution group prevent the use of the head element. It simply provides a mechanism for allowing elements to be used instead of the head element. Furthermore, the substitution group mechanism is based on element names, since substitutable elements are differentiated from their head element by their name and not by their type, which is always the same.

Prevent the usage of substitution groups

XML Schema also provides a mechanism to prevent substitution groups from being used on particular types or elements. A business document modeler may prevent the substitution of a type or element by using the `block` attribute on `xs:complexType` or `xs:element`. The allowed values for the block attribute are `extension`, `restriction`, `substitution`, and `#all`. If the `block` attribute is set to `extension` or `restriction`, all instances of extended/restricted types are prohibited from being substituted. Setting it to `substitution` generally prevents replacing an element or complex type with one from its substitution group. `#all` subsumes the first three characteristics.

10.3 Alternative strategies for a bottom-up approach

As shown in Listing 10.8, a new schema is created for the telecom application domain. In line 297 the original ebInterface schema is imported and assigned with its original `targetNamespace`. Consequently, line 298 defines a new `LineItem` element which may serve as a substitutable element for the original ebInterface element `eb:LineItem`. The new `LineItem` element is defined in the target namespace `http://www.ebinterface.at/ext/telecom` and adds the three elements `NumberOfCalls`, `CallingTime`, and `DataVolume` to the original sequence.

```
296 <xs:schema xmlns:xs='http://www.w3.org/2001/XMLSchema' xmlns:eb='
      http://www.ebinterface.at/schema/3p0/' xmlns:tco='http://www.
      ebinterface.at/ext/telecom' targetNamespace='http://www.
      ebinterface.at/ext/telecom' elementFormDefault='qualified'
      attributeFormDefault='unqualified'>
297   <xs:import namespace='http://www.ebinterface.at/schema/3p0/'
        schemaLocation='Invoice.xsd'/>
298   <xs:element name='LineItem' substitutionGroup='eb:LineItem'>
299     <xs:complexType>
300       <xs:complexContent>
301         <xs:extension base='eb:LineItemType'>
302           <xs:sequence>
303             <xs:element name='NumberOfCalls' type='xs:integer' minOccurs='0
                  '/>
304             <xs:element name='CallingTime' type='xs:integer' minOccurs='0'/
                  >
305             <xs:element name='DataVolume' type='xs:decimal' minOccurs='0'/>
306           </xs:sequence>
307         </xs:extension>
308       </xs:complexContent>
309     </xs:complexType>
310   </xs:element>
311 </xs:schema>
```

Listing 10.8
SubstitutionGroup XML Schema

Listing 10.9 shows how the concept of a substitution group is reflected in an instance document. The namespace prefix `tco` in line 313 refers to the namespace `http://www.ebinterface.at/ext/telecom` and thus, it becomes apparent that the redefined `LineItem` from the telecom domain is used in this instance and not the original `LineItem` from the ebInterface schema. The two elements in line 320 and 321 also have the telecom specific namespace. All other elements are in the original ebInterface namespace `http://www.ebinterface.at/schema/3p0/`, indicated by the prefix `eb`.

```
312 <eb:Details>
313   <tco:LineItem>
314     <eb:PositionNumber>1</eb:PositionNumber>
315     <eb:Description>Calls to other providers</eb:Description>
316     <eb:Quantity eb:Unit='Units'>60.00</eb:Quantity>
317     <eb:UnitPrice>0.1</eb:UnitPrice>
318     <eb:TaxRate>20.00</eb:TaxRate>
319     <eb:LineItemAmount>6.00</eb:LineItemAmount>
320     <tco:NumberOfCalls>43</tco:NumberOfCalls>
321     <tco:CallingTime>1800</tco:CallingTime>
322   </tco:LineItem>
323 </eb:Details>
```

Listing 10.9
SubstitutionGroup XML instance document

An advantage of the substitution group approach is that the original ebInterface schema remains unchanged. All extensions or restrictions on existing types are defined in a separate schema. Thus, a flexible and module-based extension approach is enabled. In the instance document the new elements induced by the substitution group are labeled by their specific namespace prefix, e.g., tco, which equals namespace http://www.ebinterface.at/ext/telecom in Listing 10.9. Therefore, the domain-specific extensions may be easily distinguished from the original ebInterface elements.

A major shortcoming of the substitution group approach is that a refined element is placed in its own namespace. In Listing 10.9 the substituted LineItem element is assigned its own namespace tco (cf. line 313). Thus, an application which is only capable of processing original ebInterface compliant instances cannot process the instance with the telecom specific extensions, since it does not know what, e.g., the element <tco:LineItem> is. This undermines the idea of a modular approach, where all applications should be able to process the core schema.

10.3.4 xsi:type overloading

Introducing type hierarchies

An approach similar to substitution groups is introduced with the concept of xsi:type. xsi:type uses the concept of type hierarchies, where a sub-type inherits features from a super type by extension. First, a super type is created, followed by multiple specialized subtypes, meeting different requirements. Similar to the concept of polymorphism in object-oriented technologies, a derived type may be used wherever a base type is expected. A type of an element may be explicitly specified using xsi:type. Through this mechanism it is possible to specify a certain type of an element, although the specified type is not defined in the actual schema, but defined in another schema. The XML parser validates that the type, which is specified in the xsi:type attribute, is derived from the originally expected base type. Thus, the concept of xsi:type fits very well for extending a core schema with domain-specific amendments.

In the XML Schema community the xsi:type construct is debated controversially – some even state that it is evil [27]. Although the extensive use of xsi:type constructs can make an XML Schema quite complex, it fits very well for extending a core schema with domain-specific amendments.

Before we may apply an xsi:type we have to extend a given base type. As shown in Listing 10.10, we define a

10.3 Alternative strategies for a bottom-up approach

new complex type called `tco:LineItemType` (cf. line 326) by extending the base type `eb:LineItemType` (cf. line 328). Before the complex type is refined, the necessary type definitions are made available by importing the original ebInterface schema in line 325. Note that the new complex type is defined in the target namespace `http://www.ebinterface.at/ext/telecom`, specific to the telecom application domain. In the actual XML instance document the `xsi:type` attribute in a given element is used to indicate of which type the given element is.

```
324<xs:schema xmlns:xs='http://www.w3.org/2001/XMLSchema' xmlns:eb='
       http://www.ebinterface.at/schema/3p0/' xmlns='http://www.
       ebinterface.at/ext/telecom' targetNamespace='http://www.
       ebinterface.at/ext/telecom' elementFormDefault='qualified'
       attributeFormDefault='unqualified'>
325   <xs:import namespace='http://www.ebinterface.at/schema/3p0/'
           schemaLocation='Invoice.xsd'/>
326   <xs:complexType name='LineItemType'>
327     <xs:complexContent>
328       <xs:extension base='eb:LineItemType'>
329         <xs:sequence>
330           <xs:element name='NumberOfCalls' type='xs:integer' minOccurs='0'
                 />
331           <xs:element name='CallingTime' type='xs:integer' minOccurs='0'/>
332           <xs:element name='DataVolume' type='xs:decimal' minOccurs='0'/>
333         </xs:sequence>
334       </xs:extension>
335     </xs:complexContent>
336   </xs:complexType>
337</xs:schema>
```

Listing 10.10
xsi:Type XML Schema

Listing 10.11 shows an XML document instance, using an `xsi:type` construct. The `xsi:type` attribute in line 339 indicates that `LineItem` is of type `tco:LineItemType`. The two additionally used elements, defined in `tco:LineItemType`, are defined in the telecom specific namespace `http://www.ebinterface.at/ext/telecom` as indicated by the prefix `tco` (cf. 346 line and 347).

```
338<eb:Details>
339   <eb:LineItem xsi:type='tco:LineItemType'>
340     <eb:PositionNumber>1</eb:PositionNumber>
341     <eb:Description>Calls to other providers</eb:Description>
342     <eb:Quantity eb:Unit='Units'>60.00</eb:Quantity>
343     <eb:UnitPrice>0.01</eb:UnitPrice>
344     <eb:TaxRate>20.00</eb:TaxRate>
345     <eb:LineItemAmount>6.00</eb:LineItemAmount>
346     <tco:NumberOfCalls>43</tco:NumberOfCalls>
347     <tco:CallingTime>1800</tco:CallingTime>
348   </eb:LineItem>
349</eb:Details>
```

Listing 10.11
xsi:Type XML instance document

By comparing Listing 10.8 and 10.10, the similarities between the `substitution group` and `xsi:type` extension approach become apparent, except that substitution group is based on element names and `xsi:type` is based on type names.

Comparing substitutionGroup and xsi:type

By using the `xsi:type` approach, a clear distinction between the core elements and the extension elements of the ebInterface schema is made. The extension elements are in-

Advantages

10 Extensions for bottom-up standard approaches

dicated, using the `tco` namespace (line 346 to 347), but the extended element `LineItem` remains in the original namespace. The only indication that `LineItem` is a specialized type is given by the `xsi:type` attribute in line 339. In regard to schema modularity, this approach is superior to all the other introduced approaches. If a software application has been designed to process only the core ebInterface standard, it is still able to receive a document including extensions, but it processes only the core and ignores the extensions.

Minor shortcomings of xsi:type

The `xsi:type` extension mechanism has a set of minor shortcomings as well. First of all, it assumes that the receiver has the XML Schema for the instance document. In case the receiver uses alternative XML instance validation mechanisms such as RELAX NG [123], the `xsi:type` mechanism does not work. However, since the ebInterface standard relies on a well defined XML Schema and every recipient of an instance document is supposed to have the relevant ebInterface schema definition, including any necessary extension element definitions, this argument does not hold. Second, some experts critically argue that the inclusion of the abstract type (i.e., the `xsi:type`) into the XML instance violates the paradigm of the separation of data (XML instance document) and data definition (XML Schema). Although this argument might hold for XML purists, the superiority of the `xsi:type` approach in regard to XML Schema extension is evident. The last and probably major criticism of the `xsi:type` approach is in terms of processability of such schema constructs by tools, because not all XML parsers support `xsi:type`.

10.4 Final assessment

Evaluation criteria

In this Chapter we have analyzed four different approaches to extend the existing ebInterface standard with domain-specific extensions. Thereby, we evaluated every extension approach in regard to four key criteria: i) core schema integrity ii) core schema compatibility iii) extension control, and iv) guarantee of validity. *Core schema integrity* refers to the fact, whether an extension alters the original core schema definition. If an instance document with domain-specific extensions is still compatible with the core schema definition it meets the criteria of *core schema compatibility*.

10.4 Final assessment

Extension control refers to the fact, whether the extension mechanism allows for a governance of different extensions by a standardization body. If the core schema together with the domain-specific extensions may still be validated, it meets the criteria of *guaranteed validity*.

The results of our study are aggregated in Table 10.1. The first three examined extension mechanisms used the concept of custom sections (A1-A3).

	A1	A2	A3	B	C	D
Core schema integrity	-	-	-	+	+	+
Core schema compatibility	-	-	-	-	-	+
Extension control	-	+	-	+	+	+
Guarantee of validity	+/-	+/-	+/-	+	+	+

Table 10.1 *Comparison matrix A1 - xs:any and any namespace; A2 - xs:any and defined namespaces; A3 - multiple custom sections; B - Redefine; C - Substitution Group; D - xsi:type*

As clearly shown in Table 10.1, neither A1 (xs:any and any namespace), nor A2 (xs:any and defined namespaces), nor A3 (multiple custom sections) preserve the integrity of the core schema or ensure backward compatibility to the original schema. Extension control, that is the ability of a standardization organization to prescribe what XML elements to use in an extension, is only possible if using A2. Whether the overall validity of the core schema plus the extension may be guaranteed, depends on how the **process-Contents** attribute is set. If it is set to **strict**, validity may be ensured. Thus, neither of the three approaches (A1-A3) using the concept of custom sections meets the requirements for an appropriate extension mechanism of a bottom-up schema.

Using **redefine** (B), it is possible to guarantee extension control and validity of the overall schema. Since a redefine statement imports the original schema and alters its elements in a new file, the original schema remains untouched. However, a **redefine** statement may alter any of the elements of the original schema, thus, obstructing backward compatibility to the core standard schema.

The same problem occurs if using the concept of substitution groups (C) for the extension of a core bottom-up schema. Although integrity of the original schema as well as extension control and validity is ensured, backward compatibility is violated. Eventually, the only remaining extension mechanism, meeting all four requirements for the successful extension of a bottom-up business document standard, is **xsi:type**.

xsi:type remains the most promising approach

11 Mapping bottom-up to top-down standards

In the previous Sections we have examined two business document standard examples: UN/CEFACT's Core Components as a representative example for a top-down standardization approach and ebInterface as a representative example for a bottom-up standard. In particular the core component standard may be used in a two-fold manner namely in a forward engineering and a backward engineering approach. In a forward-engineering approach, new business document definitions are created from scratch from an existing CCTS compliant model. Such a scenario may be applied for new solutions and examples have been given in this thesis (cf. Chapter 5 and 8). In case existing business document definitions already exist, they must be mapped to the CCTS compliant model. We refer to such an approach as backward engineering. In this Chapter we examine a backward engineering example, where a bottom-up standard definition is mapped to top-down core components.

Examining the mapping to core components

The remainder of this Chapter is structured as follows: Section 11.1 gives an overview of the basic idea behind the mapping of bottom-up standard definitions to top-down core components. In Section 11.2 the basic mapping mechanisms for core components are examined and Section 11.3 examines advanced mapping concepts. Finally, Section 11.5 concludes the Chapter with a final assessment.

11.1 Introduction

In a backward engineering approach, existing business document definitions are aligned to a common document format. In contrast to forward engineering, backward engineering approaches impose a set of challenges on the business document modeler. In our case the common document format is represented by a core component compliant model. Con-

Backward engineering of core components

11 Mapping bottom-up to top-down standards

sequently, a set of predefined rules is necessary, to allow for a seamless mapping of existing business document definitions to a common conceptual core component model. Such mapping mechanisms are still missing and not provided by UN/CEFACT. In this Chapter we are addressing this gap, by analyzing potential mappings from existing document definitions to conceptual core component models. For a detailed discussion on mapping of schemas see for example Legler and Naumann [89]. They present a classification of correspondences that may arise, as well as proper tooling, available in this research area.

Using EUDIN to show mapping principles

We motivate our mappings using the accompanying example from the waste management domain. We already outlined that the EU-sponsored project EUDIN uses the Core Components Technical Specification (CCTS) concepts to model the exchanged information in a cross-border waste transport scenario. Even if a central data model is created with the use of core components, the different local authorities and involved companies still have their own, internal data structure for the different transport documents. In the following Sections we examine different strategies on how to map existing business document definitions to a core component-based model. We use a simple core component scenario of a consignment item with different delivery and despatch parties, as it would be used in a cross-border waste transport process. First, we start with basic mapping principles and consequently elaborate on more sophisticated approaches.

11.2 Basic Mapping

UN/CEFACT Naming and Design Rules specify basic mapping mechanisms

The Core Component Technical Specification (CCTS) defines the basic concepts for specifying business document models on an implementation neutral level. UN/CEFACT releases Naming and Design Rules (NDR) [171], allowing for a unique mapping of core component-based business document models to an XML Schema representation. Figure 11.1 illustrates the mapping spaces, relevant for CCTS-based model integration.

In this Chapter we do not elaborate on the instance layer and the accompanying task of instance mapping and instance transformation. The mapping between CCTS and

11.2 Basic Mapping

*Figure 11.1
Mapping spaces in CCTS-based document model integration*

		CCTS Space	XML Space	Mapping Space	Example
NDR based	Metamodel Layer	CCTS	XML Schema	Metamodel Mapping	BBIE ↔ element
Modeling based	Model Layer	CCTS Model	XML Schema Instance	Model Mapping	Person Concept ↔ Party Concept
	Instance Layer	XML Instance	XML Instance	Instance Mapping	Philipp ↔ Research Studios

XML Schema is specified by UN/CEFACT's Naming and Design rules [171] and happens on the meta-model layer as depicted in Figure 11.1. This mapping specification ensures that all conforming models may be imported and exported by tools building upon the CCTS. The basic mappings as specified by the Naming and Design Rules (NDR) [171] are summarized in Figure 11.2. One may easily see by looking at the concepts involved in column XML Schema that this is only a minimal set of all XML Schema concepts which are available. Therefore, we provide additional mapping definitions apart from the Naming and Design Rules for CCTS in the following Chapter.

BIE Concept	mapsTo	XML Schema	Comment
Business Data Type (BDT)	<->	simpleType or complexType	
Basic Business Information Entity (BBIE)	<->	element	local declaration
Aggregate Business Information Entity (ABIE)	<->	complexType and element	global declaration
Association Business Information Entity (ASBIE)	<->	element	global and local declaration

*Figure 11.2
Mapping of CCTS to XML Schema components*

Note that the Naming and Design Rules define mappings for business information entities only. The underlying core component concepts are not participating in the serialization process, except as optional annotations. For the generation of an XML Schema, corresponding core components may be neglected. But for the use of these schemas or the import in a tool, one needs to know the corresponding dependencies to retrieve the semantics of the given business information entities. Without this knowledge we maintain meaningless data capsules, loosing every advantage of the general top-down approach of CCTS. The very basic method for retrieving the underlying core component definition of a business information entity is to decompose the name of a business information entity into single terms. Recall, that a

Naming and Design Rules consider business information entities only

business information entity's name must contain the name of the underlying core component as well. Thus, traceability between core components and business information entities is also ensured on the XML Schema level. By simple name matching we may then get an understanding of the contextualized core components, by looking at the defined semantics in the core component library.

Model mapping

The second mapping space (cf. Figure 11.1 modeling-based) we are interested in, is concerned with the models themselves, which constitutes the actual mapping task carried out manually by users. By mapping two models, one of which is CCTS in our case, we have to ensure that model structures and semantics are preserved. Heuristics for model mapping are presented in Section 11.3.2.

Figure 11.3 *Distinguishing BBIEs from ASBIEs*

```
<xsd:schema xmlns:xsd="http://www.w3.org/2001/XMLSchema"
    xmlns:tns="http://foo.bar/doc"
    xmlns:bdt="http://foo.bar/doc"           ❷
    targetNamespace="http://foo.bar/doc"
    ... >

<xsd:include schemaLocation="BusinessDataType_1.xsd"/>

<xsd:complexType name="Waste_ConsignmentItemType">
    <xsd:sequence>
        <xsd:element name="Waste_Identification"
                     type="bdt:Waste_IdentifierStringType" />
        ...                    ❶    ❸
        ...
        <xsd:element name="Waste_DeliveryWaste_Party"
                     type="tns:Waste_PartyType" />
    </xsd:sequence>
</xsd:complexType>

<xsd:element name="Waste_ConsignmentItem"
             type="Waste_ConsignmentItemType"/>

<xsd:complexType name="Waste_PartyType">
    <xsd:sequence>
        <xsd:element name="Waste_Name"
                     type="bdt:Waste_TextStringType" />
        ...
    </xsd:sequence>
</xsd:complexType>

<xsd:element name="Waste_Party"
             type="tns:Waste_PartyType"/>
</xsd:schema>
```

ASBIE/BBIE distinction

Another problem occurs when it comes to identifying association business information entities (ASBIE) in XML Schema, because both basic business information entities (BBIE) and ASBIEs local declarations map to the schema concept **element** (see Figure 11.3, mark 1). Generally, this problem may not be resolved very elegantly because the Naming and Design Rules promote the use of a homogeneous namespace design approach with a single target namespace (see Figure 11.3, mark 2). Nevertheless, we solve the problem via the namespace prefix of the type property of the two Schema elements for the corresponding BBIEs and ASBIEs, respectively (see Figure 11.3, mark 3). So far we elaborated on the CCTS driven mapping method, but more interesting is the mapping from arbitrary XML Schema-based document models to CCTS.

11.3 Advanced Mapping

In the previous Section we introduced different approaches, involved in CCTS driven mapping. However, the Naming and Design Rules (NDR) do not provide sufficient definitions on how to handle arbitrary business document standards, based on XML Schema. Therefore, we examine how different XML Schema concepts may be mapped to CCTS and evaluate how to preserve semantics of model elements during the mapping of two schemas. For explanatory purposes the different mappings are outlined using the UML Profile for Core Components (UPCC).

Advanced mapping concepts

11.3.1 Meta-model Layer Mapping

To illustrate the shortcomings of the NDR we identify a number of XML Schema concepts and evaluate their applicability in regard to being mapped to core components. Furthermore, we introduce a set of rules to map XML Schema concepts to core components. In the following we elaborate on the XML Schema concept of complex types. In particular the mappings of complex types' content definitions, complex type extensions, as well as complex type restrictions are discussed in more detail in the following.

Examining meta-model layer mappings

Reusable Groups

Reusable groups are used for defining a group of reusable elements or attributes. An example is the use of a model group to define a sequence of elements, which in turn may be used to define the content of a complex type. In general, there are three different kinds of model groups including sequence, choice, and all. Each listed model group is elaborated in more detail in the following.

sequence. The model group sequence is used for defining elements in a certain order, such as the order of elements within a complex type definition. An example, illustrating the use of the model group sequence within a complex type definition, is illustrated in Figure 11.4, mark A.

xsd:sequence

11 Mapping bottom-up to top-down standards

Figure 11.4
Reusable group sequence

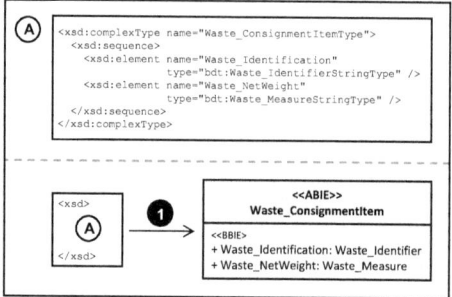

The approach of creating an adequate model representation is straightforward, since all elements of the model group may be mapped to BBIEs (see Figure 11.4, mark 1). Therefore, the resulting model representation of the illustrated example equals an ABIE named `waste_ consignment item` containing the BBIEs `waste_ identification` and `waste_ netweight`.

xsd:choice   **choice.** The model group choice allows the grouping of elements, whereas only one of the defined elements may occur. Again, the model group may be used for defining the content of a complex type. An example, utilizing the model group, is illustrated in Figure 11.5, mark A.

Figure 11.5
Reusable group choice (alternative 1)

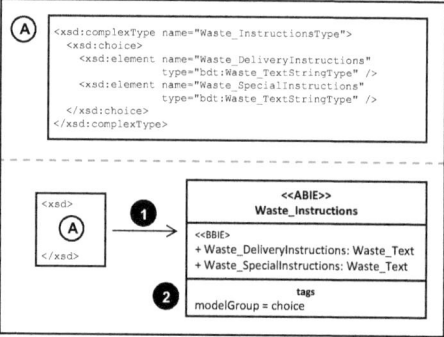

Lack of support for xsd:choice in CCTS   However, creating an adequate model representation is not feasible, without the loss of semantic meaning regarding the characteristics of the model group **choice**. Although the model representation allows specifying minimum and maximum cardinalities, the concept of an exclusive-OR is

11.3 Advanced Mapping

currently not supported in CCTS and consequently it is not supported in the UML Profile for Core Components (UPCC) either. We may overcome this limitation by extending UPCC to allow that both elements within the model group are represented as BBIEs (see Figure 11.5, mark 1). We introduce an additional tagged value named *modelGroup* in ABIEs, indicating that the BBIEs within the ABIE are exclusive (see Figure 11.5, mark 2).

Another common use case of the model group choice is to define element groupings, enabling all elements to appear in any desired order as well as in an unlimited number of occurrences. The key to define such a model group is setting the model group's maximum number of occurrences to unbounded. An according example is illustrated in Figure 11.6, mark A.

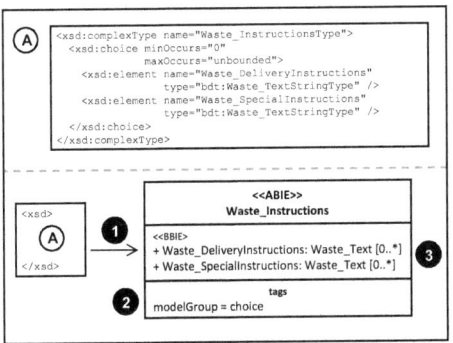

Figure 11.6
Reusable group choice (alternative 2)

The approach to create an adequate model representation is similar to the approach, introduced for the model group sequence. All element declarations may be mapped directly to BBIEs (see Figure 11.6, mark 1). The definition of the maximum number of occurrences for the model group itself may be reflected through the cardinalities of BBIEs. Therefore, each BBIE has a minimum cardinality of zero as well as an unlimited maximum cardinality (see Figure 11.6, mark 3).

However, one drawback of the proposed solution is that when serializing the model representation to an XML Schema, not all semantics are preserved. According to the Naming and Design Rules an ABIE is serialized into a complex type definition, utilizing the model group sequence with according minimum and maximum occurrences for each BBIE. Hence, the resulting XML Schema is not the same as the schema used to create the model representation. However, using our introduced tagged value *modelGroup*, as illustrated in Figure 11.6, mark 2, the correct semantics are preserved.

xsd:all **all.** The third kind of model group, named `all`, allows to define that all element declarations within the model group may appear in any order, but each element may occur only once. An example is shown in Figure 11.7, mark A.

Figure 11.7 Reusable group all

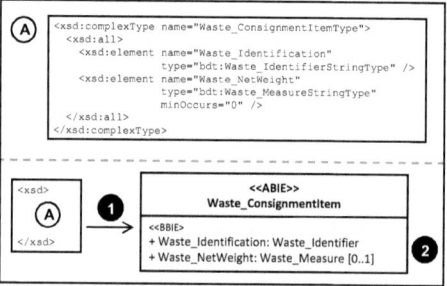

The process for creating an adequate model representation of the model group is proposed the following way. First of all, each element declaration within the model group may be mapped directly to a BBIE (see Figure 11.7, mark 1). Furthermore, the minimum occurrences and maximum occurrences of the element declarations may be reflected through the cardinalities of the BBIEs (see Figure 11.7, mark 2). Applied to the example in Figure 11.7, this would mean that the element `waste_ identification` is represented through a BBIE with a minimum cardinality of one and the element `waste_ net weight` is represented through a BBIE as well whereas the minimum cardinality of the BBIE `waste_ net weight` equals zero.

Extensions and Restrictions

xsd:redefine **redefine.** The redefine mechanism may be applied to types and groups and is used to alter existing types and groups. The types include simple types as well as complex types, whereas redefine must extend or restrict the type. Groups include attribute and model groups. Applied to groups, a

11.3 Advanced Mapping

redefine must subset or superset the original group. An example, utilizing the redefine mechanism, is illustrated in Figure 11.8, mark A. In addition to the complex type definition, Figure 11.8, mark B, shows the redefinition of the complex type.

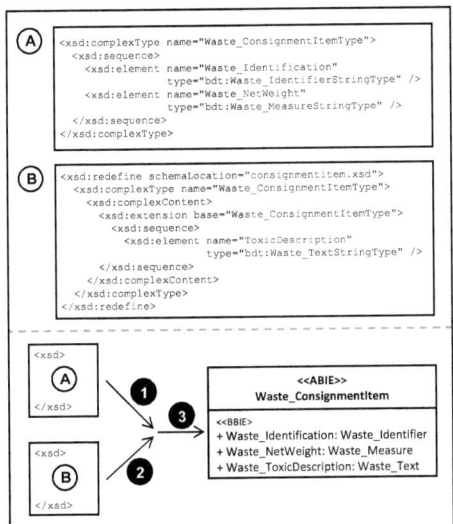

Figure 11.8 redefine mechanism

The complex type definition of `waste_ consignment item type` consists of the original type definition as well as the type redefinition. For the creation of a correct and complete model representation of the complex type, it is necessary to process both, the original type definition as well as the type redefinition. The suggested approach is to first process the complex type definition (see Figure 11.8, mark 1) and second adapt the complex type definition, according to the redefinition (see Figure 11.8, mark 2). The cumulated complex type may then be mapped to an ABIE, whereas each element of the complex type is simply mapped to a BBIE of the ABIE (see Figure 11.8, mark 3).

substitution group. The purpose of substitution groups is to add flexibility to content models, which are for example used in complex type definitions. A substitution group consists of a head element as well as one or more member elements, which together form a hierarchy. One constraint these hierarchies must fulfill is, that all member elements

substitutionGroup

are derived from the head element either by restriction or extension. A well defined substitution group then allows to substitute every head element, used in a content model, by one of the defined member elements. An example, illustrating a head element and substitutable member elements, is illustrated in Figure 11.9, marks A and B. In addition, substitution groups also allow the use of abstract head elements. Compared to non-abstract head elements described above, the use of an abstract head element enforces that the head element is replaced by one of the member elements. An example for an abstract head element definition is illustrated in Figure 11.9, mark C.

Figure 11.9
Substitution group mechanism (1/3)

Using an abstract head element

First, we detail a substitution group, defined using an abstract head element. To represent the relationship between the abstract head element and its derived member elements, the following approach is suggested. The head element is mapped to an ACC (see Figure 11.10, mark 1) and all member elements are mapped to ABIEs, which are based on the particular ACC (see Figure 11.10, mark 2).

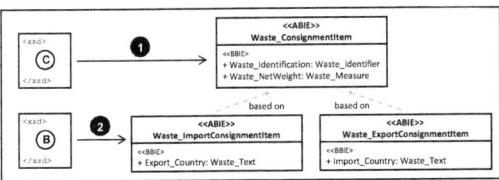

*Figure 11.10
Substitution group
mechanism (2/3)*

Careful readers might notice that the approach suggested is not valid since UPCC supports derivation by restriction only, whereas the member elements are derived from the head element by restriction or extension. Another encountered problem is the issue of representing hierarchies, consisting of multiple levels. An example is that a member element is at the same time the head element for another member element. These hierarchies are also not supported in UPCC, hence they cannot be represented at all.

On the contrary, substitution groups may be defined using a non-abstract head element. In this case, the suggested approach is that the head element as well as the member elements are represented as ABIEs in the model representation. However, also the second approach is not entirely suitable, since hierarchy information is lost.

*Using a
non-abstract head
element*

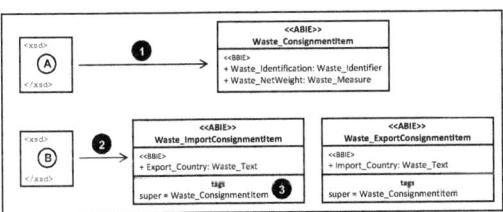

*Figure 11.11
Substitution group
mechanism (3/3)*

An alternative approach to allow the extension and restriction of member elements as well as to preserve the hierarchies within a substitution group, is introduced in the following. The suggested approach introduces an additional tagged value for ABIEs named *super*. At first, the head element as well as the member elements are mapped to ABIEs in the model representation (see Figure 11.11, marks 1 and 2). Second, a tagged value named *super* is used to maintain the hierarchy information by storing a reference from each member element to its head element in the tagged value (see

Figure 11.11, mark 3). In the following, we further concentrate on model layer mappings.

11.3.2 Model Layer Mappings

Introducing heuristics for concrete model element mappings

In the previous Section we described how XML Schema constructs, which do not explicitly occur in UPCC, may be dealt with. Additionally, we now focus on concrete model elements and how their semantics may be preserved during the mapping of two schemas, i.e., some XML Schema-based document model and UPCC. The following problem statements may not only be seen as mapping heuristics, but also to a certain extend as modeling guidelines for UPCC. For now, there do not exist modeling guidelines for UPCC, raising also issues for future work in this area. The aim of this Section is to show how XML Schema-based document parts may be mapped to the existing Core Components Library (CCL) and how extensions to the CCL may be incorporated by some lightweight extension mechanisms. The general mapping heuristic for mapping arbitrary XML Schema models, core components and business information entities, defined in the CCL, comprises the following steps:

1. Find an ACC, which includes most of the concepts modeled within a complex type.
2. Create a corresponding ABIE, which restricts on those BBIEs needed.
3. In case 1. and 2. cannot be fully applied, the following specific heuristics and problems may be considered:

Combination of different ACCs

ACC Combination Mappings. The mapping from one XML Schema complex type to only one corresponding ACC may sometimes not be sufficient. Instead, we may have to map one XML Schema complex type to more than one ACC. Thus, the mapping on the CCL side involves a combination of predefined building blocks. In practice this will most likely entail mappings from element declarations to BBIEs (cf. Figure 11.12, mark 1 for a generic visualization). For example, the information for a complex type called ConsignmentItem may be contained in an ACC Consignment and ACC Item from the CCL. This combination information must be stored within a mapping model for later use in XML Schema generation, to produce well

11.3 Advanced Mapping

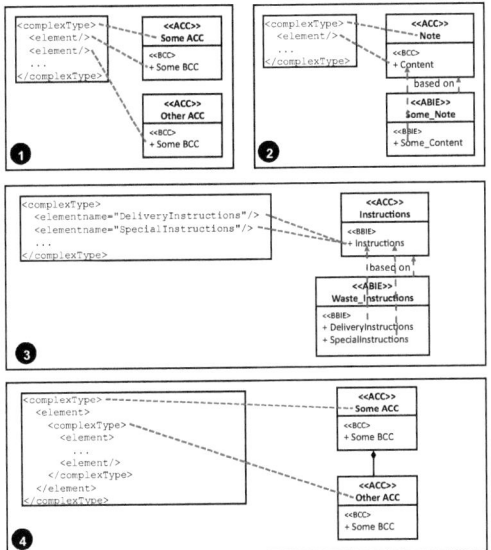

Figure 11.12
Conceptual illustration of model mappings

defined schema documents. Otherwise, more than one complex type would be generated in the schema.

Generic Content Containers. The CCL provides some generic ACCs such as Note with BCCs for content, subject, identification, and others. Wrapped in a business context of a BIE library, these components may be mapped to XML Schema elements (see Figure 11.12, mark 2). However, one has to be careful with data types of such BCCs as they might not match the ones used in the XML Schema. This may lead to type conversion problems. Also, generic core components have to be used with care and should not lead to constructs whose meaning is no longer clear or ambiguous.

Using generic core components

Semi-Semantic Loss. Some BCCs in the CCL are so generic that they may be used for more than one contextualized BBIE. Multiple identifiers of some sort in an invoice document are a good example, where the reuse of a BCC makes sense. The distinction of the BBIEs, based on just one BCC, is achieved through qualifiers, stating the specific business context. By using this BCC *overloading* we are able to map two different elements on one BCC that evolves into two BBIEs on the business information entity layer.

Dealing with semi-semantic loss

11 Mapping bottom-up to top-down standards

Thus, the basic semantic of each BBIE is defined through the *based on* dependency to the underlying core component, but the semantic of the specifics of that element is not defined. Hence, it is lost during the mapping and modeling task. An example in the waste management context is given in Figure 11.12, mark 3.

Applying negative mapping concepts

Negative Mapping. In some cases concepts defined within a schema may not be mapped to any of the reusable building blocks, provided by the CCL. In such cases we propose to allow the creation of completely new business information entities, which are not based on any existing ACCs. The meaning of the newly created and mapped ABIEs is not specified. This extension mechanism should be used wisely or interoperability issues may arise.

Dealing with extensive element nesting in a schema file

XML Schema Nesting. Both XML and XML Schema documents often show deeply nested structures. Especially XML Schema documents may contain complex types, which contain elements with complex types, which may again contain complex types, and so on. The same applies to sequences and choices, which further complicates the mapping to UPCC concepts. The problem is basically the inverse of the problem statement *ACC Combination Mappings*. The mapping task is to find suitable core components for each of the complex types if possible, to reproduce the structure of the XML Schema. The nesting of the mentioned XML Schema elements equals the use of aggregation and composition associations in the UPCC model (cf. Figure 11.12, mark 4). If some mappings cannot be established, the structure will be flattened on the UPCC side, resulting in less ACCs. Again, this information has to be stored in a suitable mapping model, capturing the individual structure of an XML Schema-based document model.

Easing UPCC restrictions. Assume we encounter some composite structures in XML Schema, which are differently nested and composed through the aggregation relationship of ACCs in the CCL. Strictly following the UPCC approach, it would not be possible to pertain these relationships because ASBIEs need to be based on some ASCC. However, in practice we may relax this restriction of the UPCC standard. For the composition of document parts on the business information entities layer, ASBIEs without corresponding ASCCs may be created.

11.4 Implementation and Case Study

This mapping approach is currently the basis for implementation in our business document engineering tool VIENNA Add-In (Visualizing Inter ENterprise Network Architectures) [180]. Our work is accompanied by a broader case study involving the Austrian e-Billing standard ebInterface [8] for small to medium-sized companies and public services.

Evaluation of our mapping rules

11.5 Final assessment

In this Chapter we addressed the gap between existing business document definitions and core components by introducing a well defined heuristic for the mapping of arbitrary document models, based on XML Schema, to the UPCC-based and thus core component conforming document models. The results of our evaluation are illustrated in Table 11.1. In particular all the XML Schema constructs are listed, for which we provided a mapping strategy. Accordingly, the Table illustrates the core component concept that the XML Schema construct has been mapped to, as well as if necessary, an extension enabling successful mapping. Furthermore, the usability of the different mapping strategies is illustrated.

Closing the gap between existing document standards and Core Components

XSD Concept	CCTS Concept	Tagged Value	Usability
xs:all	BCC/BBIE	modelgroup = all	+
xs:any	ABIE/BBIE	-	-
xs:choice	BCC/BBIE	modelgroup = choice	+
xs:group	BCC/BBIE	modelgroup = custom	+
xs:redefine	BCC/BBIE	-	o
xs:sequence	BCC/BBIE	-	++
xs:substitutionGroup	ACC/ABIE	super	-
xsi:type	-	-	- -

Table 11.1 Overview on the Usability of the different Mapping Strategies

We conclude that in general no easy straightforward 1:1 mapping between arbitrary XML Schema and core component artifacts is possible. Recall, that XML Schema is a meta-language for the definition of new XML formats. Thus, its expressiveness goes far beyond the restricted core component concepts. However, we have shown how mapping rules

11 Mapping bottom-up to top-down standards

and mapping heuristics may be used to map XML Schema constructs to predefined core components, defined in the Core Component Library (CCL). The only XML Schema construct that cannot be mapped to core components is the `xsi:type` construct. Successful mapping of the construct is inhibited due to various reasons including the following. First of all, the `xsi:type` meta construct is used in actual XML document instances. Furthermore, the `xsi:type` construct cannot be comprehended unless having the ebInterface specification at hand. Also, the construct has an inherent derivation-by-extension mechanism, which is not supported by core components.

Shortcomings of the Core Component Library

We conclude that the Core Component Technical Specification provides a sound foundation for the mapping of arbitrary XML-based business document standards. However, the imperative compliance of core component artifacts to the Core Component Library imposes several restrictions in regard to mappings. In particular finding a pertinent core component in the Core Component Library is a difficult task, since only a limited amount of predefined core component definitions is available at the moment. UN/CEFACT is currently working on the inclusion of additional core components in the Core Component Library.

12 Process choreographies and document definitions

In the previous Chapters we outlined the importance of an agreement on a common business document definition. However, as already mentioned in the introduction of this thesis, a two-fold agreement is necessary before two business partners may engage in an automated business interaction. First, an agreement on the business document structure has to be negotiated. Second, the exact exchange order of the business documents must be agreed upon. We refer to the order, in which documents are exchanged in an inter-organizational business process, as business process choreography.

Common agreement on process choreography and business document definition

In this Chapter we introduce a well accepted method for capturing requirements of an inter-organizational business process choreography, namely UN/CEFACT's Modeling Methodology (UMM) [174]. We introduce the basics of UMM using our accompanying example from the waste management domain. Finally we show how both, a business process choreography, based on UMM and a business document specification, based on the UML Profile for Core Components (UPCC) [172], may be used to provide a requirements engineering methodology for inter-organizational processes.

Introducing UN/CEFACT's Modeling Methodology

The remainder of this Chapter is structured as follows: Section 12.1 provides an introduction to UN/CEFACT's Modeling Methodology and consequently examines its different sub-views. Sub-section 12.1.3 shows how UMM and UPCC models may be combined on a conceptual level. Finally, Section 12.2 shows how UMM models in combination with UPCC models may be used in a model-driven manner, to generate deployment artifacts for service oriented environments. Section 12.3 concludes the Chapter with a final assessment.

12.1 Introduction to UN/CEFACT's Modeling Methodology

A requirements engineering approach for SOA

As already outlined in the introduction of this thesis, the field of EDI has undergone significant changes in recent years. A pure document centric approach for the definition of EDI requirements is not sufficient any more, since inter-organizational business processes must also be taken into account, in order to allow for seamless B2B interactions. In the context of service-oriented architectures (SOA), services are used for the realization of inter-organizational business processes. Zeithaml et al. define services as economic activities, offered to other business partners to achieve a certain benefit [195]. Realizing the services portfolio in a technical sense results in B2B information systems according to the concept of a SOA.

Capturing the collaborative space between companies

Web Services are currently the state-of-the-art technology for implementing a SOA. Evidently, a successful B2B integration does not start with manually creating Web Services artifacts, such as WSDL or BPEL code. According to Papazoglou et al. [133], the successful implementation of a SOA requires an evolutionary development process, which is similar to object-oriented and component-based software development processes and which considers business process modeling as a driving factor.

For analyzing and designing inter-organizational systems, UN/CEFACT has started to work on a development process called UN/CEFACT's modeling methodology (UMM). During the course of time this development process has changed considerably. However, the main goal of UMM [174] was always to capture the collaborative space between organizations. UMM has been developed according to the business operational view of the Open-edi reference model [78], which covers the business aspects such as business information, business conventions, agreements, and rules among organizations.

UMM as part of the ebXML specification

When UN/CEFACT and OASIS started the ebXML initiative in 1999, UMM concepts have significantly influenced the ebXML business process specification [120]. Also UMM changed during this time by adopting concepts from ebXML members, such as SWIFT, TM Forum, GS1 (EAN*UCC), and RosettaNet. In 2000 the copyrights of the company ED-

12.1 Introduction to UN/CEFACT's Modeling Methodology

IFECS on their Business Collaboration Framework (BCF), used by RosettaNet, were transferred to UN/CEFACT and the BCF was merged into UMM.

However, at this time UMM just provided guidelines for using the general purpose modeling language UML [129] and missed a formal customization of the UML meta-model. Furthermore, we recognized a step towards service orientation. Being part of the UMM project team, we addressed these challenges by developing a UML profile which integrates service-oriented concepts. A UML profile specifies a set of stereotypes, tagged values, and constraints for customizing UML. This means that the general-purpose language UML is customized for the specific purpose of inter-organizational systems. Thereby, UMM puts UML in a very strict corset. Each artifact is restricted to a number of precisely defined modeling elements (stereotypes) and the relationships among them is also fixed. As a consequence, it is easier for software engineers to act upon the resulting artifacts to bind their local systems to the public process, defined by UMM. We have been the editing team of the resulting specification 'UMM foundation module 1.0' [166] [55], which was finalized in 2006. Furthermore, we have provided an extensive user guide for UMM 1.0 [192].

A UML Profile for UMM

However, first experiences in applying the UMM in real world projects have shown some shortcomings: First, the current UMM provides rather vague means for modeling business documents – a gap which is closed by this thesis. Second, there is a lack of alternative responses in a business transaction. Third, results of a business transaction currently do not propagate changes of business entity states. Fourth, current UMM business choreographies used guards in natural language and, thus, lack information to be machine-processable. Fifth, UMM does not allow to interlink activities of two different business collaborations. Finally stakeholders have argued against the complex package structure of a UMM 1.0 model.

Shortcomings of UMM 1.0

Consequently, we propose new concepts to be adapted by UMM to overcome the limitations mentioned above. We submitted these concepts to UN/CEFACT to move the UMM foundation module towards version 2. In this Chapter we demonstrate the adapted UMM 2.0 development process, which overcomes the limitations of UMM 1.0. Thereby, we

From UMM 1.0 to UMM 2.0

12 Process choreographies and document definitions

specifically focus on the problem of how to capture business process and business document information in a single conceptual model. We go step by step through the development process of the UMM using our accompanying example from the waste management domain. Note that for explanatory purposes we present a simplified version of the waste management example.

In the following Sections we examine the three main views of UMM 2.0: *business requirements view (bRequirementsV)*, *business choreography view (bChoreographyV)*, and *business information view (bInformationV)*.

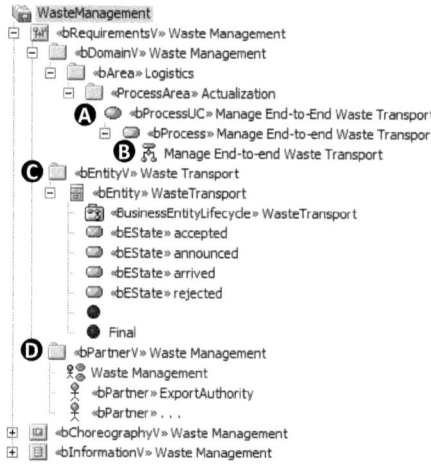

Figure 12.1
Overview of the Business Requirements View

12.1.1 Business Requirements View

The business requirements view is the first view to be constructed during the elaboration of a UMM model. Figure 12.1 shows the package structure of the *business requirements view* and its three sub-views *business domain view (bDomainV)*, *business entity view (bEntityV)*, and *business partner view (bPartnerV)*. The alphabetically numbered dots associate the example diagrams with the respective packages they belong to, e.g., Figure 12.3 shows the detailed view of A in Figure 12.1.

12.1 Introduction to UN/CEFACT's Modeling Methodology

Business Domain View

At the beginning of the UMM development process, the business analyst gathers domain knowledge and existing process knowledge of the business domain under consideration. The analyst has to capture the justification of the project and has to determine its scope. He interviews business experts and other stakeholders to get an understanding of the existing business processes in the domain. This task if often accompanied by the use of worksheets. Worksheets are structured forms for the elicitation of specific requirements and a popular mechanism to guide the interview and to capture business know-how. For a detailed discussion of worksheets see [69]. It is important that the analyst does not influence the business expert. The interview has to take place in the language of the business domain expert; technical and modeling terms should be avoided. The interviews ensure that all involved parties share a common understanding of the business domain. In this step, the analyst discovers intra- and inter-organizational business processes. A simplified example for the output of an interview, kept in a worksheet, is depicted in Figure 12.2.

Task 1: Capture the domain knowledge

Form: *BusinessProcess*	
General	
Business Process Name	Manage End-to-End Waste Transport
Definition	A waste transport taking place between an export authority and an import authority.
Description	Subject of the business process is the waste transport between different countries. The export authority of the export country pre-informs the import authority of the import country about a waste transport. Upon successful receipt of the waste transport the import authority informs the export authority.
Participants	ImportAuthority, ExportAuthority
Stakeholder	Tax Agency
Reference	Waste Management
Start/End Characteristics	
Pre-condition	The waste is ready for transport.
Post-condition	- The waste has been moved from the export country to the import country. - No waste transport took place.
Begins When	Export authority receives the order to initiate the waste transport.
Ends When	The export authority receives the transport arrival receipt from the import authority.
Actions	- Pre-inform on waste transport - Inform on waste receipt
Exceptions	-
Relationships	
Included Business Processes	none
Affected Business Entities	WasteTransport

Figure 12.2
Business Process Worksheet

The results of the interviews are transformed into a UML notation. Each worksheet, describing a business process, results in a *business process uses cases (bProcessUC)*. Business processes are classified according to UN/CEFACT's Catalog of Common Business Processes (CBPC) [165], the Supply Chain Reference Model (SCOR) [158], or Porter's Value

Task 2: Transform free-form text descriptions into UML models

12 Process choreographies and document definitions

Chain (PVC) [141]. Classifying business processes facilitates the understanding of the business domain, as well as its scope. A hierarchical composition of business areas and process areas is used to represent the classification, as shown in Figure 12.1. In this example we only show the *business area* logistics, including the *process area* actualization. In reality, a *business domain view* comprises additional *business* and *process areas*.

The business process use case manage end-to-end waste transport is assigned to the process area actualization within the business area logistics (*A* in Figure 12.1). The corresponding use case diagram is shown in Figure 12.3. In general, business partners participating in the business process and stakeholders who have an interest in the process, are associated to the business process use case. In our example, the *business partners* exporter, export authority, import authority, and importer participate in manage end-to-end waste transport, whereas the stakeholder customs authority has an interest in the inter-organizational process.

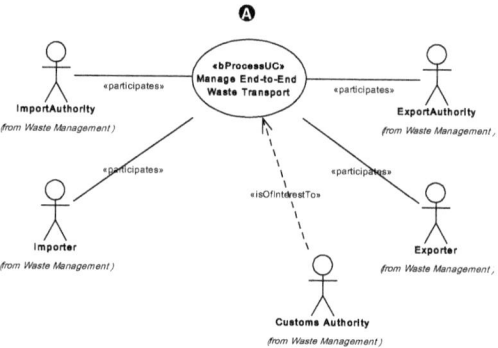

Figure 12.3
Business Process Use Case with Business Partners

Task 3: Identify relevant processes for a collaboration

Once all business processes are discovered, a review cycle is initiated to identify those which in fact have a relevance for the business collaboration to be developed. These business processes are further detailed by an activity diagram, according to the requirements specified in the respective worksheet. The activity diagram becomes a child of the *business process use case*. In our example, we show the activity diagram for manage end-to-end waste transport in Figure 12.4. According to Figure 12.1, this activity di-

12.1 Introduction to UN/CEFACT's Modeling Methodology

agram (B) is a child of the corresponding business process use case (A).

The following business semantics are kept in the activity diagram: An exporter informs the export authority about a waste transport. The export authority in turn informs the import authority about the incoming waste transport. Consequently, the import authority informs the importer. The flow of accepting or rejecting the waste transport is going into the reverse direction. In case the waste transport announcement has been accepted, the waste transport starts. Upon arrival of the waste in the import country, the flow of informing partners on its receipt is also going the reverse direction. We only show the activities between the export authority and the import authority in detail, whereas the other activities are only sketched.

The exchange of information must always lead to a synchronization of changed *business entity states* at each partner's side. Thus, the object flow between activities is denoted by a *shared business entity state*, which is further discussed in the subsection on the business entity view. The concept of *shared business entity states* denotes the need for communication between business partners. Thus, *shared business entity states* are a strong indicator for requiring information exchange in later designed business collaborations.

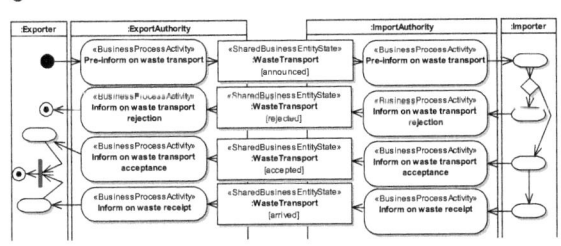

Figure 12.4
Business Process Activity Model

Business Entity View

A *business entity* is a real-world thing having business significance that is shared between two or more business partners in a collaborative business process (e.g., order, account, etc.). In our example, the information exchanged is about the *business entity* waste transport.

Task 4: Identify relevant business entities

12 Process choreographies and document definitions

A *business entity lifecycle* is described by a UML state diagram as part of the business entity view (cf. *C* in Figure 12.1). It depicts the states, a *business entity* may obtain, as well as the flow between them. The lifecycle is designed in accordance with the activity diagrams in the *business domain view*. The object flow in the activity diagrams is based on *shared business entity states* (cf. Figure 12.4). Each *shared business entity state* reflects a *business entity state* in the *business entity lifecycle* (cf. Figure 12.6). Thus, the order of changing *business entity states* in the activity diagrams must be kept in the *business entity lifecycle*.

The *business entity lifecycle* depicted in Figure 12.6 represents the states of the *business entity* `waste transport`. The business entity is created with state `announced`. The pending state `announced` is either set to `approved` or `rejected`. After the approved transport has occurred, the *business entity* is set to `arrived`. These four *business entity states* are referenced by the four *shared business entity states* of the activity diagram in Figure 12.4.

Figure 12.5
Business Entity Worksheet

\multicolumn{2}{l}{Form: *BusinessEntity*}	
General	
Business Entity Name	WasteTransport
Definition	The waste transport business entity is the list of states a waste transport can have.
Description	A waste transport is taking place between an export and an import authority.
BusinessEntityLifecycle	
Pre-condition	A waste transport exists.
Post-condition	The waste transport has been arrived or rejected.
Begins When	A waste transport is initiated.
Ends When	The waste transport has successfully arrived or has been rejected by the notifiee.
Exceptions	-
BusinessEntityState #1	
Name	announced
Definition	A waste transport is in state "announced" if the notifiee has been informed about it.
Description	Before the notifiee reports back to the notifier whether the waste transport is accepted or rejected, the waste transport is in state "announced".
Predecessing State	-
BusinessEntityState #2	
Name	accepted
Definition	A waste transport is in state "accepted" if the notifiee positively responds to the waste transport announcement of the notifier.
Description	Before the notifier is informed by the notifiee about the successful execution of the waste transport, the waste transport is in state "accepted".
Predecessing State	announced
BusinessEntityState #3	
Name	rejected
Definition	A waste transport is in state "rejected" if the notifiee negatively responds to the waste transport announcement of the notifier.
Description	If the waste transport announcement is declined, the waste transport is in state "rejected".
Predecessing State	announced
BusinessEntityState #4	
Name	arrived
Definition	A waste transport is in state "arrived" if the waste transport was successfully executed and the waste arrived in the target country.
Description	If the waste transport has been accepted by the notifiee and the transport was executed successfully, the waste transport is in state "arrived".
Predecessing State	accepted

12.1 Introduction to UN/CEFACT's Modeling Methodology

Figure 12.5 depicts a worksheet, capturing the requirements for a business entity's lifecycle, gathered during an interview between the business domain expert and the business analyst. First, definition and description of a lifecycle as well as pre- and post-conditions and begin/end characteristics are captured. Then, each state of the lifecycle is captured with its definition, description, and preceding states. Finally, the flow of the lifecycle is constructed by analyzing business entity states, together with their predecessors.

Business partners identified in the business requirements view are modeled in diagrams that belong to the business domain view. However, for the sake of an easier re-use, business partners and stakeholders are kept in a dedicated container – the *business partner view* (*D* in Figure 12.1). The business partner view may also be used to analyze relationships between the business partners and/or stakeholders in optional role models, which are not further elaborated here.

Task 5: Identify business partners

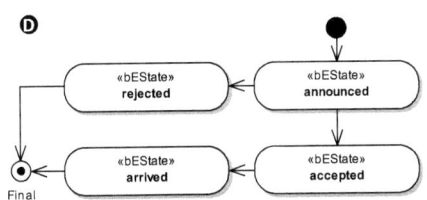

Figure 12.6
Business Entity Life Cycle: Waste Transport

12.1.2 Business Choreography View

In the *business choreography view* the analyst builds upon the previously created artifacts to develop models, describing a global choreography. According to Figure 12.7, it consists of three sub-views: *business transaction view (bTransactionV)*, *business collaboration view (bCollaborationV)*, and *business realization view (bRealizationV)*. The *business transaction view* models the basic-building blocks of a choreography, corresponding to a single business document exchange and returning an optional business document as a response. The *business collaboration view* models a global choreography built by these basic building blocks. A *business realization view* is used if the same choreography is realized between different set of business partners.

Figure 12.7
Overview of the Business Choreography View

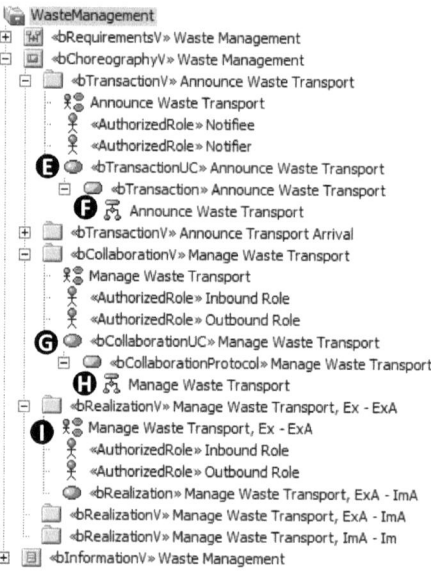

Business Transaction View

Task 6: Formalize requirements using UMM business transactions

The basic building blocks of a UMM choreography are *business transactions*. The goal of a business transaction is synchronizing the business entity states between two parties. Synchronization of states is either required in an uni-directional or in a bi-directional way. In the former case, the initiator of the *business transaction* informs the other party about an already irreversible state change the other party has to accept – e.g., the notification that the waste has arrived. It follows that responding in such a scenario is neither required nor reasonable. In the latter case, the initiating party sets a *business entity* to an interim state and the responding party decides about its final state – consider a request for a waste transport that the responder might either accept or refuse.

Business transactions synchronize business entity states

The synchronization of business entity states takes place by exchanging business information. According to the definitions above, an exchange takes always place between exactly two parties. It is either a uni-directional exchange or a bi-directional exchange, including a response. The activity diagrams, created in the business domain view (cf. Figure

12.1 Introduction to UN/CEFACT's Modeling Methodology

12.4), already indicate the need for exchanging business information to synchronize business entities by the concept of *shared business entity states*. However, these activity diagrams are not necessarily consolidated between the various parties and are just used for requirements elicitation. The business transaction has to present a consolidated and formal view on the basic information exchanges between business partners. Thus, it has to identify the commonly agreed *shared business entity states* and, possibly, aggregate two of them in a bi-directional business information exchange.

This identification and consolidation process leads to a number of *business transaction use cases* and the two *authorized roles* participating in the use case. According to Figure 12.7, each *business transaction use case* (E) and the two participating *authorized roles* are placed in their own *business transaction view*. Figure 12.8 depicts the *business transaction use case* announce waste transport, involving the participating *authorized roles* notifier and notifiee. Note that we use the abstract concepts of *authorized roles* instead of *business partners*, because *business transactions* and their use cases may be realized between different sets of *business partners*.

Figure 12.8
Business Transaction Use Case

The requirements of a *business transaction* are further elaborated using the concept of activity diagrams. For each *business transaction use case* an activity diagram is created and placed as a child underneath the respective use case, e.g., in Figure 12.7 the *business transaction use case* announce waste transport (E) is refined using the activity diagram (F).

The main purpose of a business transaction activity diagram is to formally describe a UMM business transaction. Note that a *business transaction* always follows the same pattern. Thereby, the business transaction pattern defines the type of a legally binding interaction between two decision making applications as defined in Open-edi [78] reference model. We distinguish between two one-way (information distribution, notification) and four two-way (query/response, request/response, request/confirm, commercial transaction) types of business transactions. The patterns differ in the default values of the tagged values characterizing a requesting/responding business action.

The basic building blocks of a business transaction are activity partitions, which are used to denote the authorized roles, participating in the transaction. Furthermore, a business transaction contains exactly two actions – a requesting action and a responding action – one on each business partner's side. Between the different actions, the business information exchange is denoted using the concepts of object flows and action pins. There is always exactly one object flow from the requesting action to the responding action. In a one-way business transaction there is no flow in the reverse direction. In case of a two-way business transaction, there are one or more object flows in the reverse direction. In case of two or more object flows, they are considered as alternatives. The type of the action pins in the business transaction is set using business documents from the business information view. Thus, the action pins of a business transaction are the linchpins between the business process and the business information perspective of an inter-organizational process.

Action pins are the linchpin between the business process and the business information perspective

Figure 12.9 shows the *business transaction* announce waste transport. On the left hand side the *business transaction partition (bTPartition)* of the requesting role is shown and on the right hand side the one of the responding role. The type of a *business transaction partition* is determined by the *authorized roles*, participating in the *business transaction use case*, which the *business transaction* refines. In Figure 12.9 the type of the requesting partition is set by the *authorized role* notifier and the type of the *responding partition* is set by the *authorized role* notifiee.

The *requesting partition* contains a *requesting action (ReqAction)* and the *responding partition* a *responding action (ResAction)*. In the example shown in Figure 12.9, the notifier starts the *business transaction* by sending a waste movement form to the notifiee. Since the transaction is bi-directional, the *business entity* waste transport is set to an interim state. Depending on the response of the notifiee, the *business entity* is set to its final state. After

12.1 Introduction to UN/CEFACT's Modeling Methodology

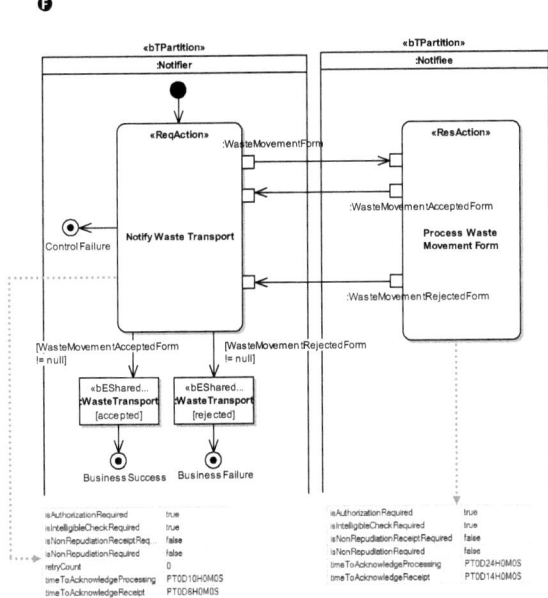

Figure 12.9
Business Transaction Announce Waste Transport

the notifiee has processed the request from the notifier, he either replies with a waste movement accepted form or with a waste movement rejected form. In the notifier's partition two *shared business entity states* waste transport are shown, together with guard conditions leading to the *shared business entity states*. Depending on the reply of the notifiee, the *shared business entity state* waste transport is either set to the final state accepted or to rejected. In case a control failure occurs during the transaction the *business transaction* results in a control failure as shown on the left hand side of Figure 12.9.

At the lower side of Figure 12.9, the tagged values containing the different business signal information of the requesting and the responding action are shown, e.g., time to acknowledge receipt indicates the maximum time within the responding party has to confirm a successful/unsuccessful syntax, grammar, and sequence validation. Further tagged values are: is authorization required, is non-repudiation required, time to perform, time to acknowledge receipt, time to acknowledge acceptance, is non-repudiation of receipt required, and retry-count. These tagged values are explained in detail in the UMM 1.0 specification [166]. As shown in Figure 12.7, the waste management example consist of exactly two business transactions: *announce waste transport* (Figure 12.9) and *announce transport arrival*. The latter is a one-way transaction and is not explained in detail here.

Business Collaboration View

Task 7: Define business collaborations representing global process choreographies

After the identification of the different *business transactions* the modeler continues with creating *business collaborations*. A *business collaboration* choreographs the execution order of different *business transactions* and *business collaborations* (since *business collaborations* may be nested recursively).

Each *business collaboration view* contains exactly one *business collaboration use case* and two *authorized roles* participating in the use case (*G* in Figure 12.7). By definition a *business collaboration* consists of different *business transactions* and/or *business collaborations*. Included *business transactions/collaborations* are denoted using the concept of *include* dependencies. Each included *business transaction* is defined in its own *business transaction view* and each included *business collaboration* is defined in its own *business collaboration view*.

As shown in Figure 12.10, the *business collaboration use case* manage waste transport includes two *business transactions*, namely
announce waste transport and announce transport arrival. Again the abstract concept of *authorized roles* is used instead of *business partners*, because *business collaborations* may be realized between different sets of *business partners*.

Figure 12.10 Business Collaboration Use Case

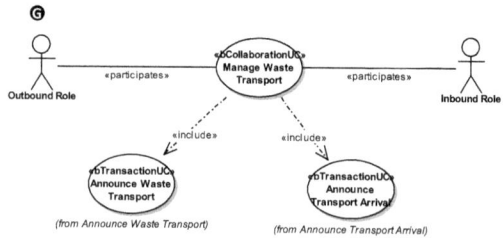

12.1 Introduction to UN/CEFACT's Modeling Methodology

Similar to the concept of a *business transaction use case*, a *business collaboration use case* is further elaborated using the concept of a *business collaboration protocol*. For each *business collaboration use case* a *business collaboration protocol* is created and placed as a child under the respective use case, e.g., in Figure 12.7 the *business collaboration use case* manage waste transport (G) is refined using the *business collaboration protocol* (H). Consequently, a *business collaboration use case* is always the parent of exactly one *business collaboration protocol*.

The main goal of a *business collaboration protocol* is to describe a *business collaboration* on a formal basis. A *business collaboration protocol* is built using *business transaction calls* and *business collaboration calls*. A *business transaction call* invokes a *business transaction* and a *business collaboration call* invokes a *business collaboration*. To depict the *authorized roles*, participating in a *business collaboration*, a *business collaboration protocol* uses the concept of partitions. For each *authorized role* exactly one partition is created. In some cases an *authorized role*, during the course of a *business collaboration*, might internally execute another *business collaboration*. In this case the concept of *nested business collaboration* is used. *Nested business collaborations* are defined in another *business collaboration view*. To denote the execution order of different *business transaction calls* and *business collaboration calls* the concept of *initFlows* and *reFlows* is used. Thereby, an *initFlow* may either lead to a partition or – in case a *nested collaboration* is used – to a *nested business collaboration*. The same applies to *reFlows*. Guard conditions, attached to the different object flows within the *business collaboration protocol*, determine the exact execution sequence.

Business collaboration protocols formalize a global process choreography

The *business collaboration protocol* in Figure 12.11 defines the exact choreography of the manage waste transport collaboration. Using the concept of two *business collaboration partitions (bCPartition)*, the two *authorized roles* outbound role and inbound role participating in the business collaboration are shown. The *business collaboration* management waste transport starts with the *business transaction* announce waste transport. The *initFlow* dependency between the outbound role and the *business transaction call* announce waste transport in Fig-

*Figure 12.11
Business
Collaboration
Protocol Manage
Waste Transport*

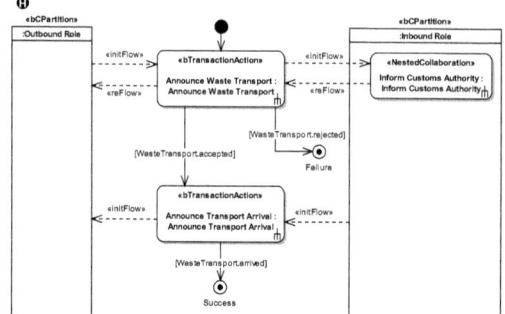

ure 12.11 indicates that the outbound role initiates the *business transaction*. Since there is a *reFlow* dependency from the *nested business collaboration* within the partition of the inbound role to the *business transaction call* and the outbound role, the *business transaction* is a two-way transaction. The inbound role informs the customs authority about the waste transport announcement of the outbound role. If the customs authority rejects the waste transport, the inbound role rejects the waste transport as well and sends a waste movement rejected form to the outbound role.

If the *business transaction* announce waste transport fails, because the inbound role or the customs authority has rejected the transport, the *business collaboration* manage waste transport also fails. In Figure 12.11 this is indicated by the control flow with the guard condition WasteTransport.rejected leading from the *business transaction call* to the final state Failure. Note that the guard conditions of the control flows directly match to the *shared business entity states* of the underlying *business transaction* (see Figure 12.9).

In case the *business transaction* announce waste transport was successful, the guard condition WasteTransport.accepted evaluates true and the *business transaction* announce transport arrival starts. Note that now the inbound role is the initiator of the *business transaction*. The inbound role has received the waste from the outbound role and now informs the *business partner* about this irreversible state. As shown in Figure 12.11, this is indicated by the *initFlow* dependency between the inbound role and

12.1 Introduction to UN/CEFACT's Modeling Methodology

the *business transaction call* announce transport arrival. The *business collaboration* finally ends with the *business entity* waste transport being in state arrived.

Business Realization View

We have seen so far that *business transactions* and *business collaborations* are executed between *authorized roles* instead of specific *business partners*. By using the concept of authorized roles, the same business collaboration/transaction may be re-used between different sets of specific business partners. This enables the standardization of business collaboration models and fosters re-use.

Binding a *business collaboration* (and implicitly the *business transactions* it consists of) to a set of *business partners* is achieved through *business realizations*. Figure 12.12 shows a possible *business realization* for the *business collaboration* manage waste transport.

Task 8: Indicating optional reuse of business collaborations

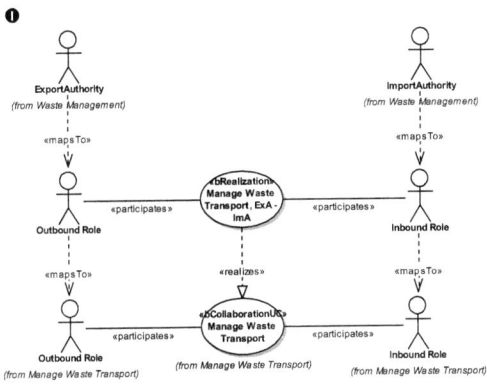

Figure 12.12
Business Realization View

At the bottom of Figure 12.12, the *business collaboration* manage waste transport is shown between the two *authorized roles* outbound role and inbound role. A *business realization* is connected to a specific *business collaboration use case* using a *realize* connection. In Figure 12.12 the *business realization* manage waste transport ExA-ImA *realizes* the *business collaboration use case* manage waste transport. The *business realization* again has two *authorized roles* outbound role and inbound role. Finally, *business partners* identified in the *business partner view* are bound

12 Process choreographies and document definitions

to *authorized roles* by connecting them via *mapsTo* dependencies.

The benefit of this concept is easily demonstrated by our example. The business collaboration between `export authority` and `import authority` is identical to the one performed between `exporter` and `export authority` as well as to the one between `import authority` and `importer`. This issue is modeled by introducing two additional business realizations, which both realize the *business collaboration use case* `manage waste transport`. One of them is performed between the `exporter` and the `export authority` and the other one between the `import authority` and the `importer`. Thus, the concept of *business realizations* evidently contributes to the re-use of modeling artifacts.

With the completion of the *business realization view* the modeler has finished the business process perspective of the UMM. In the following Section we introduce the business information view (bInformationV) of UMM and show how core component concepts may be used for modeling the business information, exchanged in business transactions. Thereby, we use the UML Profile for Core Components, which we have introduced in Chapter 5.

12.1.3 Business Information View – Combining UMM and UPCC models

Task 9: Define the exchanged business information artifacts

The final view of UMM is the *business information view*. Within the *business information view* the business documents, which are exchanged in the different *business transactions* of UMM, are defined. UMM does not mandate to use a specific business document modeling technique in this view, but leaves it up to the modeler which technology to use. However, it is strongly suggested to use UN/CEFACT's Core Components [164] for the modeling of the exchanged business documents. Since both, UMM and Core Components, are developed by UN/CEFACT and represent complementary technologies, a seamless integration of the process perspective and the data perspective is possible. In the following we use the UML Profile for Core Components to model the business documents being exchanged in the manage waste-transport example. Figure 12.13 shows the structure of the *business information view*, consisting of a *business library (bLibrary)* called `waste management data`

12.1 Introduction to UN/CEFACT's Modeling Methodology

model denoted by (J). Within a *business library* the modeler aggregates the different elements of the UML Profile for Core Components (UPCC).

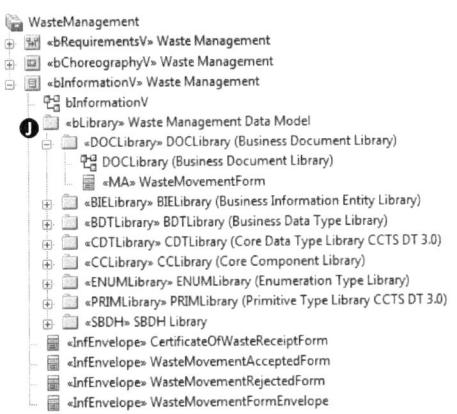

Figure 12.13
Overview of the Business Information View

At the bottom of Figure 12.13 four different *information envelopes (InfEnvelope)*, used in the manage waste transport collaboration, are shown. Above the *information envelopes* several packages are shown, which belong to the UPCC standard. Exemplarily the *information envelope* waste movement form is examined in detail.

As shown on the upper left hand side of Figure 12.14, the *information envelope* waste movement form envelope serves as the root element. Attached to the *information envelope* are the *message assemblies* and *business information entities*, representing the waste management data model for a waste movement form. Note that the waste movement form also contains a standard business document header, serving for identification purposes of technical sender and receiver, document type, etc. Standard business document headers are defined according to the Standard Business Document Header Specification of UN/CEFACT. As of 2009 the standard is currently under development.

The remaining artifacts of the data model shown in Figure 12.14, have already been thoroughly explained in Chapter 5 of this thesis. Finally, the different *information envelopes*, defined in the *business information view*, are used to set the type of the outgoing action pins of a requesting

12 Process choreographies and document definitions

Figure 12.14
Business Information View Example

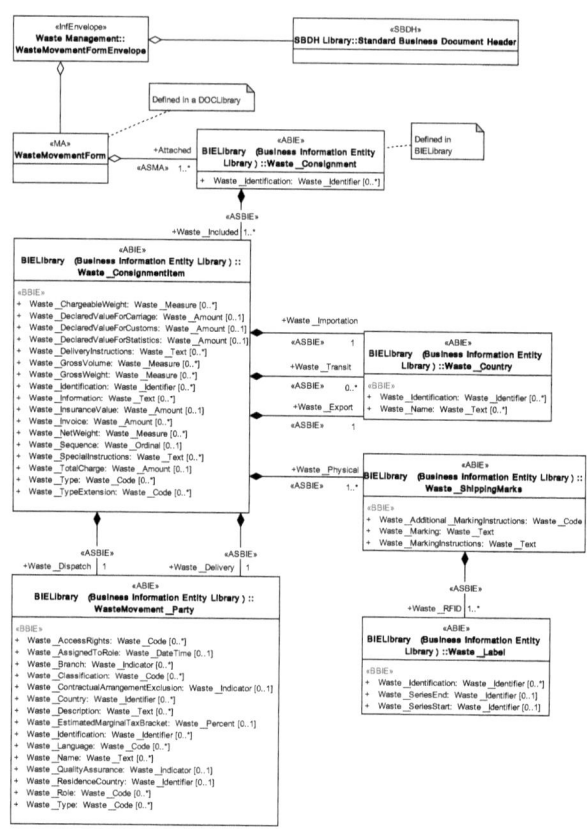

Leveraging benefits from UMM and UPCC

and responding action in a *business transaction*. (compare J in Figure 12.13 with Figure 12.9).

The benefits of combining a core component model and a UMM model are twofold. First, the business analyst is given a single model, describing the entire requirements of the inter-organizational process, i.e., the inter-organizational process model and the business document information, exchanged in the inter-organizational process. Second, the comprehensive model may serve as the basis for the derivation of deployment artifacts, which may be deployed to a service oriented architecture. In the following Section we outline a deployment artifact generation of a UMM model together with a UPCC model. Consequently, we show how the core component model and its XML representation may be inter-weaved with the XML representation of a UMM model.

12.2 Deriving code artifacts from UMM

So far, we concentrated on capturing the business requirements by means of worksheets and using the information in the worksheets for generating modeling artifacts. This helps for a better alignment of modeling artifacts and business requirements and speeds up the development process. In addition, the UMM and UPCC models should be transformed to software artifacts, which may be used to configure B2B software. This allows a straight-through development approach, starting from business requirements to code generation. We have already shown how UPCC helps to capture business document requirements and how XML Schema artifacts may be derived from UPCC models in Chapter 8.

Task 10: Derive deployment artifacts for a SOA from the UMM/UPCC model

Accordingly, a UMM model provides the foundation for deriving software artifacts, realizing the implementation of a partner's business service interface. In the following, we outline a mapping of our example UMM business process to the relevant standards of the Web Services stack – i.e., the Web Service Definition Language (WSDL) [187] and the Business Process Execution Language (WS-BPEL) [122]. Since UMM artifacts (e.g., a business transaction) follow always the same pattern, the transformation rules for code generation are generic and hence applicable to any UMM model. However, we prefer demonstrating the code generation by means of our waste management example, because showing the resulting code instead of formal transformation rules facilitates understanding.

Generating code starts with the identification of the services each participating party must offer: Each business partner must provide service operations for receiving business documents. In a one-way business transaction, there is only a single information flow from the initiator of the transaction to the responder. Thus, only the responder has to provide a service for receiving the business information. In a two-way transaction, business information is returned

Identify services each party must offer

from the responder to the initiator. Thus, the initiator has to offer a service for picking up the response message. This means a two-way business transaction is realized by two asynchronous message exchanges for business documents, instead of a single synchronous call. This is the preferred solution to avoid blocking in long-running business transactions.

Example derivation for announce waste transport business transaction

Again, we demonstrate the approach by our example *business transaction* announce waste transport, conducted between the outbound role (in the following: export authority) and the inbound role (in the following: import authority). The service interface of the import authority must be able to receive the waste movement form, defined in Figure 12.14. Similarly, the export authority has to offer services for receiving a waste movement accepted form and a waste movement rejected form. We limit our discussion to the waste movement form and do not show any details for the waste movement accepted and waste movement rejected form.

In addition to the flow of business messages, business signals are used in UMM to acknowledge the successful receipt and/or processing of a prior received business message. The exchange of exceptions for error reports on the same topic is required as well, but not detailed any further. For a complete reference of deployment artifact generation from UMM models see [101] for UMM 1.0 and [191] for UMM 2.0.

Acknowledgments are specified for each message exchange in a UMM business transaction using the quality of service parameters *time to acknowledge receipt* and *time to acknowledge processing* (cf. Figure 12.9). The former is sent, after a received business document has passed the validation of its schema, its grammar, and its sequence in the context of the process. The latter is sent, after the business document has passed checks against additional business rules and is handed over to the business application for further processing. Consequently, each party must provide two operations for receiving business signals: one for *acknowledgments of receipt* and one for *acknowledgments of processing*.

Listings 12.1 and 12.2 show stubs of WSDL port types for the service interfaces of the import authority and the export authority in the announce waste transport *business transaction*. Each of the stubs defines the operations,

12.2 Deriving code artifacts from UMM

which each business partner has to offer and what type of business document the interface accepts. Thereby, the message type definitions are derived from the business information view of the UMM model. In our example the business information, exchanged in the UMM model, has been defined using the UML Profile for Core Components. Consequently, the reference in line 352 of Listing 12.1 refers to the XML representation of the core component model shown in Figure 12.14.

```
350<portType name="ImA-PT">
351  <operation name="receiveWasteMovementForm">
352    <input message="tns:WasteMovementForm" />
353  </operation>
354  <operation name="receiveAckReceipt">
355    <input message="tns:receiveAckReceipt" />
356  </operation>
357  <operation name="receiveAckProcessing">
358    <input message="tns:receiveAckProcessing" />
359  </operation>
360</portType>
```

Listing 12.1
WSDL port type for the import authority

```
361<portType name="ExA-PT">
362  <operation name="receiveWasteMovementAcceptedForm">
363    <input message="tns:WasteMovementAcceptedForm" />
364  </operation>
365  <operation name="receiveWasteMovementRejectedForm">
366    <input message="tns:WasteMovementRejectedForm" />
367  </operation>
368  <operation name="receiveAckReceipt">
369    <input message="tns:receiveAckReceipt" />
370  </operation>
371  <operation name="receiveAckProcessing">
372    <input message="tns:receiveAckProcessing" />
373  </operation>
374</portType>
```

Listing 12.2
WSDL port type for the export authority

For the description of message exchanges of a UMM *business transaction* we use the Web Services Business Process Execution Language (WS-BPEL), which is the standard language for describing choreographies in a Web Services environment. Thus, we have to transform UMM business transactions to BPEL. UMM describes a global choreography, capturing inter-organizational requirements from an observer's perspective. Thus, is represents the single version of truth on which the business partners agreed to interact with each other. In contrary, BPEL describes a local choreography. It defines a partner-specific perspective of a business process. Hence, in our example the BPEL process of the **export authority** is not the same as the one of the **import authority**. However, the local choreographies must be complementary to each other. In other words, whenever one sends something the other one must receive something. By deriving the local BPEL choreographies from the same global UMM choreography, we ensure that resulting local choreographies are complementary. Consequently,

Deriving local choreographies from global choreographies

12 Process choreographies and document definitions

the local choreographies serve as blueprints to check the local implementations for compliance with the agreed flow.

BPEL describes a business process as a flow of Web Service interactions. The relationship between two interacting services is captured by the concept of a *partner link type*. It describes the two interacting services by their roles in the business process and the port types they have to provide. Considering our example, the *partner link type* shown in Listing 12.3 binds the services of the `export authority` and the `import authority`. Accordingly, the party that acts as the `export authority` has to provide the services described in Listing 12.2. Consequently, the services specified in Listing 12.1 correspond to the interface of the `import authority`.

Listing 12.3 Partner link type binding together the port types of export and import authority
```
375<partnerLinkType name='ImA-ExA-PLT'>
376  <role name='ExportAuthority' portType='ExA-PT'/>
377  <role name='ImportAuthority' portType='ImA-PT'/>
378</partnerLinkType>
```

In the remainder of this subsection, we elaborate on the mapping of a UMM business transaction to BPEL. We illustrate the mapping by means of the BPEL code for the `import authority` of our `announce waste transport` example transaction (see Figure 12.9). The resulting code is shown in Listing 12.4. Note that we simplified the code by removing namespaces, attribute names for activities, etc. for the purpose of enhancing its readability. The derived BPEL code describes the local choreography of the `export authority` – i.e., it captures the observable and required behavior of the `export authority` for interacting in the business transaction. It does not reveal internal implementation details how the `export authority` binds its private processes for participating in the collaborative process.

At the beginning of our example code, the *partner link* defines the role of the owner of the BPEL process and the role of the collaborating partner (starting with line 380). As said before, we show the responder's side of the business transaction. Thus, the owner of the process is the `import authority` (ImA) and the partner role is the `export authority` (ExA).

Combining UMM and UPCC derived deployment artifacts
The *partner link* definition is followed by the *variables* section. Each business document as well as each business signal occurring in the UMM business transaction is mapped to a *variable* in BPEL. Lines 386 and 387 exemplify the definitions of the business document `waste movement form`

12.2 Deriving code artifacts from UMM

and of an *acknowledgment of receipt* business signal. We omit to list all the other *variable* definitions. Of particular importance is the definition in line 386 as it refers to the XML representation which has been derived from the core component model in Figure 12.14.

The code fragment describing the control flow of the import authority's local choreography starts with line 391. According to our example in Figure 12.9, the first action of the import authority is receiving the waste movement form. This is denoted by the corresponding *receive* activity in line 392. The receipt of the waste movement request is confirmed by sending an acknowledgment of receipt (line 395). The requirement of this acknowledgment is defined in the corresponding tagged value of our UMM transaction (c.f. Figure 12.9). Similarly, the *invoke* activity in line 395, confirms that the business document is processable by transmitting an acknowledgment of processing.

The *if* block, starting with line 399, indicates that the import authority may in this step either accept or reject the waste movement – either by sending a waste movement accepted form (line 401) or a waste movement rejected form (line 405). The decision about which document to send is internal to the import authority. The condition isWasteMovementAccepted() (line 400) is an opaque function, accessing the internal decision.

In a next step, the import authority expects the export authority to confirm the receipt of the response. The import authority waits a certain duration for the acknowledgment as specified by the tagged value *time to acknowledge receipt* of the *responding business activity*. In BPEL a *pick* construct (line 410) is used to indicate that the document is expected within a certain time frame. Within the *onMessage* element, we specify the acknowledgment of receipt message the import authority is waiting for. The *onAlarm* element holds the maximum time the import authority is waiting for the acknowledgment until an error is actuated. According to our example, this time frame is 14 hours. Upon receipt of the acknowledgment within the agreed time frame, no additional action is required in this step of the local choreography and we move on to the next message exchange. If it is not received, an exception handling is required. This exception handling triggers the

12 Process choreographies and document definitions

sending of a time-out exception and requires the transaction to re-start. The code for the exception handling is not presented in Listing 12.4.

Listing 12.4
The import authority's local BPEL choreography

```
379 <process>
380   <partnerLinks>
381     <partnerLink name='ImA-ExA' partnerLinkType='ImA-ExA-PLT'
382       myRole='ImA' partnerRole='ExA'/>
383   </partnerLinks>
384
385   <variables>
386     <variable name='WasteMovementForm' .../>
387     <variable name='AckReceipt' .../>
388     ...
389   </variables>
390
391   <sequence>
392     <receive partnerLink='ImA-ExA' portType='ImA-PT'
393       operation='receiveWasteMovementForm'
394       variable='WasteMovementForm' />
395     <invoke partnerLink='ImA-ExA' portType='ExA-PT'
396       operation='receiveAckReceipt' variable='AckReceipt'/>
397     <invoke partnerLink='ImA-ExA' portType='ExA-PT'
398       operation='receiveAckProcessing' variable='AckProcessing'/>
399     <if>
400       <condition>isWasteMovementAccepted()</condition>
401       <invoke partnerLink='ImA-ExA' portType='ExA-PT'
402         operation='receiveWasteMovementAcceptedForm'
403         inputVariable='WasteMovementAcceptedForm' />
404       <else>
405         <invoke partnerLink='ImA-ExA' portType='ExA-PT'
406           operation='receiveWasteMovementRejectedForm'
407           inputVariable='WasteMovementRejectedForm' />
408       </else>
409     </if>
410     <pick>
411       <onMessage partnerLink='ImA-ExA' portType='ImA-PT'
412         operation='receiveAckReceipt'
413         variable='ReceivedAckReceipt'>
414         <empty />
415       </onMessage>
416       <onAlarm>
417         <for>PT14H</for>
418         <!-- throw exception -->
419       </onAlarm>
420     </pick>
421     <pick>
422       <onMessage partnerLink='ImA-ExA' portType='ImA-PT'
423         operation='receiveAckProcessing'
424         variable='ReceivedAckProcessing'>
425         <empty />
426       </onMessage>
427       <onAlarm>
428         <for>PT24H</for>
429         <!-- throw exception -->
430       </onAlarm>
431     </pick>
432   </sequence>
433 </process>
```

We already know that the **import authority** waits for an **acknowledgment of processing** after picking up the **acknowledgment of receipt** message. The receipt of both types of acknowledgments is handled in a similar way. Thus, we use an analogue *pick* construct for modeling the receipt of the **acknowledgment of processing** (line 421). In this case the agreed time frame corresponds to 24 hours (see *time to acknowledge processing* in Figure 12.9). After the receipt of the **acknowledgment of processing**, the choreography of our example *business transaction* ends successfully.

We outlined that a complex UMM business collaboration is composed of a flow of several business transactions.

It follows that the BPEL representation of a UMM business collaboration corresponds to a combination of the BPEL mappings of the composed business transactions. This example briefly introduced the potential of a UMM model together with a UPCC model to derive artifacts for a service oriented architecture. For further readings we would like to direct to [53] and [74] where we proposed a mapping of UMM to ebXML BPSS and to [52] and [56] where we outlined mappings to BPEL. Furthermore, a mapping of UMM to Windows Workflow Foundation has been proposed in [190].

12.3 Final assessment

Before two business partners may engage in an automated B2B interaction, an agreement on the inter-organizational business process (i.e., global process choreography) and on the exchanged business document information is needed. In this Chapter we have introduced UN/CEFACT's Modeling Methodology (UMM) as a means of capturing requirements of a global process choreography. We have demonstrated the different views and artifacts of UMM, using the accompanying example from the waste management domain. One of the shortcomings of the UMM specification is its limited expressiveness in regard to the exchanged business information. UMM does not mandate a specific technology for the description of business information, but allows in principle any representation method of choice. In this Chapter we have provided a complementary solution for the definition of business documents in the business information view of UMM, based on the UML Profile for Core Components (UPCC).

Combining process choreography and business information models

We have shown how artifacts from the UPCC may be used to model the information, being exchanged in UMM business transactions. Thereby, UPCC artifacts seamlessly integrate in the business information view of UMM. Finally, we have shown how the final model capturing both, the business process and business document requirements, may be used to derive deployment artifacts for service oriented architectures.

Deriving deployment artifacts from conceptual models

Given our comprehensive solution, a model-driven approach for artifact generation for a service-oriented architecture is provided. We fulfill the requirements of the Open-edi

Meeting Open-edi requirements

reference model [78] and capture requirements on an implementation neutral level. Consequently, we use the technology independent model to derive deployment artifacts such as XML Schema, WSDL, and WS-BPEL.

Future directions   In this Chapter we have exemplarily used UML and its two profiles UMM and UPCC for the definition of inter-organizational process requirements. Future work will concentrate on how to use other technologies such as Domain-Specific Languages (DSL) to capture inter-organizational process and business document requirements. Consequently, it must be examined how the DSL-based conceptual models may be employed in order to derive deployment artifacts.

In regard to UMM itself, the integration of value-based requirements engineering into the business requirements view is currently investigated. In value-based requirements engineering the focus is laid on business models – being well distinguished from business process models – to survey the economic justification for e-business systems. Prominent approaches for analyzing business models are the e3-Value methodology [44], the Resource-Event-Agent (REA) theory [41], or the business model ontology (BMO) [132].

13 Related Work

In this Chapter we discuss related work, according to the different contribution areas of this thesis.

13.1 Business Document Standard Overview

A general introduction into the domain of document engineering is given by [43]. Glushko and McGrath provide a thorough overview about current approaches for business document modeling, document model interoperability, and integration into business processes.

Related work of Chapter 3

Several surveys have already been conducted, focusing on business document models and frameworks. Probably one of the first surveys on electronic data interchange has been conducted by Ramamurthy et al. [143] in 1995. The study examines the role of key innovation and organizational factors in influencing the extend, to which EDI is diffused within organizations. The study provides valuable insights into EDI specific aspects, but naturally does not consider markup-based standards since it was conducted in the pre-XML era.

Survey on EDI impacts

A survey on business-to-business e-commerce has been conducted by Shim et al. [153] in 2000. The authors identify the heterogeneity of different technical standards as the main obstacle towards seamless B2B integration. Nevertheless, the authors do not provide a technical solution, but provide a comparison of different standards, aiding decision makers in choosing the right standard for their business domain.

Nurmilaakso et al. [117] compare several XML-based e-business frameworks and analyze them, according to seven distinct variables. Three of the frameworks are assessed regarding their properties and features and four in regard to standardization. The outcome has been measured in the

E-business framework comparison

form of commonalities, differences, and regularities. Built upon this work, the PhD thesis of Kotinurmi [86] identifies the relationship between e-Business Frameworks and B2B integration. The author argues that the simple availability of XML or EDI standards is not sufficient for successful B2B integration, but an e-Business Framework is needed. RosettaNet [146] is used as an accompanying example.

In [82] Kim et al. study four major B2B e-service platforms, i.e., RosettaNet, eCo, BizTalk and E-Speak, and give a brief overview of these platforms. They identify eight relevant criteria and evaluate each of the four environments. A very similar survey has been conducted by Dogac and Cingil [25] who concentrate on five XML-based B2B frameworks and analyze them by seven characteristics.

In our survey, provided in Chapter 3 of this thesis, we overcome limitations of previous approaches which focused only on a specific set of business document standards. In our approach we identify clusters of related business document standards instead of evaluating single standard definitions. Thus, an business document modeler is given an overview of potential standard categories, helping to chose the right business document standard family, based on criteria such as acceptance, business messaging compatibility, etc. Furthermore, our research has shown that several of the available business document standard surveys are outdated and do not provide up-to-date information.

13.2 Core component concepts

Related work of Chapter 4 Between the core component concepts, introduced in Chapter 4, and the ISO/IEC 11179 Metadata registry [80] model exists a strong interdependency. Similar to core components, the ISO initiative aims at the semantically unambiguous definition of data. Thereby, the ISO 11179 standard consists of six different parts: framework, classification, registry meta-model and basic attributes, formulation of data definition, naming and identification principles, and registration. Figure 13.1 gives an overview of the basic structure of an ISO 11179 data element, which may be compared to a core component or a business information entity.

The ISO standard distinguishes between an *object class*, a *property* of an object class, and the *representation* of the

13.2 Core component concepts

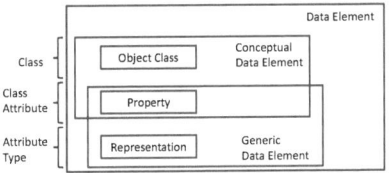

Figure 13.1
ISO 11179 data element – core concepts

property term. The UML class diagram equivalents of the different concepts are shown on the left hand side of Figure 13.1. The property and the representation term together form the concept of a *generic data element*. This generic data element is equivalent to the concept of a *basic core component property (BCC property)* and the concept of a *basic business information entity property (BBIE property)* in the core component standard. In addition to the ISO model, the core component standard introduces the concepts of *association core component properties (ASCC property)* and *association business information entity properties (ABIE property)*.

In the ISO 11179 standard an object class and a property term together constitute a *conceptual data element*. These conceptual data elements do not have a specific value domain and are reusable by applying different representations. Thus, conceptually similar, but distinct data elements are created. This concept is currently not directly supported by the core component standard. However, it is up to an implementer to preserve the structure of a conceptual data element, when implementing the core component technical specification.

As shown on the right hand side of Figure 13.1, the ISO 11179 `object class`, `property term` and `representation term` together form a `data element`. In UN/CEFACT core component terms, these data elements are equivalent to *basic core components (BCC), association core components (ASCC), basic business information entities (BBIE),* and *association business information entities (ASBIE)*.

13.3 Conceptual business document modeling with UML

Related work of Chapter 5

The conceptual modeling of data has existed for a while, and forms an integral part of data engineering. One of the most important methodologies for data modeling is the entity relationship model [18], used to design a relational database model. The entity relationship model (ER) provides its own modeling methodology, consisting of entities, attributes belonging to entities, and relationships between the different entities. A database modeler uses the entity relationship model to derive the appropriate data definition language (DDL) artifacts for creating the database model. The main goal of a database is to reliably store information and to enable information retrieval from it. If a hierarchical business document is stored in a database, it is first broken up into the relational model and then stored in the appropriate database tables. Retrieving the document means querying the database for the relevant information parts, and reassembling the business document. The relational database model has therefore less context than the business document model, because its main goal is to store and retrieve pure information, while avoiding inconsistencies and redundancy.

Business document modeling compared to relational data modeling

Both, the business document model and the relational database model [18] serve their own purpose. On the one hand, the relational model focuses on a multitude of business documents and not on a single instance, since its goal is the consistent storage of normalized data in the large scale. On the other hand, a business document is assembled using a set of reusable components, forming a hierarchical model. The avoidance of data redundancy is an integral part of the relational model. However, in some cases business document models must deliberately allow data redundancy, due to the requirements of a given business case. As an example an `invoice bundle` is taken, grouping `invoices` of the same enterprise. The left hand side of Figure 13.2 shows an `invoice bundle`, containing multiple instances of `invoices` numbered 1, 2 and 3. Each instance of the `invoice` contains the same `tax number` (3), although all `invoices` are of the same enterprise and hence the `tax number` is the same for each `invoice`. Since the `invoice` itself has to be a self contained document, the `tax number`

13.3 Conceptual business document modeling with UML

cannot be stored in the embracing `invoice bundle`, but must be part of the `invoice`.

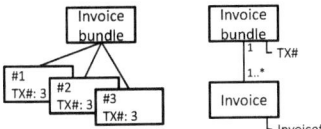

Figure 13.2
Business document model vs. relational model

In comparison, the right hand side of Figure 13.2 shows the relational model for the same scenario. An `invoice bundle` groups multiple `invoices` of the same enterprise. Since the data is stored in a normalized and redundancy free manner, the `tax number` is part of the `invoice bundle` and not of the `invoice`. It follows that the relational model is not the best method for business document modeling.

With the inception of the eXtensible Markup Language (XML) [184], a new and powerful mechanism for the definition of business documents was provided. However, the efficient representation of XML documents on a conceptual and graphical level is still a major challenge. A survey of different conceptual modeling approaches for XML is given by Nečaský [115]. Related work in the field of conceptual XML Schema modeling concentrates on two main fields. On the one hand, research is conducted in the area of forward engineering, i.e., deriving XML Schema artifacts from conceptual models such as UML. On the other hand, a lot of effort is invested in the reverse engineering approach, i.e., generating conceptual models such as UML class diagrams from XML Schema artifacts.

An overview of research on the reverse engineering of XML schemes to conceptual models such as UML class diagrams is given by Yu and Steele [189]. The authors examine reverse engineering approaches and assess their applicability to UML diagrams. Although several techniques for a forward engineering from conceptual models to XML representations exist today, only a few solutions are available for transformations in the opposite direction. The generation of UML models out of XML Schema data proves to be difficult, since not all of the features of an XML Schema may be represented in a UML diagram by default. UML does for instance not support the concept of inheritance by restriction,

Reverse engineering of XML Schema documents

as XML Schema does. Another open issue is the ordering of attributes, which is important in an XML Schema, but not supported by UML class diagrams by default. A thorough solution for a reverse engineering approach is presented by Salim et al. [149]. Using a set of transformation rules for the corresponding XML Schema elements, the authors present appropriate representation solutions in UML. However, the authors do not address the representation of <xs:restriction>, which cannot be depicted in UML.

Forward engineering of XML Schema documents

In contrast to the reverse engineering of conceptual UML models from XML Schema, several approaches exist for the forward engineering approach. Combi et al. [20] introduce the UXS model (UML & XML Schema), based on UML. UXS is a methodology for designing XML documents, using a set of graphical elements, corresponding to the appropriate XML Schema components. Furthermore, a translation mechanism is introduced, allowing the generation of XML Schema artifacts according to the three well known patterns *Russian Doll*, *Salami Slice*, and *Venetian Blind* [107].

Semantic data modeling aspects

Although several approaches for the conceptual modeling of XML Schema exist, only a few consider semantic data modeling aspects. A mutation analysis model, used to verify the general semantic correctness of an XML Schema, is introduced by Li and Miller [92]. Using their approach, the authors compare different XML Schema validators in regard to their effectiveness in finding semantic errors within XML Schemas. A formalization for a data modeling approach is introduced by Mani et al. [108], also taking the semantic dependencies between the different elements within an XML Schema into account. The introduced methodology, called *XGrammar*, allows for a precise definition of necessary features for data modeling such as n-ary relationships, generalizations, etc. The application of the Active XML Schema approach for the semantic enrichment of XML Schema documents is discussed by Bernauer et al. [13]. The authors examine the trade-off between the semantic enrichment of an XML Schema using the Active XML Schema approach and the loss of XML Schema interoperability caused by such an enrichment.

Other data modeling approaches

In regard to domain-specific business standards, several initiatives have been started in recent years. RosettaNet Implementation Framework [146] is an initiative of the electronic components and telecommunications industry. In the insurance domain the ACORD [2] standard plays a significant role, and CIDX [19] is pursing document standardization for the chemical industry. Other initiatives include SWIFT [160] from the finance industry, HL7 [49] from the health care industry, Papinet [73] from the forest and paper industry, and PIDX [5] from the oil and gas industry. However, none of these initiatives provide a formalized conceptual representation as introduced with the UML Profile for Core Components (UPCC) [172] or the Domain-Specific Language for Core Components [97].

As outlined, there exists several approaches for the conceptual modeling of XML and the forward and reverse engineering thereof. Although applicable to the general purpose of XML modeling, the different approaches do not consider the business semantics and business requirements, necessary for business document modeling. Even if dedicated business document standards with clear semantics and business requirements are provided, they do not offer a conceptual representation for the business document format. The Core Component Technical Specification (CCTS), introduced in this thesis, helps to overcome these limitations by providing a sound technical foundation and a conceptual representation format based on the Unified Modeling Language and Domain-Specific Languages.

13.4 Domain-Specific Language Approaches

Domain-Specific Languages (DSL) have been used for one of our three exemplary implementations of the Core Components Technical Specification [170]. The concept of domain-specific development is not new, but has already been introduced in 1976 by Parnas [134] through the concept of program families. The approach included the definition of a program generator, which is able to produce program family members. Thus, the general idea of Parnas is comparable to Software Factories as used today. In 1985, Bentley [11] discussed the possibility of viewing the work of programmers as the constant invention of *little languages*. His article concluded that essentially these little languages are designed to solve problems of a particular kind. Thus, Bentley had an

Related work of Chapter 6

Early views related to the concept of a DSL

early idea of Domain-Specific Languages, long before they were actually invented.

Gamma, Helm, Johnson, and Vlissides, who are also known as the *gang of four*, discussed the use of the *interpreter* pattern in their well known book on design patterns [40]. According to the authors, the intent of the interpreter pattern is:

> "Given a language, define a representation of its grammar along with an interpreter that uses the representation to interpret sentences in the language".

Essentially, the grammar representation may be defined by a DSL definition and the interpreter, using the representation is defined by the DSL generated model designer.

Model-driven development   The concept of domain-specific development is also closely related to model-driven development (MDD). In a MDD approach, a model is first built using a graphical language such as the Unified Modeling Language (UML) [129]. The models, together with a code generator, are used to transform the conceptual static as well as dynamic system representation into executable code artifacts. One of the most important initiatives in this field is the Model Driven Architecture (MDA) initiative [126], founded by the Object Management Group (OMG). Nevertheless, a UML-based approach has several shortcomings compared to a DSL-based approach, as we outlined in Chapter 6 of this thesis.

Model driven approaches, based on Domain-Specific Languages, have gained considerable popularity in recent years. Several approaches aim at streamlining the DSL definitions to provide modelers with an easy to use DSL. Mikkonen et al. [139] present a lightweight model-driven approach using Domain-Specific Languages, where a lightweight DSL is used to bootstrap a more heavyweight DSL. Another incremental approach towards defining a DSL is presented by Bierhoff et al. [15].

DSL approaches for service oriented architectures   In particular in a service oriented context, model driven approaches may help to overcome changing requirements. A study on different DSL-based approaches for service oriented architectures has been conducted by Oberortner et al. [125]. The authors provide a thorough overview of different DSL approaches and evaluate the identified DSLs using prototyping experiments. Another approach to model services, based on a Domain-Specific Language, is presented by Achilleos et al. [1]. The authors realize service creation through the phases of Domain-Specific Language definition, model definition and validation, model-to-model transformation, and model-to-code generation. However, their proposed solution does not consider the definition of the exchanged data in a service oriented environment.

We conclude that most of the work currently being pursued in the area of Domain-Specific Languages does not consider business document definitions. In this thesis we successfully addressed this gap by providing a Domain-Specific Language for the definition of business documents, based on the Core Components Technical Specification.

13.5 Semantic approaches

An early approach to abstract from the pure syntactical definition of EDI messages and implement an ontology on top of EDI, has been presented by Foxvog et al. [38] using ANSI X12 [6] as an example. In their proposed solution the authors first aim to define an ontology for the EDI syntax, i.e., specify the meaning of data elements, segments, etc. In a next step, the authors address the issue of defining an ontology for EDI itself, i.e., define the meaning of EDI messages. In regard to our proposed approach of defining a common conceptual business document model based on OWL, the ontology for EDI messages may be used as the basis for mappings to the common business document model.

Related work of Chapter 7

A document ontology, based on UN/CEFACT's Modeling Methodology (UMM) [174] and its business information view, has been presented by Hofreiter [51]. In her approach, Hofreiter proposes to bind business documents to a business document ontology based on RDFS [182]. This middle layer would later serve as the intermediate representation format for mappings to other document specification formats. Since the used ontology is based on RDFS, the author encounters several limitations for which they provide workarounds. E.g., it is not possible to state that each core data type has exactly one content component and may have one to many supplementary components using only an RDFS representation.

Selected ontologies for document standards

13 Related Work

Another approach for dynamic data mediation has been presented by Bouras et al. [17], called Enterprise Interoperability Ontology. The authors propose a mediation approach, based on ontologies for heterogeneous data representation formats of enterprise applications. Eventually, the enterprise interoperability ontology allows for a mediation of different formats between different business partners. An architecture, adopting a mediator-wrapper approach based on OWL, is also proposed by Suwanmanee et al. [159].

During the project Harmonise, funded by the European Union, an ontology-based mediation was developed by Fodor and Werthner [36]. The goal of the mediation approach was to allow tourism organizations with different data standards to exchange information seamlessly, without having to change their proprietary data schemas. Thus, Fodor and Werthner pursue a similar approach to the one presented in this thesis, although they do not take core components into account.

Due to the multitude of different ontologies which are currently available, the aforementioned ontologies are just the tip of the ontology iceberg. However, we conclude that most of the proposed ontologies are isolated solutions without an alignment to a globally defined common ontology. In our approach we address this limitation by (i) using a well accepted common ontology, based on the Core Component Technical Specification (CCTS) and (ii) using pre-defined and generic building blocks for assembling business documents, based on the Core Component Library (CCL).

Other related standardization approaches

Apart from business document centric standardization efforts, other approaches have sought a harmonization of business related data as well. Product data catalog ontologies have gained considerable attention in the semantic community in the last few years. In short, the goal of product data ontologies is the reuse of product data across enterprise boundaries. Using a unified view on commerce related data on the web allows for complex semantic search queries, which go beyond traditional approaches. A quantitative analysis of different product categorization standards has been conducted by Hepp et al. [50]. In their analysis the authors examine different categorization standards namely, eCl@ss, United Nations Standard Product and Services Code (UN/SPSC), Electronic Open Technical Directory (eOTD), and the RosettaNet Technical Directory.

Another promising approach towards the definition of a common product ontology is the Good Relations Ontology [110]. The ontology aims at the definition of a universal and free Web vocabulary for product related data. The vision is to provide a single schema for a consolidated view on electronic commerce data. Currently, a successful implementation of the Good Relations Ontology is provided for Yahoo! SearchMonkey.

GoodRelations Ontology

13.6 From conceptual models to XML Schema artifacts

A related approach to UN/CEFACT's Core Components is pursued by the Universal Business Language (UBL) [121]. The UN/CEFACT and UBL standardization committees based their standardization work on the core component specification part of the ebXML framework [124]. Due to this common basis, UBL and the core component technology share many characteristics, but are not entirely the same. UBL focuses exclusively on the development of business information entities and their realization in XML. Thus, the UBL meta-model only defines business information entity specific concepts. UBL also releases UBL Naming and Design Rules, unambiguously defining guidelines for the representation of UBL concepts using XML Schema artifacts. However, due to the meta-model differences of UBL and core components, the two Naming and Design Rules are not the same and produce XML Schema artifacts which are related to each other, but are still incompatible. A merger of the UBL initiative with the core components initiative of UN/CEFACT has been agreed upon during the UN/CEFACT forum meeting 2007 in Stockholm, with the goal to eliminate redundancies in standardization and leverage collaboration synergies.

Related work of Chapter 8

13.7 B2B registry approaches

The requirement of defining a registry specification for storage and retrieval of artifacts has been addressed by several

Related work of Chapter 9

research initiatives. Thereby, two main registry initiatives have evolved: UDDI (Universal Description, Discovery, and Integration) [118] and ebXML registry (Electronic Business XML registry) [119]. Based on the two specifications, several approaches for the definition of a B2B capable registry have been developed.

ebXML-based approaches   Most of the ebXML-based approaches use the ebXML registry information model (ebRIM) and extend it with domain-specific amendments to meet user-defined requirements. A multi-layer registry approach has been introduced by Huemer et al. [68], covering the business, business process, and deployment artifact perspective of an electronic business interaction between business partners in a service oriented context. For the business process layer artifacts, the authors use a dedicated business collaboration registry model, introduced by Hofreiter [58]. However, the registry model does not consider the business document information, being exchanged in an electronic business interaction.

Semantic extensions to ebXML   In the field of registry research, several other initiatives have built their solutions on top of the ebRIM. One of the first attempts to map ebXML classification hierarchies and semantic technologies has been presented by Dogac et al. [26]. A similar ontology based registry classification model is presented by Liu et al. [106]. Both authors abstract from the original ebXML classification approach and present a Web Ontology Language (OWL) based registry classification model. Another approach towards the integration of semantic technologies and the ebRIM is provided by Roh et al. [144]. The authors show how to embed OWL semantics in an ebXML registry by providing a new registry information model, called semantic information model (SIM). Zeng et al. [196] introduce a reference ontology for registries, aiming at ontology-based semantic interoperability between different registry models. Thus, most of the related semantic registry publications aim at interoperability of registry models by providing appropriate semantic representation mechanisms. However, none of the semantically enriched registries specifically reflects the storage and retrieval of information related artifacts for the definition of service interfaces.

UDDI-based approaches   In the field of Universal Description, Discovery, and Integration (UDDI) registries, an extension for user-defined attributes has been proposed by [4]. Shaikh et al. introduce the UDDIe standard, extending the currently three page (white, yellow, green) UDDI standard by a fourth page, called *blue page*. Using the blue page, user-defined attributes such as lease timestamps, indicating how long a service definition is valid, may be attached without altering backward compatibility to the original UDDI standard definition. However, we conclude that the UDDI initiative in general failed to provide a central registry on a global level due to several reasons such as fake entries in the registry and a too strong focus on Web Service definitions.

Currently, the Information Content Management Group (ICG) of UN/CEFACT develops a dedicated UN/CEFACT Core Component registry implementation specification [168], which is largely based on the ebRIM specification. However, for the time being no implementation of this registry exists yet.

Dedicated core component registries

13.8 Bottom-up standard extensions

The development of business document standards has been widely influenced by the introduction of XML [91], [162]. A literature review shows that in particular XML Schema has been subject to much controversy in regard to its expressiveness and complexity [109]. Nevertheless, it has become the de facto standard for defining data exchange formats in particular in the context of Web Services [181]. Pasley [135] examines the potential risks, if wildcard extension mechanisms such as `xs:any` are used in XML Schema definitions. The author provides a set of best practices to XML Schema design, helping to cope with changing schema requirements and schema extensions. However, most of the recommendations aim at changing the core schema and thus they are not applicable to the bottom-up extension scenario presented in this thesis, where the core schema must remain unchanged.

Related work of Chapter 10

Another important field, in particular in regard to business document standardization, is the research area of XML evolution [157], [46], [45]. The developed methods aim at automatically adapting XML instance documents, in case the associated XML Schema is extended or restricted by additional elements. Although several academic approaches for XML evolution exist, their integration level in B2B tools remains rather low. Generally, if schemas evolve and several versions of a schema are developed, a set of problems, e.g., revalidation issues occur [142], [10], [9].

Our presented approach aims at circumventing error-prone and time-consuming re-validation tasks of multiple schema versions by providing a single, but flexible business document solution. In our solution, interoperability on the core standard level is provided at any time. Interoperability at the level of domain-specific amendments is provided, if both partners support the domain-specific extension.

13.9 Mapping business document model to core components

Related work of Chapter 11

Mapping and interoperability issues are not new and a considerable amount of work has already been done in this field. Concerning our work, presented in this thesis, we identify three different areas of related work, i.e, schema mapping and ontology alignment, metadata standards and interoperability frameworks.

Schema mappings and ontology alignment

Schema mapping has its roots in database integration and the need to map heterogeneous data. A formal foundation for relational schema mapping is for example presented in [84], [34], and [14]. A more general perspective of schema mappings is captured by Blouin et al. [16], who define schema mappings upon some sort of formalism, which may be a relational schema or a UML model, and present a practical mapping language fostering the generation of transformation models. Another practical approach has been implemented by Popa et al. [140], [47] within their tool Clio, which is able to map relational schemas and XML Schema to generate transformations based on several technologies for concrete data. When dealing with ontologies, mappings are often not the basis for transformations and created manually, but computed automatically based on similarities – see [29]. Here, the mapping task results more or less in a matching task. All this work is closely related to ours in the sense that semantic equivalent elements are to be precisely mapped. However, we focus on preserving the structure of the mapped schemas to support round-trip engineering. Because of the very different structures of the incorporated schemas, we apply heuristics upon the mappings, to transform instances of the schemas.

13.10 Capturing inter-organizational process requirements

In regard to metadata standards, there exist several technologies and frameworks for the support of metadata and metadata registries [48]. Most related to the UN/CEFACT's CCTS is the ISO 11179 [80] standard for metadata registries, which we have already outlined before. Another popular metadata framework in Model Driven Development to support modeling and registry tasks, is the Eclipse Modeling Framework with its meta-modeling language Ecore [156]. The framework is closely related to the Meta Object Facility (MOF) [128], another metadata standard, managed by the OMG.

Metadata standards

In the ontology domain, there also exist approaches to manage metadata. See for example the W3C recommendation SAWSDL [185] or the Dublin Core Metadata Initiative [75]. However, these technologies do not provide a standardized library of reusable, on a conceptual level defined, elements.

Interoperability issues arise, because of the use of different technologies and data models. Therefore, lots of research to solve these issues has been undertaken. Saekow et al. [148] present an interoperability framework, which shall close the gap between conceptual and practical interoperability approaches. In [23] the authors describe how the ISO 11179 standard may be interpreted and extended to overcome certain restrictions of this standard, and maintain multiple views on the same data elements.

Interoperability Frameworks

13.10 Capturing inter-organizational process requirements

Over the last couple of years, several methodologies for modeling inter-organizational business processes have been developed. Surveys comparing different types of business process modeling languages are provided in [103], [85], and [154]. Some of these approaches are based on special notations, i.e., Architecture of Integrated Information Systems (ARIS) [151], Integrated DEFinition for Process Description Method (IDEF3) [111], Business Process Modeling Notation (BPMN) [127], and Petri-Nets [178]. Others customize the Unified Modeling Language (UML) [129] for business process modeling needs [105]. Most of these UML approaches are based on activity diagrams [147] and they either provide

Related work of Chapter 12

just guidelines on using activity diagrams for this special purpose or they specify a UML profile.

Traditionally process modeling focused on internal processes

Traditionally, business process modeling focuses on modeling business processes internal to an organization, fulfilling customer needs [137]. More recent approaches also take inter-organizational business processes into account [83] [87]. Due to the growing importance of XML and Web Services, several XML-based notations, describing the orchestration and choreography of executable business processes, have been developed. For a detailed discussion on choreography and orchestration of Web Services see [136]. The most popular languages in this area are the Business Process Execution Language for Web Services (WS-BPEL) [122] [81] and the Business Process Specification Schema (BPSS) [120]. Solutions for a straight-forward transformation of UMM business transaction models already exists for WS-BPEL [56] [52] [53], BPSS [74], and Windows Workflow Foundation [190].

Inter-organizational processes are complexer than their internal counterparts

The complexity of designing collaborative business processes is higher than designing business processes internal to a company. The reasons are manifold – for example the resulting specification needs to be accepted and understood among participating business partners. Furthermore, a consistent and platform-independent implementation of derived B2B software artifacts is required [145]. Code transformations are necessary to ensure a straight-forward approach from business process models to executable software artifacts. Model-driven concepts, such as Model Driven Architecture (MDA) [126], provide a persistent, interoperable, and semi-automated transformation of business process models. However, as stated by Folmer et al. [37], current state-of-the-art business process modeling methodologies do not or not fully provide such a integrated development process. According to the comparison, UN/CEFACT's Modeling Methodology (UMM) [174] is currently the only approach which deals with all required modeling and domain aspects to design collaborative business processes. Furthermore, Folmer et al. concludes that UMM may be easily integrated into a model-driven design process as stated in [37].

Petri-Nets

A more formal and mathematical approach to business process modeling is provided by Petri-Nets [113]. Petri-Nets

13.10 Capturing inter-organizational process requirements

are used to model both, business processes [178] as well as workflow systems [176]. Several approaches are using Petri-Nets for the modeling of inter-organizational processes. Lee [88] has contributed an implementation of the choreography aspects of ISO's Open-edi reference model [78]. Several other approaches by different authors use Petri-Nets for inter-organizational modeling [90] [104] [177]. One major problem a modeler using Petri Nets is facing, is the increasing complexity of a net if complex business processes are modeled. Hence, its applicability in the field of inter-organizational business processes is rather limited, since the resulting net becomes illegible for non-technicians.

A more recent approach is the Business Process Modeling Notation (BPMN) [127], which is developed by the Object Management Group. One major goal of the BPMN initiative is to create a single graphical modeling notation understandable by as many stakeholders as possible – from the business analyst to the application developer. Thereby, BPMN incorporates several concepts from existing modeling notations such as UML activity diagram [129], RosettaNet [146], ebXML BPSS [120], and IDEF [111].

Business Process Modeling Notation (BPMN)

All of the aforementioned approaches do not, or only to a limited extend, consider the exchanged business information. In this thesis we address this limitation by providing a combination of UN/CEFACT's Modeling Methodology (UMM) and the UML Profile for Core Components (UPCC).

14 Conclusion and open research issues

In this thesis we addressed shortcomings in the domain of B2B interactions between enterprises. Conventional approaches as known from the field of electronic data interchange (EDI) are not sufficient to cope with the requirements of today's inter-organizational business processes. Business-to-business interactions require an integrated view on inter-organizational business processes capturing both, the information and the process perspective. With this thesis we have addressed several gaps in current research which we summarize in the following.

Since the inception of EDIFACT [163], a multitude of different business document standards have been developed. Today, a business document expert may choose from hundreds of different document definitions, each dedicated to a certain application area or industry domain. Although several surveys on business document standards have been provided over the years, most of them focus on a certain subset of available standards. Due to the fast development of business document standards, caused by the introduction of XML, several of the surveys are simply outdated and do not provide actual information. In this thesis we abstracted from specific business document standards and provided a survey, based on business document clusters. Each cluster represents certain business document standards, sharing the same characteristics. Based on our survey results, a business document expert may assess a certain standard in regard to its business messaging compatibility, technology features, potential user groups, as well as acceptance on an industry, national, and international level.

Contemporary overview of business document standards

One of the most promising efforts in the field of business document standardization in recent years is UN/CE-FACT's Core Component Technical Specification (CCTS) [163]. Using the core component technology, a business doc-

Insight into UN/CEFACT's Core Components

14 Conclusion and open research issues

ument modeler may assemble a business document, based on reusable buildings blocks to which we refer as core components. Core components are standardized by UN/CEFACT and represent the common semantic foundation of all business documents which have been constructed based on core components. In this thesis we abstracted from the rather complicated Core Component Technical Specification standard and provided a concise and clear introduction into the basic concepts of the CCTS.

Overcoming implementation neutrality of core components

One of the strengths of core components is the implementation neutral manner in which they are defined. Thus, it is up to an implementer to provide an appropriate representation format for core components, to allow for an integration of the concepts into tools. Unfortunately, such a formalized representation format is still missing. In this thesis we provided three reference representation formats for core components: (i) a UML Profile for Core Components (UPCC) [95] (ii) a Domain-Specific Language (DSL) for Core Components [97] and (iii) a Web Ontology Language representation for Core Components [96].

UML Profile for Core Components is now a UN/CEFACT standard

The UML Profile for Core Components (UPCC) transfers implementation neutral core component concepts to the Unified Modeling Language (UML). Using a UML profile mechanism, the generic UML meta model is tailored to the specific needs of core component modeling. Thus, core components may be assembled on a conceptual level and UML-based core component models may easily be communicated between different stakeholders. This is of particular importance for inter-organizational processes, where usually several stakeholders are involved. Consequently, the conceptual core component model provides the basis for further processing of core components such as the derivation of deployment artifacts for IT systems. The resulting UML Profile for Core Components (UPCC) has been submitted to UN/CEFACT for standardization.

Domain-Specific Language for Core Components

The second reference implementation for core components has been realized using a Domain-Specific Language (DSL). In contrast to a UML Profile, which tailors the generic UML meta-model to the specific needs of core component modeling, a Domain-Specific Language defines a dedicated meta-model for core components. Thus, several shortcomings of a UML Profile may be circumvented and a business document modeler is provided with a specialized core component modeling environment. The DSL representation for core components provides similar benefits like the UML-based core component representation. A business document modeler is able to assemble a core component model on a conceptual level. Consequently, the core component model may be used to derive XML deployment artifacts for the configuration of IT systems.

The third reference implementation we provided in this thesis is a Web Ontology Language (OWL) for Core Components. Thereby, the meta-model concepts as defined in the Core Component Technical Specification (CCTS) are transferred to OWL. We refer to this OWL representation as the global reference ontology. Using the ontology, standardized core components of UN/CEFACT may be depicted using OWL – we refer to this ontological representation as the common business document model. OWL representations of other business document standards may then be mapped to the common business document model, which serves as the intermediate format for mappings. The main advantage of the OWL mapping, in contrast to regular, e.g., XML-based mappings, is the use of Semantic Web Technologies such as reasoners and ontology mapping concepts, facilitating the mapping process.

Web Ontology Language for Core Components

With the UML Profile for Core Components (UPCC) and the Domain-Specific Language for Core Components a business document modeler is able to define core components on a conceptual level. However, conceptual models may not be used for the configuration of IT interfaces, e.g., in a service oriented architecture. Thus, appropriate mechanisms for the derivation of deployment artifacts from conceptual core component models must be provided. In this thesis we showed how conceptual core component models, based on UML may be used to derive XML Schema deployment artifacts.

Configuring IT systems using core components

The main principle behind the core component approach is the reuse of existing building blocks for business documents. Thus, the general availability of core components is an important prerequisite for core component compliant modeling. A library of reusable core components is provided by UN/CEFACT with the Core Component Library (CCL) [173]. Currently, a new core component library, based on a

A registry for core components

14 Conclusion and open research issues

regular spread sheet, is released twice a year. Unfortunately, the spread sheet based representation of core components is a major obstacle towards the seamless integration of core components into conceptual modeling tools. To successfully integrate core components, e.g., in UML or DSL-based modeling environments, a single access point for core components must be established using a registry. The core component registry must allow for the easy search and retrieval of core component information. Furthermore, standardization organizations such as UN/CEFACT may use the registry to maintain existing core component information or to add new core components to the library. Unfortunately, such a registry does not exist. In this thesis we introduced a registry information model for core components. The information model unambiguously defines the relationships between the different artifacts and their metadata in the registry. A core component registry may be implemented based on the registry information model.

Adding flexibility to bottom-up standard The second major business document standardization paradigm, next to top-down definitions such as the core component approach, are bottom-up standard definitions. Instead of finding a superset of all requirements of the involved stakeholders, as it is the case with top-down standards, a bottom-up standard aims at finding a subset of the most important requirements. In contrast to top-down standards, a bottom-up standard does not require an agreement on a subset of the standard prior to an automated business document exchange, as it is usually the case with top-down standards. Thus, bottom-up standards are easy to implement into commercial-of-the-shelf-software (COTS), providing interfaces for the import and export of standardized business documents. Nevertheless, in certain cases extensions of a bottom-up standard are still required to allow for partner-specific or domain-specific amendments of the standard. Several of the business document standards available on the market provide extensions points. However, these extension points leave it up to the business document modeler what to include in the extension and, thus, no control of the different extensions is possible. In this thesis we provided an evaluation of different XML Schema extension mechanisms and assessed their applicability for the definition of bottom-up standard extensions in regard to (i) core schema integrity

(ii) core schema compatibility (iii) extension control and (iv) guarantee of validity.

Core component models are typically used in a forward engineering manner, where a new core component model is created from scratch and XML Schema artifacts are derived from it with a model-driven technique. However, in certain cases existing business document formats are mapped to a core component model, serving as the intermediate format for the mapping to another standard format. Mapping bottom-up standard definitions to an existing top-down core component model requires well defined mapping rules. Until now, such mapping rules have not been available. In this thesis we examined the mapping of an XML Schema, designed in a bottom-up manner, to a core component model. Thereby, we introduced basic mapping mechanisms and advanced mapping mechanisms. Where no clear mappings between existing XML Schema constructs and core components were possible, we provided mapping heuristics.

Closing the gap between top-down and bottom-up standards

Furthermore, this thesis provided an integrative approach for the unambiguous definition of inter-organizational business processes. Although several approaches for the definition of inter-organizational business process and business documents exist, most of the solutions focus either on the information perspective or on the process perspective. In this thesis we bridged this gap by providing an integrated approach for the definition of inter-organizational business processes based on UN/CEFACT's Modeling Methodology and UN/CEFACT's Core Components. We provided a model-driven approach, where business documents and business processes are defined on a conceptual level. Consequently, the conceptual representation may be used to derive deployment artifacts for the configuration of IT systems.

Providing an integrative approach for inter-organizational business processes

Open research issues

This thesis provides contributions to the field of business document definitions for inter-organizational business processes. However, some open research issues still remain and are subject to further research.

Validation of the survey based on field research

In this thesis we provided a survey on business document standards using standard clusters. The results of this sur-

14 Conclusion and open research issues

vey are based on our experiences gathered in the last four years of active standardization work in the field of business documents and inter-organizational business processes. Furthermore, we have reviewed current state-of-the-art literature for the survey. In a consecutive step, a field-research study must be conducted, evaluating and proving the results of the desk research study. The field research study is yet to be done.

Integration of information and process models based on DSL

In this thesis we outlined that the integrated view on an inter-organizational business process covering both, the information and the process perspective, is of crucial importance to allow for seamless B2B interactions. As a main contribution of this thesis we have shown how inter-organizational business process models and business document models may be combined on an conceptual level to unambiguously capture the requirements of inter-organizational business processes. As an example we have used the UML Profile for Core Components and UN/CEFACT's Modeling Methodology. The second reference implementation format for core components, we introduced in this thesis, is the Domain-Specific Language (DSL) for Core Components. Consequently, future research must examine how DSL models for the information and the process perspective may be combined to capture inter-organizational requirements on a conceptual level. In a next step the model-driven generation of other artifacts than Business Process Execution Language (BPEL) [173] and XML Schema should be examined – e.g., how to combine core component based XML Schema with UMM-based Windows Workflow Foundation [190] concepts.

Model versioning for the core component registry

As a main contribution for a core component registry, this thesis has provided a core component registry model. One of the key application scenarios, we envision for a core component registry, is the maintenance of core component artifacts. As soon as UN/CEFACT releases an updated core component definition or a new core component definition, the changes must be reflected in the registry. Additionally, business information entity definitions may be retrieved from the registry from two different business partners at the same time. If both business partners alter the same business information entity and try to store it back to the registry, versioning conflicts will occur. For such scenarios appropriate versioning and conflict management mechanisms must be provided, which is still an open research issue.

In this thesis we have provided several innovations and improvements to the domain of inter-organizational business processes and business documents in detail. However, we conclude that although the core component concepts provide a powerful mechanism for the definition of business documents, one significant shortcoming remains: tool support. Only if tool vendors adapt the core component technology in their applications, a broad adoption of the standard may be guaranteed. Furthermore, we identify the provision of an electronic core component registry as crucial for the success of the entire core component approach. Generally, these issues may be subsumed by a so called *network effect*. The more companies are using the core component standard, the stronger is the value created by the standard for all companies.

Tool availability as the key to success

List of Figures

1.1	Single business document standard	6
1.2	Scope of this thesis	8
1.3	Overview of the contributions of this thesis	9
2.1	EUDIN example use case	22
2.2	EUDIN paper form	24
2.3	EUDIN – example waste movement form	26
3.1	Overview of different standards	29
3.2	Top-down standardization	31
3.3	Message implementation guide	32
3.4	Bottom-up standardization	34
3.5	Hybrid standardization	37
3.6	ebXML architecture	42
4.1	Core component architecture	61
4.2	Overview of core component concepts	63
4.3	Basic core component naming conventions	64
4.4	Association core component naming conventions	65
4.5	Overview of core data type concepts	66
4.6	Core data type naming conventions	66
4.7	Overview of primitive types	67
4.8	Overview of business information entity concepts	69
4.9	Basic business information entity naming conventions	71
4.10	Association business information entity naming conventions	72
4.11	Overview of business data type concepts	74
4.12	Business data type naming conventions	75
4.13	Overview of core component implementations	77
5.1	UPCC meta-model	82
5.2	UPCC example package structure	87
5.3	Core component library example	88
5.4	Core data type library example	90
5.5	Primitive type library example	90

List of Figures

5.6	UPCC meta-model cut-out	91
5.7	Enumeration type library example	92
5.8	Business information entity library example	94
5.9	Business data type library example	95
5.10	Business document library example	97
6.1	Technical foundations of the DSL approach	102
6.2	Domain model for core components	104
6.3	Consignment item core component DSL instance	108
6.4	Consignment item business information entity DSL instance	110
6.5	Waste movement form DSL instance	110
7.1	Necessary mappers for business document formats	120
7.2	Top-down vs. bottom-up standardization	122
7.3	Overview of the common reference ontology	125
7.4	Core component ontology in detail	127
7.5	Overview of ontology mapping principles	128
7.6	Simplified core component example	129
7.7	Ontology mapping example	130
8.1	Open-edi reference model	134
8.2	Transformation concepts of UPCC to XML Schema components	136
8.3	XML Schema deployment artifacts	137
9.1	Motivating business scenario for a registry	146
9.2	UPCC meta-model	150
9.3	Cut-out: core component registry meta-model	151
9.4	Sample business information entity model	152
9.5	Core component registry example	153
9.6	Federated registry approach	157
10.1	A cut-out of the ebInterface standard	161
10.2	The details section of ebInterface	162
10.3	Excerpt from example invoice	162
10.4	Excerpt from itemized bill	163
11.1	Mapping spaces in CCTS-based document model integration	179
11.2	Mapping of CCTS to XML Schema components	179
11.3	Distinguishing BBIEs from ASBIEs	180
11.4	Reusable group *sequence*	182
11.5	Reusable group *choice* (alternative 1)	182
11.6	Reusable group *choice* (alternative 2)	183

List of Figures

11.7	Reusable group *all*	184
11.8	*redefine* mechanism	185
11.9	*Substitution group* mechanism (1/3)	186
11.10	*Substitution group* mechanism (2/3)	187
11.11	*Substitution group* mechanism (3/3)	187
11.12	Conceptual illustration of model mappings	189
12.1	Overview of the Business Requirements View	196
12.2	Business Process Worksheet	197
12.3	Business Process Use Case with Business Partners	198
12.4	Business Process Activity Model	199
12.5	Business Entity Worksheet	200
12.6	Business Entity Life Cycle: Waste Transport	201
12.7	Overview of the Business Choreography View	202
12.8	Business Transaction Use Case	203
12.9	Business Transaction Announce Waste Transport	205
12.10	Business Collaboration Use Case	206
12.11	Business Collaboration Protocol Manage Waste Transport	208
12.12	Business Realization View	209
12.13	Overview of the Business Information View	211
12.14	Business Information View Example	212
13.1	ISO 11179 data element – core concepts	223
13.2	Business document model vs. relational model	225

Nomenclature

ABIE	Aggregate Business Information Entity
ACC	Aggregate Core Component
ANSI	American National Standards Institute
ASBIE	Association Business Information Entity
ASCC	Association Core Component
ASMA	Association Message Assembly
BBIE	Basic Business Information Entity
BCC	Basic Core Component
BDT	Business Data Type
BIE	Business Information Entity
BIELibrary	Business Information Entity Library
bLibrary	Business Library
BOV	Business Operational View
CC	Core Component
CCL	Core Component Library
CCLibrary	Core Component Library
CCTS	Core Components Technical Specification
CDT	Core Data Type
CDTLibrary	Core Data Type Library
CON	Content Component
COTS	Commercial-of-the-shelf software
DEN	Dictionary Entry Name
DOCLibrary	Business Document Library
DSL	Domain-Specific Language
ebRIM	ebXML Registry Information Model
ebXML	Electronic Business XML
EDI	Electronic Data Interchange
EDIFACT	Electronic Data Interchange For Administration, Commerce and Transport
ENUM	Enumeration Type
ENUMLibrary	Enumeration Type Library
ERP	Electronic Resource Planning
FSV	Functional Service View
IDSCHEME	Identifier Scheme Type
MA	Message Assembly

Nomenclature

MIG	Message Implementation Guide
NDR	Naming and Design Rules
OCL	Object Constraint Language
PRIM	Primitive Type
PRIMLibrary	Primitive Type Library
SOA	Service-Oriented Architectures
SUP	Supplementary Component
UMM	UN/CEFACT's Modeling Methodology
UN/CEFACT	United Nations Center for Trade Facilitation and Electronic Business
UN/ECE	United Nations Economic Commission for Europe
UPCC	UML Profile for Core Components

Bibliography

[1] Achilleas Achilleos, Kun Yang, and Nektarios Georgalas. *A Model Driven Approach to Generate Service Creation Environments*. In *Proceedings of the IEEE Global Telecommunications Conference (GLOBECOM), November 30 - December 4, New Orleans, LA, USA*, pages 1673–1678. IEEE, 2008.

[2] ACORD. *ACORD Insurance Data Standards*, http://www.acord.org, 2007.

[3] AIAG. *Automotive Industry Action Group (AIAG)*, http://www.aiag.org, 2009.

[4] Ali Shaikh Ali, Omer F. Rana, Rashid Al-Ali, and David W. Walker. *UDDIe: an extended registry for Web services*. In *Proceedings of the Symposium on Applications and the Internet, January 27-31, Orlando, FL, USA*, pages 85–89. IEEE, 2003.

[5] American Petroleum Institute. *Petroleum Industry Data Exchange (PIDX)*, http://www.pidx.org, 2007.

[6] ANSI ASC. *ANSI ASC X12*, http://www.x12.org, 1983.

[7] ANSI ASC. *Context Inspired Component Architecture (CICA)*, http://www.disa.org/x12org/meetings/x12trimt/cica.cfm, 2002.

[8] AustriaPRO. *ebInterface*, http://www.ebinterface.at/, 2009.

[9] Andrey Balmin, Yannis Papakonstantinou, and Victor Vianu. *Incremental validation of XML documents*. ACM Transactions on Database Systems, 29(4):710–751, 2004.

[10] Denilson Barbosa, Alberto O. Mendelzon, Leonid Libkin, Laurent Mignet, and Marcelo Arenas. *Efficient Incremental Validation of XML Documents*. In *Proceedings of the 20th International Conference on Data Engineering (ICDE04), March 30 - April 2, Boston, MA, USA*, pages 671–682. IEEE, 2004.

[11] Jon Bentley. *Programming pearls: little languages.* Communications of the ACM, 29(8):711–721, 1986.

[12] John Berge. *The EDIFACT Standards.* Blackwell Publishers, 1994.

[13] Martin Bernauer, Gerti Kappel, and Gerhard Kramler. *Approaches to implementing active semantics with XML Schema.* In *Proceedings of the 14th International Workshop on Database and Expert Systems Applications (DEXA03), September 1-5, Prague, Czech Republic*, pages 559–565. Springer, 2003.

[14] Philip A. Bernstein and Howard Ho. *Model Management and Schema Mappings: Theory and Practice.* In *Proceedings of the 33rd International conference on Very Large Data Bases (VLDB '07), September 23-27, Vienna, Austria*, pages 1439–1440. VLDB Endowment, 2007.

[15] Kevin Bierhoff, Edy S. Liongosari, and Kishore S. Swaminathan. *Incremental Development of a Domain-Specific Language That Supports Multiple Application Styles.* In *Proceedings of the 6th OOPSLA Workshop on Domain Specific Modeling, October 22, Portland, OR, USA*, pages 67–78. Springer, 2006.

[16] Arnaud Blouin, Olivier Beaudoux, and Stéphane Loiseau. *Malan: A Mapping Language for the Data Manipulation.* In *Proceedings of the 2008 ACM Symposium on Document Engineering, September 16-19, Sao Paulo, Brazil*, pages 66–75. ACM, 2008.

[17] Thanassis Bouras, Panagiotis Gouvas, and Gregoris Mentzas. *Dynamic Data Mediation in Enterprise Application Integration.* In *Proceedings of the eChallenges Conference (eChallenges2008), October 22-24, Stockholm, Sweden*, pages 1–8, 2008.

[18] Peter Pin-Shan Chen. *The Entity Relationship Model: Towards a unified view of data.* ACM Transactions on Database Systems, 1(1):9–36, 1976.

[19] CIDX. *Chemical Industry Data Exchange Standard (CIDX)*, http://www.cidx.org/, 2007.

[20] Carlo Combi and Barbara Oliboni. *Conceptual modeling of XML data.* In *Proceedings of the ACM*

symposium on applied computing (SAC06), April 23-27, Dijon, France, pages 467–473. ACM, 2006.

[21] Commerce One. *xCBL - XML Common Business Library*, http://www.xcbl.org, 1997.

[22] Steve Cook, Gareth Jones, Stuart Kent, and Alan Cameron Wills. *Domain-Specific Development with Visual Studio DSL Tools.* Addison-Wesley, 2007.

[23] Jim Davies, Steve Harris, Charles Crichton, Aadya Shukla, and Jeremy Gibbons. *Metadata Standards for Semantic Interoperability in Electronic Government.* In *Proceedings of the 2nd International Conference on Theory and Practice of Electronic Governance (ICEGOV '08), December 1-4, Cairo, Egypt*, pages 67–75. ACM, 2008.

[24] Jim Dawson and John Wainwright. *Pro Mapping in BizTalk Server 2009.* Apress, 2009.

[25] Asuman Dogac and Ibrahim Cingil. *A Survey and Comparison of Business-to-Business e-Commerce Frameworks. ACM SIGecom Exchanges*, 2(2):16–27, 2001.

[26] Asuman Dogac, Yildiray Kabak, and Gokce B. Laleci. *Enriching ebXML Registries with OWL Ontologies for Efficient Service Discovery.* In *Proceedings of the 14th International Workshop on Research Issues on Data Engineering (RIDE), March 28-29, Boston, MA, USA*, pages 69–76. ACM, 2004.

[27] Paul Downey. *xsi:type is Evil.* http://blog.whatfettle.com/2006/11/29/xsitype-is-evil/, 2006.

[28] EDIBUILD Europe. *EDIBUILD*, http://www.edibuildeurope.dataexchangestandards.info/, 2009.

[29] Marc Ehrig and York Sure. *Ontology Mapping - An Integrated Approach.* In *Proceedings of the First European Semantic Web Symposium (ESWS'04), May 10-12, Heraklion, Greece*, pages 76–91. Springer, 2004.

[30] Christian Eis, Christian Huemer, Philipp Liegl, Christian Pichler, and Michael Strommer. *A Framework for Managing the Complexity of Business Document Integration.* In *Proceedings of the*

eChallenges e-2009 Conference and Exhibition, October 21-23, Istanbul, Turkey, pages 1–8, 2009.

[31] Christian Eis, Philipp Liegl, Christian Pichler, and Michael Strommer. *An Evaluation of Mapping Strategies for Core Components*. In *Proceedings of the International Workshop on Service Computing for B2B (SC4B2B), September 21-25, Bangalore, India*, pages 140–149. IEEE, 2009.

[32] EPS Banks. *EPS e-payment standard*, http://www.eps.or.at, 2002.

[33] European Committee for Banking Standards. *Electronic Payment Initiator (ePI), V 1.1*, http://www.stuzza.at/1229_DE.61A32C51747b3904dfa3250139a5203ba6a340e0, 2003.

[34] Ronald Fagin, Phokion G. Kolaitis, Alan Nash, and Lucian Popa. *Towards a Theory of Schema-Mapping Optimization*. In *Proceedings of the twenty-seventh ACM SIGMOD-SIGACT-SIGART symposium on Principles of database systems (PODS '08), June 9-12, Vancouver, Canada*, pages 33–42. ACM, 2008.

[35] Patrick Feng. *Studying standardization: a review of the literature*. In *Proceedings of 3rd IEEE Conference on Standardization and Innovation in Information Technology, October 22-24, Delft, Netherlands*, pages 99–112. IEEE, 2003.

[36] Oliver Fodor and Hanner Werthner. *Harmonise: A Step Toward an Interoperable E-Tourism Marketplace. International Journal of Electronic Commerce*, 9(2):11–39, 2005.

[37] Erwin Folmer and Joris Bastiaans. *Methods for Design of Semantic Message-Based B2B Interaction Standards*. In *Enterprise Interoperability III*, pages 183–196. Springer London, 2008.

[38] Douglas Foxvog and Christoph Bussler. *Ontologizing EDI Semantics*. In *Proceedings of the International Conference on Advances in Conceptual Modeling (ER2006), November 6-9, Tucson, AZ, USA*, pages 301–311. Springer, 2006.

[39] FpML standards committee. *Financial products Markup Language (FpML)*, http://www.fpml.org, 2001.

[40] Erich Gamma, Richard Helm, Ralph Johnson, and John M. Vlissides. *Design Patterns: Elements of Reusable Object-Oriented Software*. Addison-Wesley Professional, 1994.

[41] Guido L. Geerts and William E. McCarthy. *The Ontological Foundation of REA Enterprise Information Systems*. Technical report, Michigan State University, 2000.

[42] Joachim Geisler. *Handbuch E-Money, E-Payment & M-Payment*. In *Erfolgsfaktor Standardisierung am Beispiel vom eps e-payment standard (in german)*, pages 407–418. Physica-Verlag HD, 2006.

[43] Robert Glushko and Tim McGrath. *Document Engineering*. The MIT Press, 2005.

[44] Jaap Gordijn and Hans Akkermans. *Value based requirements engineering: Exploring innovative e-commerce idea*. Requirements Engineering Journal, 8(2):114–134, 2003.

[45] Giovanna Guerrini and Marco Mesiti. *X-Evolution: A Comprehensive Approach for XML Schema Evolution*. In *Proceedings of the 19th International Conference on Database and Expert Systems Application (DEXA '08), September 1-5, Turin, Italy*, pages 251–255. IEEE, 2008.

[46] Giovanna Guerrini, Marco Mesiti, and Daniele Rossi. *Impact of XML Schema evolution on valid documents*. In *Proceedings of the 7th annual ACM international workshop on Web information and data management (WIDM '05), November 5, Bremen, Germany*, pages 39–44. ACM, 2005.

[47] Laura M. Haas, Mauricio A. Hernández, Howard Ho, Lucian Popa, and Mary Roth. *Clio Grows Up: From Research Prototype to Industrial Tool*. In *Proceedings of the 2005 ACM SIGMOD international conference on Management of data (SIGMOD '05), June 14-16, Baltimore, Maryland*, pages 805–810. ACM, 2005.

[48] Steve Harris, Jeremy Gibbons, Jim Davies, Andrew Tsui, and Charles Crichton. *Semantic Technologies in Electronic Government*. In *Proceedings of the 2nd International Conference on Theory and Practice of Electronic Governance (ICEGOV '08), December 1-*

4, Cairo, Egypt, pages 45–51. ACM, 2008.

[49] Health Level Seven. *Health Level Seven (HL7)*, http://www.hl7.org, 1987.

[50] Martin Hepp, Joerg Leukel, and Volker Schmitz. *A Quantiative Analysis of Product Categorization Standards: Content, Coverage, and Maintance of eCl@ss, UNSPSC, eOTD, and the RosettaNet Technical Directory. Knowledge and Information Systems*, 13(1):77–114, 2006.

[51] Birgit Hofreiter. *Binding UMM Business Documents to a Business Document Ontology*. In *Proceedings of the Inaugural Conference on Digital Ecosystems and Technologies (DEST07), February 21-23, Cairns, Australia*, pages 666–671. IEEE, 2007.

[52] Birgit Hofreiter and Christian Huemer. *Transforming UMM Business Collaboration Models to BPEL*. In *Proceedings of the OTM Conferederated International Workshops and Posters (OTM2004), October 25-29, Agia Napa, Cyprus*, pages 507–519. Springer, 2004.

[53] Birgit Hofreiter, Christian Huemer, and Ja-Hee Kim. *Choreography of ebXML business collaborations. Information Systems and e-Business Management*, 4(3):221–243, 2006.

[54] Birgit Hofreiter, Christian Huemer, Philipp Liegl, Rainer Schuster, and Marco Zapletal. *UMM Add-In: A UML Extension for UN/CEFACT's Modeling Methodology*. In *Proceedings of the European Conference on Model Driven Architecture (ECMDA'06), July 10-13, Bilbao, Spain*, pages 618–619. Springer, 2006.

[55] Birgit Hofreiter, Christian Huemer, Philipp Liegl, Rainer Schuster, and Marco Zapletal. *UN/CEFACT's Modeling Methodology (UMM): A UML Profile for B2B e-Commerce*. In *Proceedings of the 2nd International Workshop on Best Practices of UML (ER BP-UML'06), November 6-9, Tucson, AZ, USA*, pages 19–31. IEEE, 2006.

[56] Birgit Hofreiter, Christian Huemer, Philipp Liegl, Rainer Schuster, and Marco Zapletal. *Deriving executable BPEL from UMM Business Transactions*. In *Proceedings of the IEEE International Conference*

on *Services Computing (SCC2007), July 9-13, Salt Lake City, UT, USA*, pages 178–186. IEEE, 2007.

[57] Birgit Hofreiter, Christian Huemer, Philipp Liegl, Rainer Schuster, and Marco Zapletal. *The UMM Add-In - Demo*. In *Proceedings of the International Conference on Services Oriented Computing (ICSOC2007), September 17-20, Vienna, Austria*, pages 618–619. Springer, 2007.

[58] Birgit Hofreiter, Christian Huemer, and Marco Zapletal. *A Business Collaboration Registry Model on Top of ebRIM*. In *Proceedings of the IEEE International Conference on e-Business Engineering (ICEBE06), October 24-26, Shanghai, China*, pages 392–400. IEEE, 2006.

[59] Ken Holman. *UBL Catalogue analysis*. http://markmail.org/message/o3ra6fffiw6mu7jw, 2008.

[60] HR-XML Consortium. *HR-XML*, http://www.hr-xml.org, 1999.

[61] Christian Huemer. *Electronic data interchange (EDI), standards, shortcomings, solutions*. PhD thesis, University of Vienna, 1997.

[62] Christian Huemer and Philipp Liegl. *A UML Profile for Core Components and their Transformation to XSD*. In *Proceedings of the 2nd International Workshop on Services Engineering (SEIW 2007), April 16, Istanbul, Turkey*, pages 298–306. IEEE, 2007.

[63] Christian Huemer, Philipp Liegl, Thomas Motal, Rainer Schuster, and Marco Zapletal. *The Development Process of the UN/CEFACT Modeling Methodology*. In *Proceedings of the 10th International Conference on Electronic Commerce (ICEC08), August 19-22, Innsbruck, Austria*, pages 1–10. ACM, 2008.

[64] Christian Huemer, Philipp Liegl, and Christian Pichler. *A registry model for UN/CEFACT's Core Components*. In *Proceedings of IEEE International Conference on Service-Oriented Computing and Applications (SOCA'09), December 14-15, Taipei, Taiwan*. IEEE, 2009.

Bibliography

[65] Christian Huemer, Philipp Liegl, Rainer Schuster, Hannes Werthner, and Marco Zapletal. *Inter-organizational Systems: From Business Values over Business Processes to Deployment*. In *Proceedings of the 2nd International IEEE Conference on Digital Ecosystems and Technologies (DEST2008), February 26-29, Phitsanulok, Thailand*, pages 294–299. IEEE, 2008.

[66] Christian Huemer, Philipp Liegl, Rainer Schuster, and Marco Zapletal. *Modeling Business Entity State Centric Choreographies*. In *Proceedings of the IEEE Joint Conference on E-Commerce Technology (CEC07), July 23-26, Tokyo, Japan*, pages 393–400. IEEE, 2007.

[67] Christian Huemer, Philipp Liegl, Rainer Schuster, and Marco Zapletal. *Worksheet Driven UMM Modeling of B2B Services*. In *Proceedings of the IEEE International Conference on e-Business Engineering (ICEBE 2007), October 24-26, Hongkong, China*, pages 30–38. IEEE, 2007.

[68] Christian Huemer, Philipp Liegl, Rainer Schuster, and Marco Zapletal. *A 3-level e-Business Registry Meta Model*. In *Proceedings of the IEEE International Conference on Services Computing (SCC2008), July 8-11, Honolulu, HI, USA*, pages 451–450. IEEE, 2008.

[69] Christian Huemer, Philipp Liegl, Rainer Schuster, and Marco Zapletal. *B2B Services: Worksheet-Driven Development of Modeling Artifacts and Code. Computer Journal*, 2009. (to appear).

[70] Christian Huemer, Philipp Liegl, Rainer Schuster, Marco Zapletal, and Birgit Hofreiter. *Service-Oriented Enterprise Modeling and Analysis*. In *Handbook of Enterprise Integration*, pages 307–322. Auerbach Publications, 2009.

[71] Thomas Hughes. *Networks of Power: Electrification in Western Society, 1880-1930*. The Johns Hopkins University Press, 1983.

[72] IBM. *General Markup Language (GML)*, http://www.sgmlsource.com/history/G320-2094/G320-2094.htm, 1973.

[73] papiNet IDEAlliance. *papiNet*, http://www.papinet.org, 2007.

[74] Michael Ilger and Marco Zapletal. *An Implementation to transform Business Collaboration Models to executable Process Specifications*. In *Proceedings of the Conference on Service-Oriented Electronic Commerce at the Multikonferenz Wirtschaftsinformatik (MKWI'06), Feburary 20-22, Passau, Germany*, pages 9–23. GI, 2006.

[75] Dublin Core Metadata Initiative. *Dublin Core Metadata Initiative Abstract Model*, http://dublincore.org/documents/abstract-model/, 2007.

[76] ISO. *ISO 3166 List of country names and code elements*, http://www.iso.org/iso/country_codes/background_on_iso_3166/what_is_iso_3166.htm, 1974.

[77] ISO. *Standard General Markup Language (SGML)*, http://www.w3.org/MarkUp/SGML/, 1986.

[78] ISO. *Open-edi Reference Model*, http://standards.iso.org/ittf/PubliclyAvailableStandards/c037354_ISO_IEC_14662_2004(E).zip, 2004.

[79] ISO. *Universal Financial Industry Message Scheme (UNIFI)*, http://www.iso20022.org/, 2005.

[80] ISO/IEC. *ISO/IEC 11179 Information Technology - Metadata registries*, http://metadata-standards.org/11179/, 2009.

[81] Rania Khalaf, Alexander Keller, and Frank Leymann. *Business processes for web services: principles and applications*. IBM Systems Journal, 45(2):425–446, 2006.

[82] Dan Jong Kim, Manish Agrawal, Bharat Jayaraman, and H. Raghav Rao. *A Comparison of B2B e-Service Solutions*. Communications of the ACM, 46(12):317–324, 2003.

[83] HyoungDo Kim. *Conceptual Modeling and Specification Generation for B2B Business Processes based on ebXML*. ACM SIGMOD Record, 31(1):137–145, 2002.

[84] Phokion G. Kolaitis. *Schema Mappings, Data Exchange, and Metadata Management.* In *Proceedings of the twenty-fourth ACM SIGMOD-SIGACT-SIGART symposium on Principles of database systems (PODS '05), June 13-15, Baltimore, MD, USA*, pages 61–75. ACM, 2005.

[85] Birgit Korherr and Beate List. *An Evaluation of Conceptual Business Process Modelling Languages.* In *Proceedings of the ACM Symposium on Applied Computing (SAC'06), April 23-27, Dijon, France*, pages 1532–1539. ACM, 2006.

[86] Paavo Kotinurmi. *E-Business Framework Enabled B2B Integration.* PhD thesis, Helsinki University of Technology, 2007.

[87] Gerhard Kramler, Elisabeth Kapsammer, Gerti Kappel, and Werner Retschitzegger. *Towards Using UML 2 for Modelling Web Service Collaboration Protocols.* In *Proceedings of the First International Conference on Interoperability of Enterprise Software and Applications (INTEROP-ESA'05), February 23-25, Geneva, Switzerland*, pages 227–238. Springer, 2005.

[88] Ronald M. Lee. *Documentary Petri Nets: A Modeling Representation for Electronic Trade Procedures.* In *Business Process Management: Models, Techniques, and Empirical Studies*, pages 359 – 375. Springer, 2000.

[89] Frank Legler and Felix Naumann. *A Classification of Schema Mappings and Analysis of Mapping Tools.* In *Proceedings of Datenbanksysteme in Business, Technologie und Web (BTW 2007), March 5-9, Aachen, Germany*, pages 449–464. GI, 2007.

[90] Kirsten Lenz and Andreas Oberweis. *Inter-organizational Business Process Management with XML Nets.* In *Petri Net Technology for Communication-Based Systems*, pages 243–263. Springer, 2003.

[91] Haifei Li. *XML and Industrial Standards for Electronic Commerce. Knowledge and Information Systems*, 2(4):487–497, 2000.

[92] Jian Bing Li and James Miller. *Testing the Semantics of W3C XML Schema*. In *Proceedings of the 29th Annual International Computer Software and Applications Conference (COMPSAC2006), July 26-28, Edinburgh, U.K.*, pages 443–448. IEEE, 2005.

[93] Philipp Liegl. *The strategic impact of service oriented architectures*. In *Proceedings of the 14th Annual IEEE International Conference and Workshop on the Engineering of Computer Based Systems (ECBS 2007), March 26-29, Tucson, AZ, USA*, pages 475–484. IEEE, 2007.

[94] Philipp Liegl. *Business documents in a service oriented context*. In *Proceedings of the 10th International Conference on Electronic Commerce (ICEC08), August 19-22, Innsbruck, Austria*, pages 1–5, 2008.

[95] Philipp Liegl. *Conceptual Business Document Modeling using UN/CEFACT's Core Components*. In *Proceedings of the 6th Asia-Pacific Conference on Conceptual Modeling (APCCM2009), January 20-23, Wellington, New Zealand*, pages 59–69. Australian Computer Society, 2009.

[96] Philipp Liegl, Christian Huemer, and Marco Zapletal. *Towards a global business document reference ontology*. In *Proceedings of the Third IEEE International Conference on Semantic Computing (ICSC2009), September 14-16, Berkeley, CA, USA*, pages 355–360. IEEE, 2009.

[97] Philipp Liegl and Dieter Mayrhofer. *A Domain Specific Language for UN/CEFACT's Core Components*. In *Proceedings of the International Workshop on Service Computing for B2B (SC4B2B), September 21-25, Bangalore, India*, pages 123–131. IEEE, 2009.

[98] Philipp Liegl, Robert Mosser, Rainer Schuster, and Marco Zapletal. *Modeling e-Government processes with UMM*. In *Proceedings of the VIP Symposia on Internet related research (VIPSI2007), June 7-10, Opatija, Croatia*, pages 1–11, 2007.

[99] Philipp Liegl, Thomas Motal, and Rainer Schuster. *An Add-In for UN/CEFACT's Modeling Methodology 2.0*. In *Proceedings of the 10th International*

Conference on Electronic Commerce (ICEC08), August 19-22, Innsbruck, Austria, pages 1–2, 2008.

[100] Philipp Liegl, Rainer Schuster, Robert Mosser, and Marco Zapletal. *Modeling e-Government processes with UMM*. Informatica Journal - An International Journal of Computing and Informatics, 31(4):407–417, 2007.

[101] Philipp Liegl, Rainer Schuster, and Marco Zapletal. *A UML Profile and Add-In for UN/CEFACT's Modeling Methodology*. Master's thesis, University of Vienna, 2006.

[102] Philipp Liegl, Rainer Schuster, Marco Zapletal, Christian Huemer, Hannes Werthner, Michael Aigner, Martin Bernauer, Bjoern Klinger, Michaela Mayr, Ramin Mizani, and Martin Windisch. *[vem:xi:] - A methodology for process based requirements engineering*. In *Proceedings of the 17th IEEE International Requirements Engineering Conference (RE09), August 31 - September 4, Atlanta, GA, USA*, pages 193–202. IEEE, 2009.

[103] Fu-Ren Lin, Meng-Chyn Yang, and Yu-Hua Pai. *A generic structure for Business Process Modeling*. Business Process Management Journal, 8(1):19–41, 2002.

[104] Sea Ling and Seng Wai Loke. *Advanced Petri Nets for Modelling Mobile Agent Enabled InterorganizationalWorkflows*. In *Proceedings of the 9th IEEE International Conference and Workshop on the Engineering of Computer-Based Systems (ECBS 2002), April 8-11, Lund, Sweden*, pages 245–252. IEEE, 2002.

[105] Beate List and Birgit Korherr. *A UML 2 Profile for Business Process Modelling*. In *Proceedings of the International Conference on Conceptual Modeling (ER 2005), October 24-28, Klagenfurt, Austria*, pages 85–96. Springer, 2005.

[106] Wei Liu, Keqing He, and Wudong Liu. *Design and realization of ebXML registry classification model based on ontology*. In *Proceedings of the International Conference on Information Technology: Coding and Computing (ITCC), April 4 - 5, Las Vegas, NV, USA*, pages 809–814. ACM, 2005.

[107] Ayesha Malik. *XML Schemas in an Object Oriented Framework*. http://xml.sys-con.com/node/40580, 2003.

[108] Murali Mani, Dongwon Lee, and Richard R. Muntz. *Semantic Data Modeling Using XML Schemas*. In *Proceedings of the 20th International Conference on Conceptual Modeling (ER 2001), November 27-30, Yokohama, Japan*, pages 149–163. Springer, 2001.

[109] Wim Martens, Frank Neven, Thomas Schwentick, and Geert Jan Bex. *Expressiveness and complexity of XML Schema*. ACM Transactions on Database Systems, 31(3):770–813, 2006.

[110] Martin Hepp. *GoodRelations: An Ontology for Describing Web Offers*, http://www.heppnetz.de/projects/goodrelations/primer/, 2008.

[111] Richard Mayer, Christopher Menzel, Michael Painter, Paula deWitte, Thomas Blinn, and Benjamin Perakath. *Information Integration for Concurrent Engineering (IICE) IDEF3 Process Description Capture Method Report*. Technical report, Knowledge Based Systems Incorporated, 1995.

[112] Mirth Corporation. *Mirth Connect*. http://www.mirthcorp.com/products/mirth-connect, 2009.

[113] Tadao Murata. *Petri nets: Properties, analysis and applications*. Proceedings of the IEEE, 77(4):541–580, 1989.

[114] Klaus-Dieter Naujok and Christian Huemer. *Case Study: Designing ebXML: The Work of UN/CEFACT*. In *Ontologies-Based Business Integration*, pages 79–93. Springer, 2008.

[115] Martin Nečaský. *Conceptual Modeling for XML: A Survey*. In *Proceedings of the Annual International Workshop on Databases, Texts, Specifications, and Objects (DATESO2006), April 26-28, Desna, Czech Republic*, pages 40–53, 2006.

[116] New York Stock Exchange. *Vendor Reporting Extensible Markup Language (VRXML)*, http://www.nyxdata.com/vrxml, 2002.

[117] Juha-Miikka Nurmilaakso, Paavo Kotinurmi, and Hannu Laesvuori. *XML-based e-Business Frameworks and Standardization. Computer Standards and Interfaces*, 28(12):585–599, 2006.

[118] OASIS. *Universal Description, Discovery, and Integration (UDDI)*, http://www.uddi.org/pubs/uddi_v3.htm, 2004.

[119] OASIS. *ebXML Registry Technical Specification 3.0*, http://docs.oasis-open.org/regrep/v3.0/regrep-3.0-os.zip, 2005.

[120] OASIS. *ebXML Business Process Specification Schema Technical Specification 2.0.4*, http://docs.oasis-open.org/ebxml-bp/2.0.4/ebxmlbp-v2.0.4-Spec-os-en.html, 2006.

[121] OASIS. *Universal Business Language 2.0 (UBL)*, http://docs.oasis-open.org/ubl/os-UBL-2.0/UBL-2.0.html, 2006.

[122] OASIS. *Web Services Business Process Execution Language Version 2.0 (WS-BPEL)*, http://docs.oasis-open.org/wsbpel/2.0/OS/wsbpel-v2.0-OS.html, 2007.

[123] OASIS. *RELAX NG*, http://relaxng.org/, 2009.

[124] UN/CEFACT OASIS. *ebXML - Technical Architecture Specification 1.4*, http://www.ebxml.org/specs/ebTA.pdf, 2001.

[125] Ernst Oberortner, Uwe Zdun, and Schahram Dustdar. *Domain-Specific Languages for Service-Oriented Architectures: An Explorative Study*. In *Proceedings of the First European ServiceWave Conference (ServiceWave), December 10 - 13, Madrid, Spain*, pages 159–170. Springer, 2008.

[126] Object Management Group. *Model Driven Architecture (MDA)*, http://www.omg.org/mda, 2003.

[127] Object Management Group. *Business Process Modeling Notation 1.1 (BPMN)*, http://www.bpmn.org/Documents/BPMN1-1Specification.pdf, 2006.

[128] Object Management Group. *Meta Object Facility (MOF)*, http://www.omg.org/mof/, 2006.

[129] Object Management Group. *Unified Modeling Language: Superstructure 2.2 (UML)*, http://www.omg.org/spec/UML/2.1.1/Superstructure/PDF/, 2009.

[130] Odette International. *ODETTE*, http://www.odette.org, 1984.

[131] Open Applications Group. *OAGIS Canonical Model for Integration*, http://www.openapplications.org/, 1994.

[132] Alexander Osterwalder and Yves Pigneur. *An e-Business Model Ontology for Modeling e-Business*. In *Proceedings of the 15th Bled Electronic Commerce Conference, June 17-19, Bled, Slovenia*, pages 1–12. EconWPA, 2002.

[133] Mike P. Papazoglou, Paolo Traverso, Schahram Dustdar, and Frank Leymann. *Service-Oriented Computing: State of the Art and Research Challenges*. IEEE Computer, 40(11):38–45, 2007.

[134] David L. Parnas. *On the design and development of program families*. IEEE Transactions on Software Engineering, 2(1):193–213, 1976.

[135] James Pasley. *Avoid XML Schema wildcards for Web service interfaces*. IEEE Internet Computing, 10(3):72–79, 2006.

[136] Chris Peltz. *Web Services Orchestration and Choreography*. Computer, 36(10):46–52, 2003.

[137] Magnus Penker and Hans-Erik Eriksson. *Business Modeling With UML: Business Patterns at Work*. Wiley, 2000.

[138] Christian Pichler, Michael Strommer, and Philipp Liegl. *On Mapping Business Document Models to Core Components*. In *Proceedings of the Hawaii International Conference on System Sciences (HICSS-43), January 5-8, Kauai, HI, USA*, pages 1–10. IEEE, 2010.

[139] Risto Pitkänen and Tommi Mikkonen. *Lightweight Domain-Specific Modeling and Model-Driven Development*. In *Proceedings of the 6th OOPSLA Workshop on Domain Specific Modeling, October 22, Portland, OR, USA*, pages 159–168. Springer, 2006.

[140] Lucian Popa, Yannis Velegrakis, Mauricio A. Hernández, Renée J. Miller, and Ronald Fagin.

Translating Web Data. In *Proceedings of the 28th International Conference on Very Large Data Bases (VLDB '02), August 20-23, Hongkong, China*, pages 598–609. VLDB Endowment, 2002.

[141] Michael E. Porter. *Competitive Advantage: Creating and Sustaining Superior Performance*. Free Press, 1998.

[142] Mukund Raghavachari and Oded Shmueli. *Efficient Revalidation of XML Documents*. IEEE Transactions on Knowledge and Data Engineering, 19(4):554–567, 2007.

[143] K. Ramamurthy and G. Premkumar. *Determinants and outcomes of electronic data interchange diffusion*. IEEE Transactions on Engineering Management, 42(4):332–351, 1995.

[144] Yohan Roh, Hangkyu Kim, Hak Soo Kim, Myoung HoKim, and Jin Hyun Son. *Semantic Business Registry Information Model*. In *Proceedings of International Conference on Convergence Information Technology (ICCIT07), November 21-23, Gyeongju, Republic of Korea*, pages 2142–2145. ACM, 2007.

[145] Stephan Roser and Bernhard Bauer. *A Categorization of Collaborative Business Process Modeling Techniques*. In *Proceedings of the Seventh IEEE International Conference on E-Commerce Technology (CEC2005), July 19-22, Munich, Germany*, pages 43–51. IEEE, 2005.

[146] RosettaNet. *RosettaNet Implementation Framework: Core Specification*, http://www.rosettanet.org/cms/sites/RosettaNet/Standards/RStandards/rnif/, 2002.

[147] Nick Russell, Wil M.P. van der Aalst, Arthur H.M. ter Hofstede, and Petia Wohed. *On the Suitability of UML 2.0 Activity Diagrams for Business Process Modelling*. In *Proceedings of the Third Asia-Pacific Conference on Conceptual Modelling (APCCM2006), January 16-19, Hobart, Australia*, pages 95–104. Australian Computer Society, 2006.

[148] Apitep Saekow and Choompol Boonmee. *Towards a Practical Approach for Electronic Government Interoperability Framework (e-GIF)*. In *Proceedings*

of the 42nd Hawaii International Conference on System Sciences (HICSS '09), Wikoloa, HI, USA, pages 1–9. IEEE, 2009.

[149] Flora Dilys Salim, Rosanne Price, Shonali Krishnaswamy, and Maria Indrawan. *UML Documentation Support for XML Schema*. In *Proceedings of the Australian Software Engineering Conference (ASWEC2004), April 13-16, Melbourne, Australia*, pages 211–220. IEEE, 2004.

[150] Willie Schatz. *EDI: putting the muscle in commerce and industry*. In *Management information systems: readings and cases: a managerial perspective*, pages 104–112. Scott, Foresman & Co., 1990.

[151] August-Wilhelm Scheer. *ARIS - Business Process Modeling*. Springer, 2000.

[152] Harald Schömburg, Gerrit Hoppen, and Michael H. Breitner. *Expertenbefragung zur Rechnungseingangsbearbeitung: Status quo und Akzeptanz der elektronischen Rechnung*. Technical report, Institut für Wirtschaftsinformatik Universität Hannover, 2008.

[153] Simon S.Y. Shim, Vishnu S. Pendyala, Meera Sundaram, and Jerry Z. Gao. *Business-to-business e-commerce frameworks*. Computer, 33(10):40–47, 2000.

[154] E. Söderström, B. Andersson, P. Johannesson, E. Perjons, and B. Wangler. *Towards a Framework for Comparing Process Modelling Languages*. In *Proceedings of the 14th International Conference on Advanced Information Systems Engineering (CAiSE '02), May 27-31, Toronto, Canada*, pages 600–611. Springer, 2002.

[155] Software & Information Industry Assocation. *Market Definition Language (MDDL)*, http://www.mddl.org, 2000.

[156] Dave Steinberg, Frank Budinsky, Marcelo Paternostro, and Ed Merks. *EMF: Eclipse Modeling Framework*. Addison-Wesley, 2009.

[157] Hong Su, Diane Kramer, Li Chen, Kajal Claypool, and Elke A. Rundensteiner. *XEM: XML Evolution Management*. In *Proceedings of the 11th*

Bibliography

International Workshop on research Issues in Data Engineering, April 1-2, Heidelberg, Germany, pages 103–110. IEEE, 2002.

[158] Supply Chain Council. *Supply-Chain Operations Reference-model (SCOR)*, http://www.supply-chain.org/, 2006.

[159] Seksun Suwanmanee, Djamal Benslimane, and Philippe Thiran. *OWL-based approach for semantic interoperability*. In *Proceedings of the 19th International Conference on Advanced Information Networking and Applications (AINA2005), March 28-30, Taipei, Taiwan*, pages 145–150. IEEE, 2005.

[160] SWIFT. *Society for Worldwide Interbank Financial Telecommunication*, http://www.swift.com, 2007.

[161] Don Tapscott, David Ticoll, and Alex Lowy. *The rise of business webs*. Ubiquity, 1(3):2, 2000.

[162] J. Tucker, W. Alcorn, and K. Kaplan. *Development of XML industry standards for information exchange and commerce [electronics recycling industry example]*. In *Proceedings of the International Symposium on Electronics and the Environment, May 19-23, Phoenix, AZ, USA*, pages 281–286. IEEE, 2004.

[163] UN/CEFACT. *United Nations Electronic Data Interchange For Administration, Commerce and Transport (UN/EDIFACT)*, http://www.unece.org/trade/untdid/welcome.htm, 1988.

[164] UN/CEFACT. *Core Components Technical Specification 2.01 (CCTS)*, http://www.untmg.org/ccts/spec/2_01, 2003.

[165] UN/CEFACT. *UN/CEFACT Common Business Process Catalog 1.0*, http://www.uncefactforum.org/TBG/TBG14/TBG14%20Documents/cbpc-technical-specification-v1_0-300905-11.pdf, 2005.

[166] UN/CEFACT. *UN/CEFACT's Modeling Methodology 1.0 (UMM)*, http://www.unece.org/cefact/umm/UMM_Foundation_Module.pdf, 2006.

[167] UN/CEFACT. *UML Profile for Core Components Technical Specification 1.0 (UPCC)*, http://www.untmg.org/upcc/spec/1_0, 2008.

[168] UN/CEFACT. *UN/CEFACT Registry Implementation Specification*, http://www.uncefactforum.org/ICG/Documents/ICG%20Archive/UN-CEFACT_Registry_Specification_V1.3.zip, 2008.

[169] UN/CEFACT. *Core Components Data Type Catalogue 3.0*, http://www.untmg.org/ccdatatypecatalogue/spec_3_0, 2009.

[170] UN/CEFACT. *Core Components Technical Specification 3.0 (CCTS)*, http://www.untmg.org/ccts/spec/3_0, 2009.

[171] UN/CEFACT. *Naming and Desing Rules 3.0*, http://75.43.29.149:8080/display/ATG/NDR+-+XML+Naming+and+Design+Rules, 2009.

[172] UN/CEFACT. *UML Profile for Core Components Technical Specification 3.0 (UPCC)*, http://www.untmg.org/upcc/spec/3_0, 2009.

[173] UN/CEFACT. *UN/CEFACT's Core Component Library (UN/CCL)*, http://www.unece.org/cefact/codesfortrade/unccl/CCL_index.htm, 2009.

[174] UN/CEFACT. *UN/CEFACT's Modeling Methodology 2.0 (UMM)*, http://www.untmg.org/umm/spec/foundation/2_0, 2009.

[175] Falk v. Westarp, Tim Weitzel, Peter Buxmann, and Wolfgang König. The status quo and the future of EDI - results of an empirical study. In *Proceedings of the 7th European Conference on Information Systems (ECIS99), June 23-25, Copenhagen, Denmark*, pages 719–731, 1999.

[176] Wil M. P. van der Aalst. The Application of Petri Nets to Workflow Management. *Journal of Circuits, Systems, and Computers*, 8(1):21–66, 1998.

[177] Wil M. P. van der Aalst. Interorganizational Workflows: An Approach based on Message Sequence Charts and Petri Nets. *Systems Analysis - Modelling - Simulation*, 34(3):335–367, 1999.

[178] Wil M. P. van der Aalst. Making Work Flow: On the Application of Petri Nets to Business Process Management. In *Proceedings of the 23rd International Conference on Applications and*

Bibliography

Theory of Petri Nets (ICATPN 2002), June 24-30, Adelaide, Australia, pages 1–22. Springer, 2002.

[179] Eric van Heck and Peter Vervest. *Smart business networks: how the network wins.* Communications of the ACM, 50(6):28–37, 2007.

[180] VIENNA Add-In development team. *The VIENNA Add-In.* http://code.google.com/p/vienna-add-in/, 2009.

[181] Eric Wilde. *What are you talking about?* In Proceedings of the International Conference on Services Computing (SCC07), July 9-13, Salt Lake City, UT, USA, pages 256–261. IEEE, 2007.

[182] World Wide Web Consortium. *RDF Vocabulary Description Language 1.0 (RDF Schema)*, http://www.w3.org/TR/rdf-schema/, 2004.

[183] World Wide Web Consortium. *Web Ontology Language (OWL)*, http://www.w3.org/TR/owl-features/, 2004.

[184] World Wide Web Consortium. *Extensible Markup Language (XML)*, http://www.w3.org/XML/, 2006.

[185] World Wide Web Consortium. *Semantic Annotations for WSDL and XML Schema (SAWSDL)*, http://www.w3.og/TR/sawsdl/, 2007.

[186] World Wide Web Consortium. *Simple Object Access Protocol (SOAP)*, http://www.w3.org/TR/soap12-part1/, 2007.

[187] World Wide Web Consortium. *Web Services Description Language 2.0 (WSDL)*, http://www.w3.org/TR/2007/REC-wsdl20-primer-20070626/, 2007.

[188] XBRL International. *Extensible Business Reporting Language (XBRL)*, http://www.xbrl.org, 2000.

[189] Augustin Yu and Robert Steele. *An overview of research on reverse engineering XML Schemas into UML diagrams.* In Proceedings of the Third International Conference on Information Technology and Applications (ICITA 2005), July 4-7, Sydney, Australia, pages 772–777. IEEE, 2005.

[190] Marco Zapletal. *Deriving business service interfaces in Windows Workflow from UMM*

transactions. In *Proceedings of the International Conference on Service-Oriented Computing (ICSOC2008), December 1-5, Sydney, Australia*, pages 498–504. ACM, 2008.

[191] Marco Zapletal. *A UML-based Methodology for Model-Driven B2B Integration: From Business Values over Business Processes to Deployment Artifacts*. PhD thesis, Vienna University of Technology, 2009.

[192] Marco Zapletal, Philipp Liegl, and Rainer Schuster. *UN/CEFACT's Modeling Methodology (UMM) 1.0 - A Guide to UMM and the UMM Add-In*. VDM Verlag Dr. Müller, 2008.

[193] Marco Zapletal, Wil van der Aalst, Nick Russell, Philipp Liegl, and Hannes Werthner. *An Analysis of Windows Workflow's Control-Flow Expressiveness*. In *Proceedings of the European Conference on Web Services (ECOWS'09), November 9-11, Eindhoven, The Netherlands*, pages 200–209. IEEE, 2009.

[194] Marco Zapletal, Wil van der Aalst, Nick Russell, Philipp Liegl, and Hannes Werthner. *Pattern-based Analysis of Windows Workflow*. Computer Science Report 09/07, Technische Universiteit Eindhoven, 2009.

[195] Valerie Zeithaml, Mary J. Bitner, and Dwayne D. Gremler. *Services Marketing*. McGraw-Hill/Irwin, New York, NY, 2005.

[196] Cheng Zeng, Keqing He, Zhitao Yu, and Caiping Wan. *Towards Improving Web Service Registry and Repository Model Through Ontology-Based Semantic Interoperability*. In *Proceedings of the 7th International Conference on Grid and Cooperative Computing (GCC08), October 24-26, Shenzhen, China*, pages 747–752. IEEE, 2008.

List of Publications

The up-to-date list of publications can be found on
http://www.big.tuwien.ac.at/staff/pliegl.html.

Books

- Marco Zapletal, Philipp Liegl, and Rainer Schuster. *UN/CEFACT's Modeling Methodology (UMM) 1.0 - A Guide to UMM and the UMM Add-In.* VDM Verlag Dr. Müller, 2008

Book chapters

- Christian Huemer, Philipp Liegl, Rainer Schuster, Marco Zapletal, and Birgit Hofreiter. *Service-Oriented Enterprise Modeling and Analysis.* In *Handbook of Enterprise Integration*, pages 307–322. Auerbach Publications, 2009

Journal Papers

- Christian Huemer, Philipp Liegl, Rainer Schuster, and Marco Zapletal. *B2B Services: Worksheet-Driven Development of Modeling Artifacts and Code.* Computer Journal, 2009. (to appear)
- Philipp Liegl, Rainer Schuster, Robert Mosser, and Marco Zapletal. *Modeling e-Government processes with UMM.* Informatica Journal - An International Journal of Computing and Informatics, 31(4):407–417, 2007

Conference and Workshop Papers

- Christian Pichler, Michael Strommer, and Philipp Liegl. *On Mapping Business Document Models to Core Components.* In *Proceedings of the Hawaii International*

Conference on System Sciences (HICSS-43), January 5-8, Kauai, HI, USA, pages 1–10. IEEE, 2010

❏ Christian Huemer, Philipp Liegl, and Christian Pichler. A registry model for UN/CEFACT's Core Components. In Proceedings of IEEE International Conference on Service-Oriented Computing and Applications (SOCA'09), December 14-15, Taipei, Taiwan. IEEE, 2009

❏ Marco Zapletal, Wil van der Aalst, Nick Russell, Philipp Liegl, and Hannes Werthner. An Analysis of Windows Workflow's Control-Flow Expressiveness. In Proceedings of the European Conference on Web Services (ECOWS'09), November 9-11, Eindhoven, The Netherlands, pages 200–209. IEEE, 2009

❏ Christian Eis, Christian Huemer, Philipp Liegl, Christian Pichler, and Michael Strommer. A Framework for Managing the Complexity of Business Document Integration. In Proceedings of the eChallenges e-2009 Conference and Exhibition, October 21-23, Istanbul, Turkey, pages 1–8, 2009

❏ Philipp Liegl and Dieter Mayrhofer. A Domain Specific Language for UN/CEFACT's Core Components. In Proceedings of the International Workshop on Service Computing for B2B (SC4B2B), September 21-25, Bangalore, India, pages 123–131. IEEE, 2009

❏ Christian Eis, Philipp Liegl, Christian Pichler, and Michael Strommer. An Evaluation of Mapping Strategies for Core Components. In Proceedings of the International Workshop on Service Computing for B2B (SC4B2B), September 21-25, Bangalore, India, pages 140–149. IEEE, 2009

❏ Philipp Liegl, Christian Huemer, and Marco Zapletal. Towards a global business document reference ontology. In Proceedings of the Third IEEE International Conference on Semantic Computing (ICSC2009), September 14-16, Berkeley, CA, USA, pages 355–360. IEEE, 2009

❏ Philipp Liegl, Rainer Schuster, Marco Zapletal, Christian Huemer, Hannes Werthner, Michael Aigner, Martin Bernauer, Bjoern Klinger, Michaela Mayr, Ramin Mizani, and Martin Windisch. [vem:xi:] - A methodology for process based requirements engineering. In Pro-

ceedings of the 17th IEEE International Requirements Engineering Conference (RE09), August 31 - September 4, Atlanta, GA, USA, pages 193–202. IEEE, 2009

- Philipp Liegl. *Conceptual Business Document Modeling using UN/CEFACT's Core Components*. In *Proceedings of the 6th Asia-Pacific Conference on Conceptual Modeling (APCCM2009), January 20-23, Wellington, New Zealand*, pages 59–69. Australian Computer Society, 2009

- Christian Huemer, Philipp Liegl, Thomas Motal, Rainer Schuster, and Marco Zapletal. *The Development Process of the UN/CEFACT Modeling Methodology*. In *Proceedings of the 10th International Conference on Electronic Commerce (ICEC08), August 19-22, Innsbruck, Austria*, pages 1–10. ACM, 2008

- Christian Huemer, Philipp Liegl, Rainer Schuster, Hannes Werthner, and Marco Zapletal. *Inter-organizational Systems: From Business Values over Business Processes to Deployment*. In *Proceedings of the 2nd International IEEE Conference on Digital Ecosystems and Technologies (DEST2008), February 26-29, Phitsanulok, Thailand*, pages 294–299. IEEE, 2008

- Christian Huemer, Philipp Liegl, Rainer Schuster, and Marco Zapletal. *A 3-level e-Business Registry Meta Model*. In *Proceedings of the IEEE International Conference on Services Computing (SCC2008), July 8-11, Honolulu, HI, USA*, pages 451–450. IEEE, 2008

- Philipp Liegl. *Business documents in a service oriented context*. In *Proceedings of the 10th International Conference on Electronic Commerce (ICEC08), August 19-22, Innsbruck, Austria*, pages 1–5, 2008

- Philipp Liegl, Thomas Motal, and Rainer Schuster. *An Add-In for UN/CEFACT's Modeling Methodology 2.0*. In *Proceedings of the 10th International Conference on Electronic Commerce (ICEC08), August 19-22, Innsbruck, Austria*, pages 1–2, 2008

- Birgit Hofreiter, Christian Huemer, Philipp Liegl, Rainer Schuster, and Marco Zapletal. *Deriving executable BPEL from UMM Business Transactions*. In *Proceedings of the IEEE International Conference on Services Computing (SCC2007), July 9-13, Salt Lake City, UT, USA*, pages 178–186. IEEE, 2007

List of Publications

- Birgit Hofreiter, Christian Huemer, Philipp Liegl, Rainer Schuster, and Marco Zapletal. *The UMM Add-In - Demo*. In *Proceedings of the International Conference on Services Oriented Computing (ICSOC2007), September 17-20, Vienna, Austria*, pages 618–619. Springer, 2007
- Christian Huemer and Philipp Liegl. *A UML Profile for Core Components and their Transformation to XSD*. In *Proceedings of the 2nd International Workshop on Services Engineering (SEIW 2007), April 16, Istanbul, Turkey*, pages 298–306. IEEE, 2007
- Christian Huemer, Philipp Liegl, Rainer Schuster, and Marco Zapletal. *Modeling Business Entity State Centric Choreographies*. In *Proceedings of the IEEE Joint Conference on E-Commerce Technology (CEC07), July 23-26, Tokyo, Japan*, pages 393-400. IEEE, 2007
- Christian Huemer, Philipp Liegl, Rainer Schuster, and Marco Zapletal. *Worksheet Driven UMM Modeling of B2B Services*. In *Proceedings of the IEEE International Conference on e-Business Engineering (ICEBE 2007), October 24-26, Hongkong, China*, pages 30–38. IEEE, 2007
- Philipp Liegl. *The strategic impact of service oriented architectures*. In *Proceedings of the 14th Annual IEEE International Conference and Workshop on the Engineering of Computer Based Systems (ECBS 2007), March 26-29, Tucson, AZ, USA*, pages 475–484. IEEE, 2007
- Philipp Liegl, Robert Mosser, Rainer Schuster, and Marco Zapletal. *Modeling e-Government processes with UMM*. In *Proceedings of the VIP Symposia on Internet related research (VIPSI2007), June 7-10, Opatija, Croatia*, pages 1–11, 2007
- Birgit Hofreiter, Christian Huemer, Philipp Liegl, Rainer Schuster, and Marco Zapletal. *UN/CEFACT's Modeling Methodology (UMM): A UML Profile for B2B e-Commerce*. In *Proceedings of the 2nd International Workshop on Best Practices of UML (ER BP-UML'06), November 6-9, Tucson, AZ, USA*, pages 19–31. IEEE, 2006
- Birgit Hofreiter, Christian Huemer, Philipp Liegl, Rainer Schuster, and Marco Zapletal. *UMM Add-In: A UML*

Extension for UN/CEFACT's Modeling Methodology. In *Proceedings of the European Conference on Model Driven Architecture (ECMDA'06), July 10-13, Bilbao, Spain*, pages 618–619. Springer, 2006

Technical Reports

❑ Marco Zapletal, Wil van der Aalst, Nick Russell, Philipp Liegl, and Hannes Werthner. *Pattern-based Analysis of Windows Workflow*. Computer Science Report 09/07, Technische Universiteit Eindhoven, 2009

Master Thesis

❑ Philipp Liegl, Rainer Schuster, and Marco Zapletal. *A UML Profile and Add-In for UN/CEFACT's Modeling Methodology*. Master's thesis, University of Vienna, 2006

Die VDM Verlagsservicegesellschaft sucht für wissenschaftliche Verlage abgeschlossene und herausragende

Dissertationen, Habilitationen, Diplomarbeiten, Master Theses, Magisterarbeiten usw.

für die kostenlose Publikation als Fachbuch.

Sie verfügen über eine Arbeit, die hohen inhaltlichen und formalen Ansprüchen genügt, und haben Interesse an einer honorarvergüteten Publikation?

Dann senden Sie bitte erste Informationen über sich und Ihre Arbeit per Email an *info@vdm-vsg.de*.

Sie erhalten kurzfristig unser Feedback!

VDM Verlagsservicegesellschaft mbH
Dudweiler Landstr. 99　　　　　　　Telefon +49 681 3720 174
D - 66123 Saarbrücken　　　　　　　Fax　　　+49 681 3720 1749
www.vdm-vsg.de

Die VDM Verlagsservicegesellschaft mbH vertritt

Printed by Books on Demand GmbH, Norderstedt / Germany